Modern Fortran in Practice

From its earliest days, the Fortran programming language has been designed with computing efficiency in mind. The latest standard, Fortran 2008, incorporates a host of modern features, including object-orientation, array operations, user-defined types, and provisions for parallel computing.

This tutorial guide shows Fortran programmers how to apply these features in twenty-first-century style: modular, concise, object-oriented, and resource-efficient, using multiple processors. It offers practical real-world examples of interfacing to C, memory management, graphics and GUIs, and parallel computing using MPI, OpenMP, and coarrays. The author also analyzes several numerical algorithms and their implementations and illustrates the use of several open source libraries. Full source code for the examples is available on the book's website.

Arjen Markus is a senior consultant at Deltares, an institute for applied research in the field of water, subsurface and infrastructure in The Netherlands, where he develops and maintains their numerical modeling programs and the tools that accompany them. He is an active contributor to the ACM newsletter *Fortran Forum* and the comp.lang.fortran newsgroup.

D0920285

Modern Fortran
in Practice

Arjen Markus
with Foreword by Michael Metcalf

CAMBRIDGE
UNIVERSITY PRESS

32 Avenue of the Americas, New York NY 10013-2473, USA

Cambridge University Press is part of the University of Cambridge.

It furthers the University's mission by disseminating knowledge in the pursuit of
education, learning and research at the highest international levels of excellence.

www.cambridge.org
Information on this title: www.cambridge.org/9781107603479

First published 2012

A catalogue record for this publication is available from the British Library

Library of Congress Cataloguing in Publication data

Markus, Arjen.
Modern Fortran in practice / Arjen Markus, Michael Metcalf.
    pages cm
Includes bibliographical references and index.
ISBN 978-1-107-01790-0 (hardback) – ISBN 978-1-107-60347-9 (pbk.)
1. Fortran 2008 (Computer program language)   I. Metcalf, Michael.   II. Title.
QA76.73.F25M375   2012
005.26'2–dc23   2012000126

ISBN 978-1-107-01790-0 Hardback
ISBN 978-1-107-60347-9 Paperback

Additional resources for this publication at www.cambridge.org/9781107603479

"Eadem mutata resurgo"
(Loosely: though changed, I reappear as myself)
Inscription on the grave of Jacob Bernoulli,
referring to the logarithmic spiral.

In memory of my father

My parents taught me to be inquisitive.
My wife and kids teach me still other
important things.

Contents

Foreword

The applications of Fortran span, very nearly, the whole period during which computers have been in general-purpose use. This is quite remarkable and, given the demise so many other high-level languages, it is quite difficult to know why. Possibly the original design concepts of John Backus – ease of use and efficiency of execution – have been two major factors. Another might be the devotion of Fortran's user community, who labor to keep it abreast of developments in programming techniques and to adapt it to ever-more demanding requirements.

Despite all the predictions, over several decades, that Fortran is about to become extinct, the language has shown itself to be remarkably resilient. Furthermore, over the last few years, it has been subject to new rounds of standardization, and the latest standard, Fortran 2008, should again extend the language's life. Against this background, it is very regrettable that old versions of Fortran live on, both in the form of antiquated courses given by incorrigible teachers and also as an outmoded concept in the minds of its detractors. After all, modern Fortran is a procedural, imperative, and compiled language with a syntax well suited to a direct representation of mathematical formulae. Its individual procedures may be compiled separately or grouped into modules, either way allowing the convenient construction of very large programs and procedure libraries. The language contains features for array processing, abstract data types, dynamic data structures, object-oriented programming, and parallel processing. It can readily be interfaced to C. Thus, modern Fortran, as versions from Fortran 95 onwards are called, is a powerful tool. It fully supports structured programming, and the introduction of object-oriented programming into Fortran 2003, which was its most significant new feature, represented a major upgrade. Much of this is explained in this book.

Nevertheless, no Fortran standard up to and including Fortran 2003 contained any significant feature intended directly to facilitate parallel programming. Rather, this has had to be achieved through the intermediary of ad hoc auxiliary standards, in particular HPF, MPI, OpenMP, and Posix Threads. The use of MPI and OpenMP has become widespread, but HPF, ultimately, met with little success. However, now, with the advent of Fortran 2008, a particular strength of modern Fortran is its ability to support parallel programming, as this latest standard introduces a sorely needed facility: coarrays.

HPF directives took the form of Fortran comment lines that were recognized as such only by an HPF processor. An example was the ability to align three conformable (matching in shape) arrays with a fourth, thus ensuring locality of reference. Further directives allowed, for instance, aligned arrays to be distributed over a set of processors. MPI, on the other hand, is a library specification for message passing, and OpenMP, which supports multiplatform, shared-memory parallel programming, consists of a set of compiler directives, library routines, and environment variables that determine run-time behavior. Posix Threads is a library specification, for multithreading.

By contrast, the objective of coarrays is to provide a syntax, designed to make the smallest possible impact on the appearance of a program, that enables the distribution over some number of processors not only of data, as in a Single-Instruction-Multiple-Data (SIMD) model, but also of work, using the Single-Program-Multiple-Data (SPMD) model. The facility requires a programmer to learn only a modest set of new rules. Coarray handling is Fortran 2008's single most important new feature, but the *do concurrent* form of loop control is also introduced as a way of parallelizing loops. We then see how it becomes possible to achieve a significant degree of parallelization without going outside the language itself. These various paradigms are compared and contrasted in this book.

Other major new features in Fortran 2008 include: submodules, enhanced access to data objects, enhancements to I/O and to execution control, and additional new intrinsic procedures, in particular for bit processing. Fortran 2008 was published in 2010 and is the current standard. If Fortran lives on, it will be because it is well suited to applications in high-performance computing and thus, coarrays will be crucial.

But a language cannot survive without a means to learn about it. This implies the availability not only of textbooks on the language's syntax and semantics, but also of books on how to use the language in real-life situations. Somehow, experience in the use and application of a language needs to be passed on to a new generation of programmers and new features require advice on how they are best to be used. At a time when a single language is rarely used in isolation, but more often in conjunction with other languages or with various tools, *Modern Fortran in Practice* fulfills a real need for practical advice in the field.

The author has been a regular contributor to the ACM newsletter *Fortran Forum* and has given valuable and much appreciated advice on the comp.lang.fortran user newsgroup, where he has been very active as a contributor. Here, the community has been able to benefit from his experience in scientific programming in The Netherlands. His papers on topics such as generic programming and design patterns were quite novel to Fortran. Thus, he is more than amply qualified to write this book.

But *Modern Fortran in Practice* is not merely a concatenation of previous contributions. They have been woven into a coherent primer, together with original material on parallel programming in Fortran, using MPI, OpenMP and, briefly, coarrays, as well as on the use of Fortran for graphics applications and within GUIs. It is supplemented by extended examples that will be invaluable to providing a framework upon which users can build.

This book is a most worthwhile undertaking and I commend it to all Fortran practitioners. After all, as we have seen, Fortran is in for the long haul.

Michael Metcalf
Tokyo, October 2011

Preface

I have been programming in Fortran for more than 25 years, first in FORTRAN IV and somewhat later in FORTRAN 77. In the last decade of the 20th century, I attended, together with a number of colleagues, a course on Fortran 90, given by the late Jan van Oosterwijk at the Technical University of Delft. It was also around this time that I came to know the comp.lang.fortran newsgroup, and I have learned a lot by participating in that friendly community.

In a way, I am a typical Fortran programmer. My background is physics and I learned the task of programming partly during my study, but mostly on the job. In other ways, I am not because I took a fancy to the more esoteric possibilities of programming in general and sought means to apply them in Fortran. I also began writing articles for the *ACM Fortran Forum*. These articles are the groundwork for this book.

This book will not teach you how to program in Fortran. There are plenty of books dedicated to that ([22], [65]). Instead, the purpose of this book is to show how modern Fortran can be used for modern programming problems, such as how techniques made popular in the world of object-oriented languages like C++ and Java fit neatly into Fortran as it exists today. It even shows some techniques for solving certain programming problems that are not easily achieved in these languages.

If you know Fortran mainly from the days before Fortran 90, you may find the first few chapters to be a gentle introduction to array operations, overloaded operations, and other features that were introduced by that standard. You will find that Fortran has also opened the way to completely different styles of programming, normally associated with *functional* programming languages. Most chapters are dedicated to illustrating how all of these language features can be employed in practice.

In this book, I often refer to software I have written myself and published via the *SourceForge* website or to software I am involved with in some other way. This is not to promote that particular software over anything else – it is merely a consequence of knowing that software very well. I have tried to attribute all of the examples that are not my own to the people who have written them. However, as I am only human, I may have forgotten one or two names.

A book like this can hardly come into existence in isolation. Besides Michael Metcalf and Ian Chivers, the editors of the *ACM Fortran Forum*, and many people who participate in the comp.lang.fortran newsgroup, I am indebted to at least the following people, in no particular order: Bil Kleb, Paul van Delst, Rolf Ade, Henry Gardner, Simon Geard, Richard Suchenwirth, Daniel Kraft, Richard Maine, Steve Lionel, Cameron Laird, and Clif Flynt. I thank them for their discussions, reviewing my contributions, and bringing various aspects of programming, directly related to Fortran or otherwise, to my attention.

The website that accompanies this book, http://flibs.sf.net/examples_modern_fortran.html contains the full source code for the examples. I have run them using the *gfortran* and *Intel Fortran* compilers, mostly on Windows, but also on Linux. As some of these programs use the very latest features of Fortran, you will need a recent version of the compiler of your choice.

Arjen Markus
Rotterdam, November 2011

1.

Introduction to Modern Fortran

Since the publication of the FORTRAN 77 standard in 1978, the Fortran language has undergone a large number of revisions [61].[1] The changes that were introduced reflect both new insights in programming techniques and new developments in computer hardware. From the very start, the language has been designed with computing efficiency in mind. The latest standard as of this writing, Fortran 2008, puts even more emphasis on this aspect by introducing explicit support for parallel processing [71].

This first chapter gives an overview of the various standards that have appeared after FORTRAN 77. There is no attempt to be complete or even to describe all major features, as that would mean a whole book or even a series of books. Consult Metcalf [63], [65] or Brainerd et al. [36] for a detailed description of the standards.

1.1 The Flavor of Modern Fortran

The Fortran 90 standard introduced some very significant changes with respect to the widespread FORTRAN 77 standard: free form source code, array operations, modules, and derived types to name a few. To give an impression of what this means for the programmer, consider this simple problem: you have a file with numbers, one per line (to keep it simple), and you want to determine the distribution of these numbers to produce a simple histogram. In FORTRAN 77, a program that does this might look like the following:

```
*
* Produce a simple histogram
*
      PROGRAM HIST

      INTEGER MAXDATA
      PARAMETER (MAXDATA = 1000)
```

---

[1] Officially, Fortran 77 should be written as *FORTRAN 77*. Since the *Fortran 90* standard, the name is written in lowercase.

```
      INTEGER NOBND
      PARAMETER (NOBND = 9)
      REAL BOUND(NOBND)

      REAL DATA(MAXDATA)
      INTEGER I, NODATA

      DATA BOUND /0.1, 0.3, 1.0, 3.0, 10.0, 30.0,
     &            100.0, 300.0, 1000.0/

      OPEN( 10, FILE = 'histogram.data',
     *                  STATUS = 'OLD', ERR = 900 )
      OPEN( 20, FILE = 'histogram.out' )

      DO 110 I = 1,MAXDATA
          READ( 10, *, END = 120, ERR = 900 ) DATA(I)
  110 CONTINUE
*
  120 CONTINUE
      CLOSE( 10 )
      NODATA = I - 1

      CALL PRHIST( DATA, NODATA, BOUND, NOBND )
      STOP
*
*     File not found, and other errors
*
  900 CONTINUE
      WRITE( *, * ) 'File histogram.data could not be opened'
     &              'or some reading error'

      END


*
* Subroutine to print the histogram
*
      SUBROUTINE PRHIST( DATA, NODATA, BOUND, NOBND )
      REAL DATA(*), BOUND(*)
      INTEGER NODATA, NOBND

      INTEGER I, J, NOHIST

      DO 120 I = 1,NOBND
         NOHIST = 0
         DO 110 J = 1,NODATA
             IF ( DATA(J) .LE. BOUND(I) ) THEN
                 NOHIST = NOHIST + 1
             ENDIF
```

```
110     CONTINUE

        WRITE( 20, '(F10.2,I10)' ) BOUND(I), NOHIST
120 CONTINUE

    END
```

Since Fortran 90, this program can be rewritten in the so-called *free form*, using various inquiry functions and array operations:

```
! Produce a simple histogram
!
program hist
    implicit none

    integer, parameter :: maxdata = 1000
    integer, parameter :: nobnd   = 9

    real, dimension(maxdata) :: data
    real, dimension(nobnd)   :: &
        bound = (/0.1, 0.3, 1.0, 3.0, 10.0, &
                  30.0, 100.0, 300.0, 1000.0/)

    integer                  :: i, nodata, ierr

    open( 10, file = 'histogram.data', status = 'old', &
        iostat = ierr )

    if ( ierr /= 0 ) then
        write( *, * ) 'file histogram.data could not be opened'
        stop
    endif

    open( 20, file = 'histogram.out' )

    do i = 1,size(data)
        read( 10, *, iostat = ierr ) data(i)

        if ( ierr > 0 ) then
            write( *, * ) 'Error reading the data!'
            stop
        elseif ( ierr < 0 ) then
            exit ! Reached the end of the file
        endif
    enddo

    close( 10 )
    nodata = i - 1
```

```fortran
    call print_history( data(1:nodata), bound )

contains

! subroutine to print the histogram
!
subroutine print_history( data, bound )
    real, dimension(:), intent(in) :: data, bound

    integer :: i

    do i = 1,size(bound)
        write( 20, '(f10.2,i10)' ) &
            bound(i), count( data <= bound(i) )
    enddo
end subroutine print_history

end program hist
```

The main differences are:

- Fortran 90 and later allow the free form and lower-case program text, though many FORTRAN 77 compilers did allow for this as well as an extension.
- The introduction of the statement implicit none causes the compiler to check that all variables are actually declared with an explicit type, removing a whole class of programming errors.
- By using an *internal* routine (indicated by the contains statement), you can ensure that the compiler checks the correctness of the actual arguments so far as number and types are concerned.[2]
- You have no more need for the infamous GOTO statement in this program, therefore, it can be replaced by its more structured counterpart exit to terminate the do loop.
- You can use array sections (such as data(1:nodata)) to pass only that part of the array data that is of interest, and the inquiry function size() allows you to get the appropriate number of elements. This also means you can remove the two arguments that indicate the sizes.
- Finally, you have eliminated an entire do loop in the code by using the standard function count() to determine the histogram data.

Note, however, that the first program is still completely valid as far as modern Fortran standards are concerned. This is a very important aspect of Fortran. It means that you can gradually introduce modern features, rather than rewrite an entire program.

---

[2] This is actually only one effect of internal routines – (see Section 1.2).

1.2 Fortran 90

The Fortran 90 standard introduced a large number of features. The best known are perhaps those involving array operations, but there are many more:

- The `implicit none` statement requires the user to explicitly declare all variables and it requires the compiler to check this. Using this feature means typing errors are much less likely to inadvertently introduce new variables.

- *Modules*, together with the *public* and *private* statements or attributes, provide an effective means to partition the entire program into smaller units that can only be accessed when explicitly stated in the source code. Modules furthermore provide explicit interfaces. to the routines they contain, which makes it possible for the compiler to perform all manner of checks and optimizations.

  Should this not be possible (such as when dealing with routines in a different language), you can use *interface blocks*.

- The main program but also subroutines and functions can contain so-called *internal routines*. These routines have access to the variables of the containing routine but provide a new scope in which to define local variables. It is an additional method for modularizing the code.

- As modern computers allow a flexible memory management that was not at all ubiquitous when the FORTRAN 77 standard was published, several features of Fortran 90 relate to managing the memory:

  - *Recursive routines* are now allowed, making it far easier to implement recursive algorithms.
  - Via the *allocate* and *deallocate* statements, programmers can adjust the size of arrays to fit the problem at hand. Arrays whose size can be adjusted come in two flavors: *allocatable* and *pointer*. The former offers more opportunities for optimization, whereas the latter is much more flexible.
  - Besides explicit allocation, the programmer can also use *automatic* arrays – arrays that get their size from the dummy arguments and that are automatically created and destroyed upon entry or exit of a subroutine or function.

- *Array operations* are an important aspect of the Fortran 90 standard, as they allow a concise style of programming and make the optimization task much simpler for the compiler. These operations are supported in arithmetic expressions but also via a collection of generic standard functions.

  Not only can you manipulate an entire array, but you can also select a part, defined by the start, stop, and stride in any dimension.

  User-defined functions can also return arrays as a result, adding to the flexibility and usefulness of array operations.

- Besides the obsolete *fixed form* that characterized Fortran from the start, there is the *free form*, where columns 1 to 6 no longer have a special meaning. This makes source code look much more modern.

- Arrays of values can be constructed on the fly, via so-called array constructors. This is a powerful mechanism that can be put to good use to fill an array with values.

- Just as in most other modern languages, Fortran allows the definition of new data structures. The basic mechanism is that of *derived types*. Derived types consist of components of different types – either basic types, like integers or reals, or other derived types. You can use them in much the same way as the basic types – pass them to subroutines, use them as return values, or create arrays of such types.

  Moreover, you can use derived types to create linked lists, trees, and other well-known abstract data types.

- *Overloading* of routines and operations, such as addition and subtraction, makes it possible to extend the language with new full-blown types. The idea is that you define generic names for specific routines or define +, -, and so forth for numerical types that are not defined by the standard (for instance, rational numbers).

  It is in fact possible to define your own operations. A simple example: suppose your program deals with planar geometrical objects, then it may make sense to define an *intersection* operation on two such objects, `object_a .intersects. object_b`, to replace the call to a function `intersect_objects( object_a, object_b )`.

- Functions and subroutines can now have *optional* arguments, where the function `present()` determines if such an argument is present or not. You can also call functions and subroutines with the arguments in an arbitrary order, as long as you add the names of the dummy arguments, so the compiler can match the actual arguments with the dummy arguments.

  A further enhancement is that you can specify the *intent* of an argument: whether it is input only, output only, or both input and output. This is an aid to documentation as well as an aid to the compiler for certain optimizations.

- *Kinds* are Fortran's way of determining the characteristics of the basic types. For example, you can select single or double precision for real variables not via a different type (`real` or `double precision`) but via the kind:

```
integer, parameter :: double = &
    select_kind_real( precision, range )
real(kind=double)   :: value
```

- Besides the introduction of the `select/case` construct, `do while` loops and do loops without a condition, you can use a name for all control structures. This makes it easier to document the beginning and end of such structures.

  To skip the rest of a do loop's body you can now use the `cycle` statement – possibly with the name of the do loop – so that you can skip more than one do loop in a nested construction. Similarly, the `exit` statement terminates the do loop.

- The Fortran standard defines a large number of functions and subroutines:
  - Numerical inquiry functions for retrieving the properties of the floating-point model.
  - Array manipulation functions that often take an array expression as one of their arguments. For instance, you can count the number of positive elements in an array using:

```
integer, dimension(100,100) :: array
...
write(*,*) 'Number of positive elements:', &
    count( array > 0 )
```

  - Character functions and bit manipulation functions
- Enhancements of the I/O system include nonadvancing I/O. That is, rather than whole records, a program can read or write a part of a record in one statement and the rest in another one.

1.3 Fortran 95

As the Fortran 95 standard is a minor revision of the previous one, the differences mostly concern details. However, these details are important:

- In Fortran 90, variables with the *pointer* attribute could not be initialized. Their initial status was explicitly undefined: neither associated nor not associated. Fortran 95 introduces the *null()* function to initialize pointers explicitly:

```
real, dimension(:), pointer :: ptr => null()
```

- A further enhancement is that local *allocatable* variables without the *save* attribute are automatically deallocated, when they go out of scope (upon returning from a subroutine or function). It is safe for the compiler to do so, as the memory cannot be reached by any means afterwards.
- As a preparation for the next standard, a technical report describes how derived types may contain allocatable components and how functions can return allocatable results. (This technical report has become part of the Fortran 2003 standard with some additions.)
- New features in Fortran 95 are the *pure* and *elemental* routines. Elemental routines release the programmer from having to write versions of a routine for arrays of all the dimensions they want to support. Many functions and subroutines in the standard library already were elemental, meaning they work on individual elements of the arrays that are passed without regard for any order. With the advent of Fortran 95, programmers themselves can also write such routines.

  Pure routines are routines that provide the compiler more opportunities to optimize, as, roughly, they cause no side effects.

- Finally, the *forall* statement must be mentioned, known from High Performance Fortran. It was designed to enhance the capabilities of array operations, but in practice it turns out to be difficult to use properly. (In Fortran 2008, a more flexible construct, *do concurrent*, is introduced.)

1.4 Fortran 2003

Fortran 2003 is also a major revision and its main theme is the introduction of object-oriented programming.[3] However, there are more enhancements, for instance, a standardization of interacting with C routines.

- The support for **object-oriented programming** comes from several new features:
  - Derived types can now contain procedures (functions and subroutines). These are either bound to the type, so that all variables of a particular type have the same actual procedure, or they can be procedures particular to a variable. Such procedures automatically get passed the variable (or object if you like) as one of their arguments, but you can control which one. (We will discuss these matters extensively in Chapter 11.)
  - Derived types can be extended into new types. This is Fortran's inheritance mechanism. An extended type can have new components (both data and procedures), it can redefine the procedures that are bound to the parent type, but it cannot change their signature.
  - The *select* statement has been enhanced to select on the *type* of the variable. This is important if you use so-called *polymorphic* variables – pointer variables whose type comes from the variable they are associated with while the program is running. Polymorphic variables are declared via the *class* keyword instead of the *type* keyword.[4]
  - To enhance the flexibility of the extension mechanism, procedures can be characterized by *abstract interfaces*. Rather than defining a particular routine, these interfaces define what a routine should look like in terms of its argument list and return value. This can then be applied as a mold for actual routines.

- While *procedure pointers* will most often occur within derived types, you can use them as "ordinary" variables as well.
- To achieve certain special effects, the concept of *intrinsic modules* has been introduced. Examples of these special effects are the control of the floating-point environment: rounding mode, the effect of floating-point exceptions,

---

[3] Fortran 90 possesses quite a few features that allow a programmer to come close to that style of programming, but it lacks inheritance, often viewed as one of the important characteristics of object-oriented programming. Fortran 90 is, therefore, sometimes called **object-based.**
[4] Rouson and Adalsteinsson [73] compare the terminology for object-oriented concepts in Fortran and C++.

but also the interfacing to C, as that sometimes requires a different calling and naming convention.

■ Memory management has been enhanced:
  – The length of character strings can now be determined by the `allocate` statement.
  – Under some circumstances an allocatable array can be automatically reallocated to the correct size.
  – It is possible to move the allocated memory from one variable to the next via the *move_alloc* routine. This makes it easier to expand an array.

■ Another welcome new feature is that of *stream access* to files. This makes it possible to read (and write) files without attention to complete records. In particular, it makes it possible to read and write binary files that contain no intrinsic structure, unlike the traditional *unformatted* files that do have a record structure and are cumbersome to deal with in other programming languages.

■ Fortran 2003 also standardizes the access to the system's environment in the form of *environment variables* and to the command-line arguments that were used to start the program. Previously, you had to use all manner of compiler-specific solutions to access this information.

1.5 Fortran 2008

The Fortran 2008 standard is a minor revision to the language, even though it defines a rather large new feature: coarrays. These are discussed more fully in Chapter 12 [72], [71]. Besides these, the standard defines a number of new constructs and keywords as well as new standard functions:

■ Coarrays are a mechanism for parallel computing that falls in the category of *Partitioned Global Address Space* (PGAS). Essentially, it makes data available on various copies of the program without the programmer having to worry about the exact methods that have to be used to transfer the data. It is the compiler's job to generate code that does this efficiently and effectively.

■ Arrays can be defined to be *contiguous*. This enables the compiler to generate more efficient code, as the array elements are adjacent in memory.

■ The *block – end block* construct defines a local scope within a program or routine, so that new variables can be declared that are present only within that block.

■ Modules as introduced in Fortran 90 are an important mechanism to modularize a program. However, the module mechanism itself does not allow much modularization, as the entire module must be compiled. Fortran 2003 introduces *submodules* to overcome the problem of very large source files containing a large module. An additional enhancement is the *import* feature. This is used in interface blocks to import a definition from the containing module, instead of having to define a second module containing just the definitions you require.

- To further reduce the need for a GOTO statement, the *exit* statement can be used to jump to the end of if blocks and select blocks.
- The *do concurrent* statement may be regarded as a more flexible alternative to the *forall* statement/block. It indicates to the compiler that the code can be run in parallel (note that this is parallellism within the same *copy*, not between copies as with coarrays).
- *Internal procedures* may now be passed as actual arguments, thus giving access to the variables in the routine that contains them. It makes certain interface problems easier to solve (see Chapter 5).
- New standard functions include various Bessel functions and bit inquiry functions.

1.6 What Has Not Changed?

The introduction of all these new features to the Fortran language does not have consequences for existing code that adheres to one or the other standards, with the exception of a few features that have been deleted or obsoleted.[5]

Apart from such deleted, and perhaps almost forgotten features, like the assigned GOTO, old code should still work.[6]

There are in fact more *invariants* in the design of modern Fortran, besides this support for old code:

- Fortran is case-insensitive, contrary to many other programming languages in use today.
- There is no concept of a *file* as an organizational unit for the source code. In particular, there can be no code outside the program, subroutine, function, or module.
- The design of Fortran is biased to efficient execution. This is especially so in the latest Fortran 2008 standard, in which features have been added to help the compiler in the creation of fast and efficient programs.

  The details may surprise programmers who are used to languages like C (see Appendix B).
- The data type of an expression or subexpression depends solely on the operands and the operation, not on the context. This makes reasoning about a program much easier, but again it may cause surprises (Appendix B). Here is an example:

```
real :: r

r = 1 / 3
```

---

[5] The most important of these deleted features is the use of real variables to control a do loop ([68], Section 2.1.5).
[6] Most compilers continue to support such features, so that old programs can still be compiled and run.

The value of the variable r is 0.0, not 0.333333..., as the two integers are divided first, yielding a new integer. Then that integer is converted to a real.

The same separation of concern holds for array operations:

```
integer, dimension(10) :: array
array = 2 * array(10:1:-1)
```

This statement is executed (at least conceptually) as:

```
integer, dimension(10) :: array
integer, dimension(10) :: tmp
integer                :: i

! First evaluate the right-hand side and store the result
! in a temporary array
do i = 1,10
    tmp(i) = 2 * array(11-i)
enddo

! Now copy the right-hand side into the array left of the
! equal sign
do i = 1,10
    array(i) = tmp(i)
enddo
```

This means that code like the preceding simply works, even though the right-hand side involves the same array elements as the left-hand side, but in a different order.

2.

Array-Valued Functions

Along with array operations the Fortran 90 standard introduced the concept of functions returning arrays. Such functions can be used for a very compact, high-level programming style, much like what John Backus, the "father" of Fortran, advocated in his speech for accepting the ACM Award [13].

While Fortran 90 allowed the programmer to define functions that return arrays of data, Fortran 95 introduced the concept of elemental functions and procedures. In combination with several features were introduced in Fortran 2003, these have become even more powerful and easy to use.

Many of the intrinsic functions work directly on arrays and Fortran's array operations transform one array into another, without the need for explicit loops that can obscure the programmer's goal. For example, suppose you have an array of data and you want to print only those values that are larger than some threshold. One way of doing that is:

```
do i = 1,size(data)
    if ( data(i) > threshold ) then
        write( *, '(f10.4)' ) data(i)
    endif
enddo
```

If you use the pack() intrinsic function, this can be written more compactly:

```
write( *, '(f10.4)' ) pack( data, data > threshold )
```

2.1 Passing Arrays

The standard function pack() returns only those elements of an array for which the accompanying logical array elements are true. For example:

```
integer, dimension(5) :: x = (/ 1, 2, 3, 4, 5 /)

write(*,*) pack( x, x > 3 )
```

prints the numbers 4 and 5, because these are the only elements of the array x that are greater than 3. The result is always an array, even if there is only one element that fits the condition, or even no elements at all, since zero-sized arrays are allowed.

You can pass the result of pack() to another function or subroutine, such as one that determines basic statistical properties:

```
write( *, '(a,f10.4)') 'Mean of values above mean:', &
    mean( pack( data, data > mean(data) ) )
```

with mean() looking like:

```
real function mean( data )
    real, dimension(:) :: data

    mean = sum(data)/max(1,size(data))

end function mean
```

Compare this to an approach with work arrays (so that you can reuse the mean() function):

```
real, dimension(...)        :: data
real, dimension(size(data)) :: work ! Work array for selected data

meanv = mean(data)
count = 0

do i = 1,size(data)
    if ( data(i) > meanv ) then
        count = count + 1
        work(count) = data(i)
    endif
enddo

write( *, '(a,f10.4)') 'Mean of values above mean:', &
    mean( work(1:count) )
```

Or, bypass the mean() function, because it is so simple:

```
meanv = mean(data)   ! We do need to determine the threshold

sumv  = 0.0
count = 0
do i = 1,size(data)
    if ( data(i) > meanv ) then
        count = count + 1
        sumv  = sumv  + data(i)
    endif
enddo

write( *, '(a,f10.4)') 'Mean of values above mean:', &
    sumv/max(1,count)
```

In consequence, using such functions can lead to more compact, and, in many cases, clearer code. But they do have drawbacks:

- You cannot access individual elements directly. For instance, to determine the second largest element of an array, you need to first store the result of a sort function to a separate array.
- Similarly, if you need the result in more than one place, you have to copy it to an actual array or pass it to a function or subroutine.
- The functions produce intermediate arrays that need to be allocated and deallocated at appropriate times. This may influence the performance of the program.

Whether these drawbacks are a serious problem greatly depends on the context in which this feature is used. The style of programming is, at the very least, quite economic in terms of lines of code and it conveys the purpose much more clearly. Also compilers improve all the time, so performance should not be your first concern.

Performance with Array-Valued Functions   To illustrate the difference in performance, the mean value of random numbers larger than a threshold is computed using two different methods:

- Filter the data that are larger than the threshold via pack() and determine the mean from that:

```
call random_data( data )
...
call mean_pack( pack( data, data > threshold ), mean1 )
```

Implement the subroutine mean_pack as:

```
subroutine mean_pack( data, mean )
    real, dimension(:) :: data
    real               :: mean

    mean = sum(data)/max(1,size(data))

end subroutine mean_pack
```

- Pass the complete array (filled with the same random numbers) to a subroutine that selects the data and determines the sum in a do loop:

```
call random_data( data )
...
call mean_do_loop( data, threshold, mean2 )
```

Implement the subroutine in question as:

```
subroutine mean_do_loop( data, threshold, mean )
    real, dimension(:) :: data
    real               :: threshold
    real               :: mean
```

Table 2.1. Elapsed Time for Determining the Mean of an Array of Data (time in clock ticks)			
Total Number of Data	**Using a Do Loop**	**Using Array Operations**	**Ratio**
1000	16	47	2.9
10000	62	172	2.8
100000	556	1219	2.2
1000000	6594	12515	1.9

```
integer          :: i
integer          :: count

mean  = 0.0
count = 0
do i = 1,size(data)
    if ( data(i) > threshold ) then
        mean  = mean  + data(i)
        count = count + 1
    endif
enddo

mean = mean / max(1,count)

end subroutine mean_do_loop
```

The elapsed time is measured using the system_clock subroutine: the system time is requested before and after a loop in which each of the methods is called 1000 times. The difference between these times is a measure for the elapsed time (in clock ticks). The results are shown in Table 2.1.

These times are merely indications of the relative performance of the two methods. Much depends on the compiler that is used as well as the compiler options. For example, results with another compiler indicate that the ratio between the two timings may increase with increasing array size.

2.2 Elemental Functions and Automatic Reallocation

In Fortran 90, only the standard functions and the array operations can be used for arrays of any dimensions. For instance, it makes no difference if you use the sine function on a scalar, one-dimensional array, or n-dimensional array – the code remains the same. If you want to do the same for a function implementing the Bessel J_0 function, then you need a version for scalar arguments, one-dimensional array arguments, and so on as well as introduce an interface to hide the separate names.

Fortran 95 introduced the so-called *elemental* functions and subroutines. They have to satisfy a number of conditions, as the order in which the function works on the various array elements is conceptually undefined, meaning a single version suffices:

```
program test_j0
    real                     :: scalar
    real, dimension(10,10) :: matrix

    scalar = 1.0
    call random_number( matrix )
    matrix = matrix * 100.0

    write(*,*)              'J0(1) = ', j0(scalar)
    write(*,*)              'Random values x in the range (0,100):'
    write(*,'(10f10.4)' ) j0(matrix)

contains

real elemental function j0( x )
    real :: x

    j0 = ...
end function j0
end program test_j0
```

This is quite useable if the return value of the function is the same shape as the input argument(s). If not, then elemental functions cannot be used.

If you do not know in advance how many elements the result will contain, as is quite often the case with the pack() function, then it is difficult to assign the result to an array – the shapes need to match. However, a feature introduced in Fortran 2003 solves this problem rather elegantly via *allocatable* arrays:

```
    real, dimension(:), allocatable :: positive_values

    positive_values = pack( data, data > 0.0 )
```

Using this feature,[1] the array on the left-hand side of the preceding statement is reallocated automatically to the right size and shape, if that is necessary to assign the result.

2.3 Two More Advanced Examples

The following two examples are more elaborate: a number-theoretical problem and a compact implementation of the QuickSort algorithm.

---

[1] At least one compiler requires a special option to turn on this feature.

Spacing of Irrational Numbers

This first example requires a bit of explanation: it is a number-theoretical problem regarding the spacing of irrational numbers [66]. The numbers considered are (α, an irrational number):

$$V = \{x \mid x = n\alpha \ mod \ 1, n = 1 \ .. \ N\} \tag{2.1}$$

If you sort these numbers, the spacing between successive numbers takes only one of three distinct values (here the interval [0,1) is wrapped, so that 0.9 and 0.1 are 0.2 apart, not 0.8). The following program demonstrates this. It constructs an array of these numbers, sorts them (using a simple algorithm), and prints the spacings:

```fortran
program nearest_neighbors
    implicit none
    integer :: i

    write(*,'(f10.4)') &
        cdiff( sort( (/ (mod(i*sqrt(2.0),1.0) ,i=1,20) /) ) )

contains

function cdiff( array )
    real, dimension(:) :: array
    real, dimension(size(array)) :: cdiff

    cdiff = abs( array - cshift(array,1) )
    cdiff = min( cdiff, 1.0 - cdiff )
end function cdiff

function sort( array )
    real, dimension(:)              :: array
    real, dimension(size(array)) :: sort

    real                      :: temp
    integer                   :: i, j
    integer, dimension(1)     :: pos

    !
    ! Retrieve the lowest elements one by one
    !
    sort = array
    do i = 1,size(sort)
        pos    = minloc( sort(i:) )
        j      = i + pos(1) - 1
        temp   = sort(j)
```

```
        sort(j) = sort(i)
        sort(i) = temp
    enddo
end function sort
end program nearest_neighbors
```

In this example, the sort() function works by finding the position of the smallest value first and then exchanging that value with the value in the first non-sorted position. Note that the minloc() function returns an array (one element for each dimension) and that you need to correct the index returned, as it is relative to the start of the array section.

A more traditional program looks like this, adapting the contents of the array data directly:

```
program nearest_neighbors
    implicit none
    integer :: i
    integer, parameter :: n = 20
    real, dimension(n) :: data

    do i = 1,n
        data(i) = mod(i*sqrt(2.0),1.0)
    enddo

    call sort( data )
    call cdiff( data )

    write(*,'(f10.4)') data

contains

subroutine cdiff( array )
    real, dimension(:) :: array
    real, dimension(size(array)) :: work
    integer :: i

    do i = 1,size(array)-1
        work(i) = array(i+1) - array(i)
    enddo
    work(size(array)) = array(size(array)) - array(1)

    do i = 1,size(array)
        array(i) = min( abs(work(i)), abs(1.0-work(i)) )
    enddo
end subroutine
```

```
subroutine sort( array )
    real, dimension(:) :: array

    real    :: temp
    integer :: i, j

    do i = 1,size(array)
        do j = i+1,size(array)
            if ( array(i) > array(j) ) then
                temp = array(i)
                array(i) = array(j)
                array(j) = temp
            endif
        enddo
    enddo

end subroutine sort
end program nearest_neighbors
```

QuickSort

With array constructors, you can do even more surprising things. This implementation of the well-known QuickSort algorithm may not be fast (and it consumes more memory than necessary), but it is rather compact:

```
recursive function qsort_reals( data ) result( sorted )
    real, dimension(:), intent(in) :: data
    real, dimension(1:size(data))  :: sorted

    if ( size(data) > 1 ) then
        sorted = &
        (/ qsort_reals( pack( data(2:), data(2:) > data(1) ) ), &
           data(1),                                             &
           qsort_reals( pack( data(2:), data(2:) <= data(1) ) ) /)
    else
        sorted = data
    endif
end function qsort_reals
```

These eleven lines of code have two important properties:

- Arrays in Fortran can have length 0, which removes the need for a number of special cases in this function.
- The conditions are carefully chosen so that the constructed array has exactly the same length as the input array. The function should also work if the same value occurs multiple times.

Table 2.2. Tabulated Function, Illustrating Linear Interpolation in Two Dimensions. Cell Containing (12.0, I6.7) Highlighted

y\x	...	5.0	10.0	25.0	100.0	...
...	...	...	...	...	...	...
2.5	...	0.1	0.9	2.3	7.8	...
5.0	...	0.5	**2.0**	**3.5**	11.0	...
10.0	...	1.4	**3.1**	**4.7**	12.5	...
20.0	...	2.6	5.3	6.5	14.0	...
...	...	...	...	...	...	...

The construction of a more traditional version is left as an exercise. You can also experiment with a more robust version that has better worst-case behavior.

2.4 Concise Style

This style of programming is not always the best way to solve a problem: the preceding QuickSort routine creates multiple copies of the array during the recursion – roughly, $^2log\,N$ times – but if used carefully, it helps create programs that are easy to understand.

The following is another example of a concise solution to a programming problem. Suppose you have a tabulated function with three independent variables and you need to find the value for a particular triple of these variables via multidimensional linear interpolation (see Table 2.2 for an illustration of the two-dimensional case). First, you need to find the "cell" within which the triple lies and the weighing factors in each dimension (this can be done for each dimension). Say this has the indices (i1,i2,i3) to (i1+1,i2+1,i3+1), with weights (w1,w2,w3). For the interpolation only the values at the corners of this cell are required, so you can extract them into an array of $2 \times 2 \times 2$ elements:

```
real, dimension(:,:,:) :: table
real, dimension(2,2,2) :: cell

cell = table(i1:i1+1,i2:i2+1,i3:i3+1)
```

If you use an explicit formula for the interpolation, you need to write down all eight terms, and for higher dimensions even more. However, the interpolation can also be done per dimension: simply compute the values at a slice through the cell, thereby reducing the dimension by 1. Repeat until the dimension of the cell is reduced to zero. This is elegantly expressed in the Fortran code:

```
cell(:,:,1) = w3 * cell(:,:,1) + (1.0-w3) * cell(:,:,2)
cell(:,1,1) = w2 * cell(:,1,1) + (1.0-w2) * cell(:,2,1)
cell(1,1,1) = w1 * cell(1,1,1) + (1.0-w1) * cell(2,1,1)

result = cell(1,1,1)
```

It is trivial to extend this code to any number of dimensions, as long as you stay within the maximum number of dimensions that the standard allows.

3.

Mathematical Abstractions

The features of Fortran 90 and later to define operations for derived types, to use array operations, and, for Fortran 2003 and later, to store procedure pointers allow a high-level style of programming that can be likened to *functional* programming languages such as *Lisp*. We will discuss several examples: automatic differentiation, integer programming, Diophantine equations, and dynamic expressions.

3.1 Automatic Differentiation

When solving stiff differential equations or finding the roots of some function, you often use the first derivative of the functions involved. It is, of course, possible to implement the function and its derivative explicitly, but that is error-prone if the function is even mildly complicated. For example, let the function f be defined as:

$$f(x) = \frac{x}{(1 - x^2)^2} - \frac{e^{-x}}{1 + \cos^2 x} \tag{3.1}$$

Here is the first derivative:

$$f'(x) = \frac{1 + 3x^2}{(1 - x^2)^3} - e^{-x} \frac{1 + \cos^2 x - \sin 2x}{(1 + \cos^2 x)^2} \tag{3.2}$$

Determining the derivative of a function is a completely mechanical process. You just follow the basic rules. Because of this property we can automate it using overloaded operators [38].

We start with a derived type, autoderiv:

```
type autoderiv
    real :: v
    real :: dv
end type autoderiv
```

In this type, the component v represents the value of the independent variable or the function value and dv, the derivative. Summing two such variables is done using this function:

```
function add_vv( x, y ) result( z )
    type(autoderiv), intent(in) :: x
    type(autoderiv), intent(in) :: y
    type(autoderiv)             :: z

    z%v  = x%v  + y%v
    z%dv = x%dv + y%dv
end function add_vv
```

Multiplying them is a bit more complicated, as you need to use the multiplication rule for the derivative components (note the intent(in) attributes, these are required later on):

```
function mult_vv( x, y ) result( z )
    type(autoderiv), intent(in) :: x
    type(autoderiv), intent(in) :: y
    type(autoderiv)             :: z

    z%v  = x%v  * y%v
    z%dv = x%dv * y%v + x%v * y%dv
end function mult_vv
```

Likewise, you define functions for subtraction, division, and all mathematical functions you are interested in. Via interface blocks you then tie these functions to the arithmetical operations:

```
interface operator(+)
    module procedure add_vv
end interface
interface operator(*)
    module procedure mult_vv
end interface
```

Next apply this technique to the function $f(x) = \cos x / (1 + x^2) - \frac{1}{2}$:

```
function f( x ) result( z )
    type(autoderiv), intent(in) :: x
    type(autoderiv)             :: z

    z = cos(x) / (1 + x**2 ) - 0.5
end function f
```

Because of the overloading, the function looks just like a normal mathematical function, only the return type and the type of the arguments is special.

This main program prints the function value and its first derivative:

```
program print_table
    use automatic_differentiation

    type(autoderiv) :: x, y

    do i = 0,10
        x%v  = 0.1 * i
        x%dv = 1.0       ! x is the variable we differentiate to

        y = f(x)

        write(*,'(310.4)') x%v, y%v, y%dv
    enddo
contains
    function f( x ) result( z )
        ...
    end function f
end program print_table
```

You can apply the technique to find the root of equation $f(x) = 0$ using Newton's method. Mathematically, the method is expressed as:

$$x_{k+1} = x_k - \frac{f(x_k)}{f'(x_k)} \qquad (3.3)$$

where x_{k+1} is the new estimate of the root, if the iteration converges. Put into a subroutine, it looks like:

```
subroutine find_root( f, xinit, tolerance, root, found )
    use automatic_differentiation

    interface
        function f(x)
            use automatic_differentiation
            type(autoderiv), intent(in) :: x
            type(autoderiv)             :: f
        end function
    end interface

    type(autoderiv), intent(in)  :: xinit
    type(autoderiv), intent(out) :: root
    real                         :: tolerance
    logical                      :: found

    integer                      :: iter
    integer, parameter           :: maxiter = 1000
    type(autoderiv)              :: fvalue
```

```
type(autoderiv)                    :: newroot

found   = .false.
root    = xinit
root%dv = 1.0

do iter = 1,maxiter

    fvalue = f(root)

    newroot = root - fvalue%v / fvalue%dv
    found   = abs( newroot%v - root%v ) < tolerance
    root    = newroot

    if ( found .or. abs(root%v) > huge(1.0)/10.0 ) exit
enddo

end subroutine find_root
```

The interface to the function passed as an argument is non-trivial, therefore, you need to explicitly define what kind of function you are using. This is done with an interface block:[1]

```
interface
    function f(x)
        use automatic_differentiation
        type(autoderiv), intent(in) :: x
        type(autoderiv)             :: f
    end function
end interface
```

Inside an interface block, you must use the module that contains the definition of the derived type, either via a use statement or via Fortran 2003's import statement.

Note that the loop used to find the root stops on three criteria (see also Chapter 10):

- If the new estimate is within the error margin of the previous estimate.
- If the maximum number of iterations is reached.
- If the iteration does not seem to converge: the root is becoming larger and larger.

The technique is not limited to functions of one variable or to the first derivative. It is quite possible to expand it to functions of two or three variables:

```
type autoderiv_two_vars
    real :: v
    real :: dvdx
    real :: dvdy
end type autoderiv_two_vars
```

---

[1] With Fortran 2003 and later you can also use *abstract interfaces* (see Section 11.2).

As an example, the multiplication rule then becomes:

```
function mult_vv( x, y ) result( z )
    type(autoderiv_two_vars), intent(in) :: x
    type(autoderiv_two_vars), intent(in) :: y
    type(autoderiv_two_vars)             :: z

    z%v     = x%v     * y%v
    z%dvdx = x%dvdx * y%v + x%v * y%dvdx
    z%dvdy = x%dvdy * y%v + x%v * y%dvdy
end function mult_vv
```

To determine $\frac{\partial f}{\partial x}$ and $\frac{\partial f}{\partial y}$, you must use the right "vectors": $x = (x_0, 1, 0)$ and
$y = (y_0, 0, 1)$.

For the function $f(x, y) = xy$, the result will then be:

$$f\%v = x_0 \cdot y_0 \tag{3.4}$$

$$f\%dvdx = 1 \cdot y_0 + x_0 \cdot 0 = y_0 \tag{3.5}$$

$$f\%dvdy = 0 \cdot y_0 + x_0 \cdot 1 = x_0 \tag{3.6}$$

Of course, the implementation gets more complicated with higher-order derivatives and more variables, but the principle remains the same.

Numerical Aspects The technique of automatic differentiation does have a few problems. First of all, it does not work well if the function in question has a "removable" singular point, like the *sinc* function. However, more seriously, *catastrophic cancellation* can occur. Here is an example:

$$f(x) = \frac{\ln x}{x - 1} \quad (x \neq 1) \tag{3.7}$$

$$f(x) = 1 \quad (x = 1) \tag{3.8}$$

The first derivative of this function is:

$$f'(x) = \frac{1}{x(x - 1)} - \frac{\ln x}{(x - 1)^2} \tag{3.9}$$

$$= \frac{x - 1 - x \ln x}{x(x - 1)^2} \tag{3.10}$$

which tends to $-\frac{1}{2}$ for $x \to 1$.

If you compute the derivative around $x = 1$ using the automatic differentiation module, a very large relative error is observed around $x = 1.00001$ (see Figure 3.1). The cause is the fact that the two contributions to the derivative in

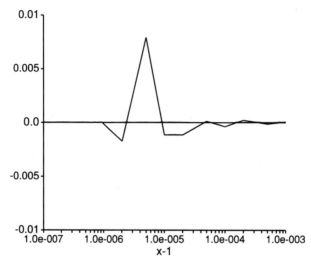

Figure 3.1. Error in determining the first derivative of the function
$f(x) = \frac{\ln x}{x-1}$ around $x = 1$

Equation 3.9 are computed separately – both are large numbers near $x = 1$ – and the two contributions are subtracted. This leads to a severe loss of accuracy.

If you use the rearranged version and approximate the logarithm with a Taylor series, the result is a well-behaved function. Such a rearrangement can not be taken care of with automatic differentiation alone.

3.2 Integer Programming

As a second example, consider the following problem: For integer $x, y \geq 0$, find the pair (x, y) for which $f(x, y) = 3x + 4y$ is maximal, subject to the constraints:

$$10x + 3y \leq 200 \tag{3.11}$$

$$3x + 7y \leq 121 \tag{3.12}$$

You can tackle this problem with brute force: Due to the constraints x must be between 0 and 20 and y lies in the range [0,17]. Therefore, looping over all pairs (x, y) within that region will give the desired answer.

Using array operations and suitable derived types you can solve this problem in a more elegant way:

```
type(integer_set)       :: xset
type(integer_set)       :: yset
type(integer_pair_set) :: c
```

```
integer, dimension(1)  :: idx

xset = range(0,20)                ! x values in the required range
yset = range(0,17)                ! ditto for y

c = cartesian_product(xset,yset) ! create all pairs
```

You first define the sets of integers you will use, xset and yset, and a set c of integer pairs that contains all pairs (x, y) with x and y in the allowed range.

Then, you impose the actual set of constraints 3.11 and 3.12 from the problem you want to solve:

```
!
! Select those pairs that fulfill the first two conditions
!
c = select( c, 10*x(c)+3*y(c) <= 200 )
c = select( c,  3*x(c)+7*y(c) <= 121 )
```

Now you have all (x, y) pairs that could possibly be candidates. The last step is to pick out the one that maximizes $f(x, y) = 3x + 4y$:

```
idx = maxloc( 3*x(c) + 4*y(c) )

write(*,*) 'Solution: ', getelem(c,idx(1))
```

Note: The auxiliary function getelem hides the details of the derived type integer_pair_set and the intrinsic function maxloc returns an array of indices, even if its argument is a one-dimensional array; x and y are functions that return the x- and y-coordinates, respectively.

Memory Management What is conveniently hidden from the user is the management of the memory involved. Rather than relying on the default assignment method for derived types a custom routine is used to set variables of the types integer_set and integer_pair_set:

- The derived type integer_set contains an array of elements that needs to be adjusted in size to fit the intended set:

```
type integer_set
    logical                          :: from_function
    integer, dimension(:), pointer :: elements => null()
end type integer_set
```

- The default assignment is overwritten by two module procedures:

```
interface assignment(=)
    module procedure assign_set
    module procedure assign_pair_set
end interface
```

- If the right-hand side in an assignment is the result of a function, the component `from_function` in the derived type is set to `.true.`, so that the memory can be pointed to instead of newly allocated:

```
subroutine assign_set( setleft, setright )
    type(integer_set), intent(inout) :: setleft
    type(integer_set), intent(in)    :: setright

    setleft%from_function = .false
    if ( associated(setleft%elements) ) then
        deallocate( setleft%elements )
    endif
    if ( .not. setright%from_function ) then
        allocate( setleft%elements(size(setright%elements)) )
        setleft%elements = setright%elements
    else
        setleft%elements => setright%elements
    endif

end subroutine assign_set
```

In Fortran 2003, you have the `move_alloc` routine, so that you can use a very similar technique for allocatable components. You can even rely on automatic reallocation:

```
if ( .not. setright%from_function ) then
    setleft%elements = setright%elements
else
    call move_alloc( setright%elements, setleft%elements )
endif
```

3.3 Enumerating Solutions of Diophantine Equations

Procedure pointers, as defined in Fortran 2003, make it possible to enumerate the solutions of Diophantine equations in a very generic way. Such equations take only integer or rational solutions. One example is Fermat's famous *last theorem* – $x^n + y^n = z^n$, which has no non-trivial solutions for $n > 2$. Pell's equation [82]:

$$y^2 = Ax^2 \pm 1 \quad (A \text{ square free}) \tag{3.13}$$

is another well-known example. Contrary to Fermat's theorem, these equations do have solutions and even an infinitude of solutions. One way of looking at this equation is: Consider the left-hand side and the right-hand side as separate sets of points (x, t) and (y, s):

$$S_1 = \{(x, t) \mid t = Ax^2 + 1, x \in N\} \tag{3.14}$$

$$S_2 = \{(y, s) \mid s = y^2, y \in N\} \tag{3.15}$$

Then consider what is the set S_3 defined as:

$$S_3 = \{(x, y) \mid (x, t) \in S_1 \wedge (y, s) \in S_2 \wedge t = s\} \qquad (3.16)$$

If you assume that t and s in these sets are increasing functions of x and y, then a simple algorithm suffices to determine the elements of S_3:

1. Set x and y to 0.
2. Determine $t = Ax^2 + 1$ and $s = y^2$.
3. If $t = s$, you have found a solution.
4. If $t < s$, increase x by 1 and go to step 2.
5. If $t > s$, increase y by 1 and go to step 2.

To implement this mathematical algorithm, use a derived type that can store the descriptions in Equations 3.14 and 3.15:

```
type enum_func
    type(enum_func), pointer                    :: f    => null()
    type(enum_func), pointer                    :: g    => null()
    procedure(enumeration), pointer, pass(t) :: enum => null()
end type enum_func
```

This type uses the feature that you can refer *recursively* to the same type. It also uses an abstract interface to define what kind of procedures enum you will deal with (see Chapter 11, which also discusses the class keyword):

```
abstract interface
    integer function enumeration( t, idx )
        import :: enum_func
        class(enum_func), intent(in) :: t
        integer, intent(in)          :: idx
    end function enumeration
end interface
```

The sets S_1 and S_2 are implemented using these two functions:

```
integer function y_square( t, idx )
    class(enum_func), intent(in) :: t    ! Not used
    integer, intent(in)          :: idx

    y_square = idx ** 2

end function y_square

integer function x_pell( t, idx )
    class(enum_func), intent(in) :: t    ! Not used
    integer, intent(in)          :: idx

    x_pell = 2 * idx ** 2 + 1

end function x_pell
```

The set S_3 requires a bit more work, but the preceding algorithm is contained in the function combine:

```fortran
integer function combine( t, idx )
    class(enum_func), intent(in) :: t
    integer, intent(in)          :: idx

    integer                      :: count, i, j, fi, gj

    count = 0
    i     = 0
    j     = 0

    fi = t%f%enum(i)
    gj = t%g%enum(j)

    do while ( count < idx )

        if ( fi == gj ) then
            count = count + 1
            i     = i     + 1
        else if ( fi < gj ) then
            i = i + 1
        else
            j = j + 1
        endif
        fi = t%f%enum(i)
        gj = t%g%enum(j)

    enddo

    combine = i - 1

end function combine
```

All you have to do now is to create the Fortran equivalent of set S_3 and to enumerate a number of its elements:

```fortran
xright = func( x_pell )
yleft  = func( y_square )

xpell  = combination( xright, yleft, combine )
ypell  = combination( yleft, xright, combine )

do i = 1,5
    x = xpell%enum(i)
    y = ypell%enum(i)
    write(*,*) '>>', i, x, y
enddo
```

where the function func() is merely a convenience function to set the enum component:

```
function func( f )
    procedure(enumeration)        :: f
    type(enum_func)               :: func

    func%enum => f

end function func
```

The output of the program is:

```
>>         1         0         1
>>         2         2         3
>>         3        12        17
>>         4        70        99
>>         5       408       577
```

By inserting other functions, such as $h(x) = x^3 + 2$, you can solve other Diophantine equations. Of course, the implementation of combine assumes that there *are* solutions and you tacitly ignore the fact that the integers you use have a finite range. However, these are mere practical details that obscure the principle, which is the reformulation of a mathematical problem into a Fortran program that closely resembles the mathematics.

3.4 Delayed Evaluation

You can take the overloading of operations one step further. Instead of running the routines that do the computations immediately, you will *store* the operation. You do this by creating an expression parse tree, so that you can evaluate it later. In this way, you can create new expressions, new functions if you like, within the running program. You cannot quite use the same syntax as ordinary functions, but you do get the effect.

Here is a simple example:

```
type(integer_operand), target    :: x
type(integer_operand), target    :: y

type(integer_relation), pointer :: relation

!
! Store the relation, NOT the result
!
relation => x + y == 0

x = 1
y = -1
write(*,*) 'x, y: 1, -1 ', integer_relation_eval( relation )
```

```
x = 2
y = -1
write(*,*) 'x, y: 2, -1 ', integer_relation_eval( relation )
```

First, set a variable `relation` that holds the relation between two variables x and y that can be considered to be place holders for integer values. Then by *assigning* an actual value to these variables, you determine whether the relation holds or not. The hard work is done by the functions `integer_relation_eval` and `integer_eval`:

```
function integer_relation_eval( relation ) result(value)
    type(integer_relation)   :: relation
    logical                  :: value

    call integer_eval( relation%first  )
    call integer_eval( relation%second )

    select case( relation%relation )
    case ( 1 )
        !
        ! Relation: equality
        !
        value = relation%first%value == relation%second%value
    case ( 2 )

        ... other relations (>, <, ...)
    end select

end function integer_relation_eval
```

The function `integer_eval` is a recursive function that looks like this:

```
recursive subroutine integer_eval( x )
    type(integer_operand)   :: x

    if ( associated( x%first  ) ) call integer_eval( x%first  )
    if ( associated( x%second ) ) call integer_eval( x%second )

    select case( x%operation )
    case ( 0 )
        ! Nothing to be done

    case ( 1 )
        x%value = x%first%value + x%second%value

    case ( 2 )
        x%value = x%first%value * x%second%value

    case ( 3 )
        x%value = x%first%value ** x%second%value
```

```
    case default
       ! Nothing to be done
    end select

end subroutine integer_eval
```

The secret is that for the derived type integer_operand you have overloaded operations that store what operation was called and with what operands, rather than do the actual computation:

```
function integer_add( x, y ) result(add)
    type(integer_operand), intent(in), target  :: x
    type(integer_operand), intent(in), target  :: y
    type(integer_operand), pointer              :: add

    allocate( add )

    add%operation =  1
    add%first      => x
    add%second     => y
end function integer_add
```

Note that the function result, defined via the result variable add, is a pointer variable – it must persist after the statement has been executed.

The previous example concerns a very simple relation, but you can extend this to Pell's equation or any relation between numbers. The following full example shows how to create a set of pairs of integers that can then be queried:

```
type(integer_operand), target   :: x
type(integer_operand), target   :: y

type(integer_pair_set)           :: set

write(*,*) 'Does the set {(x,y) | y**2 = 3*x**2 + 1} &
    &contain (1,2) or (3,3)?'

set = create_pair_set( y**2 == 3*x**2 + 1, range(x, 0, 0), &
                                           range(y, 0, 0)  )

write(*,*) '(1,2) in this set? ', has_element(set, (/1,2/))
write(*,*) '(3,3) in this set? ', has_element(set, (/3,3/))
```

The program produces the expected output:

```
Does the set {(x,y) | y**2 = 3*x**2 + 1} contain (1,2) or (3,3)?
(1,2) in this set?  T
(3,3) in this set?  F
```

Note the following important concepts:

- The function range is a means to examine all values of x and y within the given range, so that the pairs for which the relation holds can be added to a cache. In this case, with only 0 in the range, nothing will be added to that cache.
- The function has_element simply checks whether the given pair of integers is part of the set. It does this by evaluating the stored relation with the given pair as the values for the two variables x and y.

Thus, using Fortran 90 features, you can implement a style of programming that seems at first sight impossible in a compiled, statically typed language like Fortran.

4.

Memory Management

The introduction of allocatable arrays and pointers has made it much easier to create programs that can adapt their memory requirements to the problem at hand. As a side effect though, memory management, in the sense of allocating and deallocating arrays, has become an issue that needs to be addressed.

4.1 Flexible Arrays

Fortran 90 and later provides three ways of creating arrays of flexible size:

- **Automatic arrays** are created when a subroutine or function is entered and they are automatically destroyed when returning from the routine. This type of arrays is perfectly suited for work arrays. The only drawback is that they are often created on the *stack* of the program and, therefore, they should not become too large.[1]

  Something similar can be done with character strings: the length of local character variables in routines can be dynamic, as shown in Section 4.4.

- **Allocatable arrays** require an explicit `allocate` statement, but as long as they do not have the `save` attribute, the compiler will clean them up on return from a routine (from Fortran 95 on). Of course, you can deallocate such arrays explicitly if you no longer need them.

- **Pointers** are the most flexible type of memory. For instance, via a pointer you can select elements from an array that need not be contiguous:

```
real, dimension(:,:), allocatable, target :: array
real, dimension(:,:), pointer              :: ptr

allocate( array(20,20) )

ptr => array(1:20:5,3:4)
```

The variable ptr would point to the elements array(1,3), array(6,3), and so forth as:

```
ptr(1,1) => array(1,3)
ptr(2,1) => array(6,3)
...
ptr(1,2) => array(1,4)
ptr(2,2) => array(6,4)
...
```

---

[1] Some compilers offer options to control how such arrays are allocated, either from the stack (faster) or from the heap (more robust).

However, because a pointer can also point to fixed memory, or to automatic memory, it is very difficult and often impossible for the compiler to determine if it is safe to deallocate the memory that is being pointed to by such variables. In other words, if you use pointer variables, you are yourself responsible for cleaning up the memory.

From Fortran 2003 onwards, there are two more methods to consider: character strings with an allocatable length and parametrized derived types.

In the remainder of this chapter, various aspects of the previous types of arrays are discussed.

4.2 Memory Leaks with Pointers

In the following fragment, the memory allocated via the pointer variable `ptr` becomes unavailable, because the pointer disappears upon return from the routine:

```
subroutine alloc_and_forget( amount )
    integer :: amount

    real, dimension(:), pointer :: ptr    ! Local variable!

    allocate( ptr(amount) )
end subroutine alloc_and_forget
```

Such a *memory leak* can be very difficult to find, and if this routine is called often, more and more memory gets allocated and becomes unavailable until, finally, all is lost.

Tools exist that can detect this type of problem, such as *valgrind* (see Appendix A). However, in some circumstances it is not easy to prevent them, for instance, with derived types that have pointer or allocatable components (see Section 4.8).

4.3 Extending an Array

Quite often you need to grow an array as more and more values are added, such as when reading input data. Until Fortran 2003, one way to do this is:

- Create a pointer to an array of the new size.
- Copy the contents of the old array into the temporary one.
- Deallocate the old array and then make it point to the temporary array.

In actual code, this looks like:

```
real, dimension(:), pointer :: array, tmp
integer                     :: newsize, oldsize
```

```
allocate( tmp(newsize) )
tmp(1:oldsize) = array
deallocate( array )
array => tmp
```

This requires the use of *pointers* rather than allocatable arrays, lacking the advantages of the latter type. Using allocatables in this context is possible, but it requires two copy actions instead of one.

In Fortran 2003, the move_alloc routine enables you to write this as:

```
real, dimension(:), allocatable :: array, tmp
integer                         :: newsize, oldsize


allocate( tmp(newsize) )
tmp(1:oldsize) = array
deallocate( array )
call move_alloc( tmp, array )
```

In this case, you have all the benefits of allocatables.

4.4 Character Strings with Adjustable Length

Just as for arrays, locally defined character strings can have a length that is determined at runtime. This is illustrated in the following code fragment that implements an index() function to find the position of a string in another string while ignoring the case:

```
integer function index_ignore_case( stringa, stringb )
    implicit none

    character(len=*), intent(in) :: stringa, stringb

    character(len=len(stringa)) :: copya
    character(len=len(stringb)) :: copyb

    copya = stringa
    copyb = stringb

    ! Convert to uppercase
    call toupper( copya )
    call toupper( copyb )

    index_ignore_case = index( copya, copyb )

end function index_ignore_case
```

From Fortran 2003 onwards, you can allocate character strings to have a length determined at run-time (so-called *deferred-length strings*):

```
character(len=:), allocatable :: string
integer                       :: size

size = ...
allocate( character(len=size):: string )
```

This is very useful for analyzing the contents of a file or to split up a string in words. The following module uses allocatable strings and several other features to read an arbitrarily long line from a file:

```
module readline_utility
    use iso_fortran_env

    implicit none

contains

subroutine readline( lun, line, success )
    integer, intent(in)                         :: lun
    character(len=:), allocatable, intent(out) :: line
    logical, intent(out)                        :: success

    character(len=0)                            :: newline

    success = .true.

    call readline_piece_by_piece( newline )

contains

recursive subroutine readline_piece_by_piece( newline )
    character(len=*)                 :: newline

    character(len=10)                :: piece
    integer                          :: ierr
    integer .                        :: sz

    read( lun, '(a)', advance = 'no', size = sz, &
        iostat = ierr ) piece

    if ( ierr /= 0 .and. ierr /= iostat_eor ) then
        allocate( character(len=len(newline)):: line )
        line = newline
        success = .false.
        return
    endif
```

```
!
! Have we gotten to the end of the line or not?
!
if ( sz >= len(piece)  ) then
    call readline_piece_by_piece( newline // piece )
else
    allocate( character(len=len(newline)+sz):: line )
    line = newline // piece(1:sz)
    success = .true.
endif
end subroutine readline_piece_by_piece
end subroutine readline

end module readline_utility
```

The public subroutine **readline** simply provides a convenient interface to the functionality, it is the *recursive* subroutine **readline_piece_by_piece** that does the actual work:

- The **read** statement uses nonadvancing I/O to read a small piece of the current line in the file. If you reach the end of the line, then the file pointer will move to the start of the next line or to the end of the file.
- Depending on whether the end of the line is reached or not, the routine either calls itself recursively or it allocates the memory needed to store the entire string in the variable **line**. The number of characters read and stored in the variable **sz** is used as an indicator.

  When the subroutine calls itself recursively, it does so with a longer string as the argument. This string is constructed on the fly via concatenation and contains all the contents sofar.

  If it reached the end of the line, the job is finished and the routine returns successively, up to the calling routine.
- When the routine reaches the end of the file or some other error occurs, it allocates the string and stores whatever it was able to read.
- The preceding code defines **readline_piece_by_piece** to be a subroutine internal to **readline** – it appears between **contains** and the **end subroutine** statement of **readline**. It also uses the standard **iso_fortran_env** module to access the integer parameter **iostat_eor** to detect the *end of line* condition.

This is an example of how you can use various techniques for managing the memory. However, it may not actually be the most efficient way to read an arbitrarily long line from a file. An alternative is to use a do loop within which you repeatedly allocate the string to ever-increasing length. An advantage of a such a do loop is that you can release the memory of a previous iteration immediately.

4.5 Combining Automatic and Allocatable Arrays

As discussed while automatic arrays are very easy to use, large automatic arrays pose a problem. Here is a method to prevent this from happening. The algorithm for getting the median of a set of data requires sorting the data, but you do not want to disturb the original array.[2] Therefore, you need a copy of the data and then to sort that copy. As the array can be any size, you distinguish between small data arrays, for which you use an *automatic* array, and larger data arrays, for which you explicitly allocate a work array of the correct size:

```fortran
subroutine get_median( array, median )
    implicit none

    real, dimension(:), intent(in) :: array
    real, intent(out)              :: median

    ! Arbitrary threshold ...
    integer, parameter             :: threshold = 2000

    real, dimension(min(size(array), threshold)) :: auto_array
    real, dimension(:), allocatable              :: alloc_array

    if ( size(array) < threshold ) then
        auto_array = array
        call get_median_sub( auto_array, median )
    else
        allocate( alloc_array(size(array)) )
        alloc_array = array
        call get_median_sub( alloc_array, median )
    endif
contains
subroutine get_median_sub( array, median )

    real, dimension(:), intent(in) :: array
    real, intent(out)              :: median

    call sort_data( array )

    !
    ! Either the middle element or the mean of the
    ! two elements at the center
    !
    median = 0.5 * ( array((size(array)+1)/2) + &
                     array((size(array)+2)/2) )

end subroutine get_median_sub
end subroutine get_median
```

---

[2] Algorithms exist to do this without sorting, but that would defeat the purpose of this example.

The idea is to let the subroutine get_median decide what method is safe and efficient and then let an internal routine (get_median_sub) do the actual work. This way you only need to use an allocated array with the (slight) performance hit when dealing with a large number of data.

4.6 Performance of Various Types of Arrays

Common wisdom has it that arrays with the pointer attribute are more costly than other arrays, as they can point to non-contiguous memory and they can cause *aliasing* (two names for the same memory location), which hampers all manner of optimizations. To give an indication of that cost, measure the time it takes to run a simple algorithm with various types of arrays.

The basic code is this:

```
subroutine compute_mean( data, sz, mean )
    real, dimension(:) :: data
    integer            :: sz
    real               :: mean

    integer            :: i

    do i = 1,sz
        data(i) = i
    enddo

    mean = sum( data(1:sz) ) / sz
end subroutine compute_mean
```

The array data can be an automatic array, a *local* allocatable array, or a local pointer array. The latter two types are allocated explicitly, so there is some overhead due to the allocation and deallocation. A second alternative is to *pass* an array that has the allocatable or pointer attribute in the calling program, but not in the subroutine itself.

The results are shown in Figure 4.1. The numbers that were used for the figure are the result of measuring the time that had elapsed after repeating the various versions of the subroutine 10,000 times. The numbers were reproduceable within several percents. In the figure, the *mean* value per array size is used to normalize the data.

While it is difficult to draw general conclusions (the numbers vary greatly per compiler, compiler options, and per operating system), it would seem that *local* arrays with the pointer attribute require systematically 10 to 20 percent more time – which includes the overhead of allocations and deallocations. There is little difference between automatic and allocatable arrays (the triangle symbols), though this depends on the choice of platform.

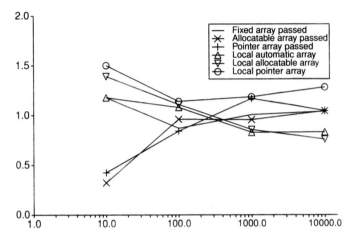

Figure 4.1. Performance of various types of arrays, normalized time as a function of the array size

If you pass arrays with various attributes to a routine where the dummy argument is declared without the attribute, the performance is quite comparable. Therefore, in this case it pays to "strip off" the pointer attribute:

```
real, dimension(:), pointer :: data
integer                     :: sz
real                        :: mean

interface
    subroutine compute_mean( array, sz, mean )
        real, dimension(:) :: array
        integer            :: sz
        real               :: mean
    end subroutine
end interface

allocate( data(sz) )

call compute_mean( data, sz, mean )
```

In general, however, pointers can refer to arrays that are not contiguous. The program will then have to copy the data into a temporary array and back into the original one.

4.7 Parametrized Derived Types

The Fortran 2003 standard adds so-called parametrized derived types to the instruments for memory management. This is in fact a generalization of the *kind* mechanism from Fortran 90 and the character lengths that are at least as old as FORTRAN 77. For example, suppose you are dealing with image processing. It would be very useful to have a derived type that stores the image data in such a way that you can hide all details, such as the image dimensions. With parametrized derived types, you can:

```
type image_data( rows, columns )
    integer, len :: rows, columns
    integer, dimension(rows,columns) :: data
end type
```

(This assumes the image data are represented as discrete intensity, hence a single integer.)

You can declare variables of this type with fixed dimensions:

```
type(image_data(100,100)) :: picture
type(image_data(5,5))       :: mask
```

You can also adapt the dimensions to the problem at hand:[3]

```
type(image_data(:,:)), allocatable :: picture
integer                            :: rows, columns
. . .
! Read the image size
read( 10, * ) rows, columns

allocate( image_data(rows, columns) :: picture )
```

If you need another variable of this type with the same parameters, then you can use *sourced allocation*:

```
type(image_data(:,:)), allocatable :: picture1, picture2

allocate( picture2, source = picture1 )
```

The effect of sourced allocation is that the newly allocated variable has the same length parameters as the source variable, and that it has the same value.[4]

Variables of a parametrized type can be passed to routines in a way similar to the length of character strings:

```
subroutine convolution( picture, mask, result )
    type(image_data(*,*)) :: picture, mask, result
    . . .
end subroutine convolution
```

---

[3] While you can use *kind* parameters as well to define a derived type, the kinds are fixed at compile-time. There is no way to redefine the kinds dynamically.

[4] Fortran 2008 introduces the option to use the source variable as a "mold" only, so that the type parameters are copied, but not the value.

or, for clarity:

```
subroutine convolution( picture, mask, result )
    type(image_data(rows=*,columns=*)) :: picture, mask, result
    ...
end subroutine convolution
```

Of course, you need to know the actual values of these type parameters to work with such parametrized types. They are simply available as implicit components:

```
write( *, * ) 'Picture dimensions: ', &
    picture%rows, picture%columns
```

4.8 Avoiding Memory Leaks with Derived Types

Derived types that have pointer components, and are also used in operations like addition or assignment, still suffer from the possibility of memory leaks. In this section, I describe a simple technique to avoid such leaks. Even when you replace the pointer attribute by the allocatable attribute, a slightly different variant of it may be beneficial.[5]

Consider three variables a, b, and c of a derived type chain with pointer components that are used in an expression like this, where .concat. is a user-defined operation:

```
a = b .concat. c
```

The derived type and its associated operations are implemented in the following module.

```
module chains
    type chain
        integer, dimension(:), pointer :: values => null()
    end type chain

    interface assignment(=)
        module procedure assign_chain
        module procedure assign_array
    end interface assignment(=)

    interface operator(.concat.)
        module procedure concat_chain
    end interface operator(.concat.)
```

---

[5] List and Car, describe a general reference counting technique for managing the memory [53].

```
contains

subroutine assign_array( ic, jc )
    type(chain),intent(inout) :: ic
    integer, dimension(:)     :: jc

    if ( associated( ic%values ) ) deallocate( ic%values )
    allocate( ic%values(1:size(jc)) )
    ic%values = jc
end subroutine assign_array

subroutine assign_chain( ic, jc )
    type(chain), intent(inout) :: ic
    type(chain), intent(in)    :: jc

    if ( associated( ic%values ) ) deallocate( ic%values )
    allocate( ic%values(1:size(jc%values)) )
    ic%values = jc%values

end subroutine assign_chain

function concat_chain( ic, jc )
    type(chain), intent(in) :: ic, jc
    type(chain)             :: concat_chain
    integer :: nic, njc

    nic = size(ic%values)
    njc = size(jc%values)

    allocate( concat_chain%values(1:nic+njc) )
    concat_chain%values(1:nic)         = ic%values(1:nic)
    concat_chain%values(nic+1:nic+njc) = jc%values(1:njc)

end function concat_chain

end module chains
```

The derived type represents a chain of integers that can be extended via the
.concat. operation. The result is a new type(chain) data item that contains
the concatenated arrays of the two operands. When you assign one variable of
this type to another, a copy is made of the array of values.

Whenever assigning a new value to a variable of this type, any old memory
must be deallocated and new memory of the right size allocated (as shown in
the subroutines assign_array and assign_chain). Otherwise, memory would
be referenced twice or get lost. The problem, however, is that the program will
not deallocate the data in the temporary object that is created via the .concat.
operation, because it does not know that it is safe to do so.

Therefore, while code like:

```
a = b .concat. c
```

is perfectly possible, it also introduces a memory leak.

One alternative to avoid this is to use subroutines instead of functions and assignments, so that there are no intermediate results, but this causes a rather awkward way of working. Compare:

```
call concatenate( a, b, c )
```

with:

```
a = b .concat. c
```

or:

```
a = concat( b, c )
```

A better solution that allows you to use such operations as .concat. almost without memory leaks is to *mark* the derived types, so that the allocated memory can be deallocated when it is no longer needed. You modify the definition of the derived type slightly:

```
type chain
   integer, dimension(:), pointer :: values => null()
   logical                        :: tmp    = .false.
end type chain
```

With this new type, the function concat_chain() can mark its result as temporary. All functions in the module now check whether their arguments are temporary and clean them up if that is the case, as they will not be used anymore:

```
function concat_chain( ic, jc )
    type(chain), intent(in) :: ic, jc
    type(chain)             :: concat_chain
    integer :: nic, njc

    nic = size(ic%values)
    njc = size(jc%values)

    allocate( concat_chain%values(1:nic+njc) )
    concat_chain%values(1:nic)        = ic%values(1:nic)
    concat_chain%values(nic+1:nic+njc) = jc%values(1:njc)

    concat_chain%tmp = .true.      ! Mark as temporary

    call cleanup( ic, .true. )     ! Clean up temporary arguments
    call cleanup( jc, .true. )
end function concat_chain
```

and similarly for the assign_array and assign_chain subroutines.

The routine `cleanup` has the task of hiding the details of deallocating the arrays:

```
subroutine cleanup( ic, only_tmp )
    type(chain) :: ic
    logical     :: only_tmp

    if ( .not. only_tmp .or. ic%tmp ) then
        if ( associated( ic%values) ) deallocate( ic%values )
    endif
end subroutine cleanup
```

To effectively avoid all memory leaks using this technique puts some burden on the programmer of these modules. The programmer must ensure that variables are appropriately initialized and memory is released when it can be done.

If the derived type has `allocatable` components instead of `pointer` components, keeping track of the temporary status is still worthwhile, even though memory leaks would not be the main reason anymore. Consider again the chain type, but now with allocatable components:

```
type chain
    integer, dimension(:), allocatable :: values
    logical                            :: tmp    = .false.
end type chain
```

Concatenating two such variables becomes simpler when using Fortran 2003's automatic allocation feature:

```
function concat_chain( ic, jc )
    type(chain), intent(in) :: ic
    type(chain), intent(in) :: jc
    type(chain)             :: concat_chain

    concat_chain%values = (/ ic%values, jc%values /)
end function concat_chain
```

However, in the assignment routine you can avoid the allocation and copying if the right-hand side is a temporary object:

```
subroutine assign_chain( ic, jc )
    type(chain), intent(inout) :: ic
    type(chain)                :: jc

    if ( jc%tmp ) then
        call move_alloc( jc%values, ic%values )
    else
        ic%values = jc%values  ! Automatic allocation
    endif

    ic%tmp = .false.
end subroutine assign_chain
```

4.9 Performance and Memory Access

Another form of memory management is *how* you access the memory. In modern computers, and, in fact, this has been the case for several decades, as witnessed by a 1982 book by Metcalf [60], the *locality* of memory access is quite often the foremost important factor in the performance of a program. This is due to the relative slowness of memory access compared to the rate of (numerical) operations. The hardware solution is to have several levels of cache memory with different sizes and speeds. It is the compiler's task to efficiently use these caches, so that the data on which the operations occur are available as fast as possible [7], [32].

The programmer can help by carefully considering the access patterns. The following program accesses the matrix elements in three different rows and columns [31]:

```fortran
program measure_matrix
    implicit none
    double complex, allocatable :: a(:,:)
    integer                     :: i, j, l, m, n
    integer                     :: t1, t2, rate

    write(*,*) 'Enter power of 2'
    read(*,*)  n

    call system_clock( count_rate = rate )

    allocate(a(n+4,n+4))

    !
    ! Avoid some caching effect that causes the first iteration
    ! to take much more time
    !
    m = n-4
    do l=1,max(1,100000000/(n*n))
        call test(a,m,n-4)
    enddo

    do m = n-4, n+4
        a = 1.0d0

        call system_clock(t1)
        do l = 1, max(1,100000000/(n*n))
            call test( a, m, n-4 )
        enddo
        call system_clock(t2)
        write(*,'(i4,f8.3)') m, (t2 - t1) / real(rate)
    enddo
```

Table 4.1. Measured Time as Function of the Matrix Size. Results for Sizes that are a Power of 2 are Highlighted

Size	Time	Size	Time	Size	Time	Size	Time	Size	Time
28	0.156	60	0.218	124	0.250	252	0.266	508	0.640
29	0.156	61	0.219	125	0.266	253	0.265	509	0.641
30	0.141	62	0.203	126	0.250	254	0.266	510	0.672
31	0.172	63	0.219	127	0.265	255	0.375	511	0.719
32	**0.156**	64	**0.391**	128	**0.500**	256	**0.656**	512	**0.750**
33	0.140	65	0.218	129	0.250	257	0.297	513	0.781
34	0.172	66	0.219	130	0.266	258	0.266	514	0.687
35	0.141	67	0.219	131	0.250	259	0.281	515	0.657
36	0.156	68	0.219	132	0.266	260	0.281	516	0.640

```
contains
subroutine test( a, m, n )
   ! goes through a in "wrong" order
   integer        :: m, n
   double complex :: a(m,m)

   integer        :: i, j

   do i = 2, n-1
      do j = 2, n-1
         a(i,j) = (a(i+1,j-1) + a(i-1,j+1)) * 0.5
      enddo
   enddo
endsubroutine
endprogram
```

Table 4.1 shows the reported run times. When the size of the matrix is a power of 2, the operation takes roughly twice as long as when it is not. This is due to **cache misses**. The size of the columns interferes with the size of the cache, which makes the temporary storage of a part of the matrix in the fastest cache inefficient.

When the column is large enough, the effect disappears, as can be seen in the last part of the Table 4.2.[6]

In this case, the problem can be solved by going through the matrix in *column first* order, instead of *row first* – or by using odd matrix dimensions.

Another example is searching in a linked list. Linked lists are quite convenient for inserting and deleting data efficiently, but there is no guarantee that the locations of the memory occupied by the various elements are close together.

---

[6] The effect depends on the compiler and the compile options you use. The results shown here were obtained with the *Intel Fortran* compiler. With the *gfortran* compiler, the run times were longer and did not show such a pronounced effect.

Table 4.2. Measured Time of Finding an Element in the List for Different Data Structures

Structure	Time (μ s)
Simple array	1.55
Compact list	2.30
List with irregularly allocated elements	4.97

This means caching blocks of memory is likely to be less efficient than with arrays. As a consequence, it can take up to two or three times as long to find an element in a linked list as to find an element in an ordinary array:

Both linked lists have list elements defined as:

```
type linked_list
    real :: value
    type(linked_list), pointer :: next => null()
end type linked_list
```

The elements for the compact list were allocated in a tight loop, whereas in the second case, the elements were allocated with extra allocations in between:

```
do i = 2,size(data)
    allocate( element )
    allocate( dummy(11*i) )
    element%value =  data(i)
    plist%next    => element
    plist         => element
enddo
```

This causes the list elements to be far away from each other in the memory and annihilates the benefits of the cache.

5.

An Interface Problem

This chapter focuses on how to make a general (computing/programming) facility generic enough to be useful for a large set of applications, but specific enough to make it practically useable. Concrete examples are: a library for integrating ordinary differential equations or a library to read XML files (see Section 7.4). To elaborate on the second example, you can read such files piece by piece and deal with the data you read directly or you can store the data in some convenient structure for later reference – the SAX and the DOM approaches.

Now examine various implementations for a somewhat simpler problem: integrating a function over a particular interval.[1] You are not interested in the numerical aspects, though they are quite interesting in their own right, but rather in the methods available for integrating a well-behaved function that depends on one or more parameters. For instance, the function f:

$$f(x) = e^{-ax} \cos bx \quad (a, b >= 0) \tag{5.1}$$

to be integrated over the interval $[0, 10]$.

A general library of suitable integration methods might contain a routine such as:

```
module integration_library

    implicit none

contains

subroutine integrate_trapezoid( f, xmin, xmax, steps, result )

    interface
        real function f( x )
            real, intent(in) :: x
        end function f
    end interface

    real, intent(in)    :: xmin, xmax
    integer, intent(in) :: steps
```

---

[1] Oliveira and Stewart [68] call this the environment problem. It is also discussed at some length by [65].

```
    real, intent(out)    :: result

    integer              :: i
    real                 :: x, deltx

    if ( steps <= 0 ) then
        result = 0.0
        return
    endif

    deltx = (xmax - xmin) / steps

    result = ( f(xmin) + f(xmax) )/ 2.0

    do i = 1,steps-1
        x        = xmin + i * deltx
        result = result + f(x)
    enddo

    result = result * deltx
end subroutine integrate_trapezoid

end module integration_library
```

The limitations of such an implementation are immediately clear: the interface of any subprogram that computes the mathematical function f is fixed and in the preceding example it does not allow any parameters like a and b in Equation 5.1 to be passed.

If you are stuck with this implementation, then you have only two options:

- Incorporate the values of the parameters directly in the implementation of the function f.
- Use a "pool of data" (a COMMON block or module variables) that is accessed from within the implementation of f and from the outside, so that you can set the parameters before invoking the integration routine.

If, however, you can revise the implementation of the library, you pass these extra parameters directly or you could use a technique like *reverse communication*.

You will now study these methods in the light of the four major standards for Fortran: FORTRAN 77, Fortran 90/95, Fortran 2003, and Fortran 2008.

5.1 Filling in the Parameters

If you are interested in only a few particular values of the parameters a and b, you could easily program specific versions of the function f and pass these to the integration routine:[2]

```
c
c Define the function
c
      real function f( x )
      real x

      real a, b
      save a, b
      data a, b / 1.0, 2.0 /

      f = exp(-a*x) * cos(b*x)
      end
```

A more sophisticated approach is to read these parameters from a file:

```
c
c Define the function
c
      real function f( x )
      real x

      logical first
      real a
      real b
      save a, b, first
      data first / .true. /

      if ( first ) then
         first = .false.
         open( 10, file = 'function_values.inp' )
         read( 10, * ) a
         read( 10, * ) b
         close( 10 )
      endif

      f = exp(-a*x) * cos(b*x)
      end
```

The drawbacks are that you cannot pass a file name and the file is read only the first time (with no way to integrate the parameterized function with different values).

---

[2] The example almost conforms to FORTRAN 77 (officially lowercase is not allowed, but in later examples names longer than 6 characters appear). This style will not be consistently used, except when emphasizing an aspect of FORTRAN 77 that has a more modern counterpart in later standards.

FORTRAN 77, however, does offer a somewhat obscure facility, the entry statement, which could be exploited here:

```
c
c Define the function
c
      real function f( x )
      real x

      logical first
      real a
      real b
      save a, b

      f = exp(-a*x) * cos(b*x)

      return
c
c Provide access to the parameters A and B
c (Set the value of the function f - a synonym for
c the function setab c for good form)
c
      entry setab( ain, bin )
      real ain, bin
      a = ain
      b = bin
      f = 0.0
      end
```

This allows access to the variables a and b by means of the alternative interface defined by the entry statement [62]. It can be used as follows:

```
      program integrate_function

      real xmin, xmax, result, dummy
      integer steps
      external f

c
c Set the parameters before calling the integration routine
c (setab is formally a function, just as f is, so call it as
c a function)
c
      dummy = setab( 1.0, 2.0 )

      xmin  =  0.0
      xmax  = 10.0
      steps = 10
```

```
call integrate_trapezoid( f, xmin, xmax, steps, result )

write(*,*) 'Result: ', result

end
```

The advantages are clear: you only need to implement the function itself, perhaps with a few extras, to make it slightly more flexible. The values of the parameters are completely private to the function.

The disadvantage is that you need to implement several specific versions or create roundabout ways to set the parameters. Also, if you need to output more information,[3] for instance, to report that you are crossing a singularity, making the result unreliable, you have very little support.

5.2 Using a Pool of Data

The example with the **entry** statement is akin to the second approach to be discussed: using COMMON blocks or module variables. In FORTRAN 77, such an approach looks like this:

```
c
c Define the function
c
      real function f( x )
      real x

      real a, b
      common /fparam/ a, b

      f = exp(-a*x) * cos(b*x)

      end
```

with the following program as a typical way to use the interfacing via COMMON blocks:

```
      program integrate_function

      real xmin, xmax, result
      integer steps
      external f

c
c We need to repeat the definition of the COMMON block
c to access the function parameters
```

---

[3] This is likely to be an important issue if you apply this approach to other types of programming/computing problems.

```
c

      real a, b
      common /fparam/ a, b

c
c Set the parameters before calling the integration routine
c
      a = 1.0
      b = 2.0

      xmin =    0.0
      xmax =   10.0
      steps = 10
      call integrate_trapezoid( f, xmin, xmax, steps, result )

      write(*,*) 'Result: ', result

      end
```

COMMON blocks have a rather bad reputation:

- You need to include the same source code defining the COMMON block in each routine that uses it.
- You are allowed to use different variable names and even different variable types for defining the same COMMON block (only the block's name is fixed), as they only provide access to a piece of memory.

Data in Modules   Module variables are much more reliable: you define them in one location – the module – and you can access them **by using** the module. A preferable implementation in Fortran 90 is:

```
module functions
    implicit none

    !
    ! Publically accessible parameters
    !
    real :: a, b
contains
real function f( x )

    real, intent(in) :: x

    f = exp(-a*x) * cos(b*x)

end function f
end module functions
```

The corresponding program to illustrate the use is as follows:

```
program integrate_function

    use integration_library
    use functions

    implicit none

    real    :: xmin, xmax, result
    integer :: steps

!
! Set the parameters before calling the integration routine
!
    a = 1.0
    b = 2.0

    xmin =    0.0
    xmax =   10.0
    steps = 10
    call integrate_trapezoid( f, xmin, xmax, steps, result )

    write(*,*) 'Result: ', result

end program integrate_function
```

Additional benefits of using modules are that the compiler can now check the number and types of all arguments and that subroutine and function names are no longer completely global. In a large program that uses many libraries, global names can cause all manner of conflicts.

Using module variables does have an important drawback though. Multi-threaded computing is more and more common these days and without measures it would be easy to have one thread mess up the values used in another thread.

The details depend on the method by which you implement multithreading but if you use OpenMP, a possible solution to this problem is this (see Chapter 12):

```
module functions
    implicit none

    !
    ! Publically accessible parameters
    ! Assume no more than 10 threads for simplicity
    !
    real, dimension(10), private :: a
    real, dimension(10), private :: b
```

```
contains
subroutine setab( ain, bin )
    real, intent(in) :: ain, bin

    integer :: thid

    thid = omp_get_thread_num()
    a(thid) = ain
    b(thid) = bin
end subroutine setab

real function f( x )

    real, intent(in) :: x

    integer :: thid

    thid = omp_get_thread_num()

    f = exp(-a(thid)*x) * cos(b(thid)*x)

end function f
end module functions
```

Instead of a single set of variables, which can be (mis)used by different threads, you use a separate set per thread. Unfortunately, it complicates the implementation, especially if a lot of parameters are involved:

```
program integrate_function

    use integration_library
    use functions

    implicit none

    real    :: xmin, xmax, result
    real    :: a, b
    integer :: steps, thid

    xmin =    0.0
    xmax =   10.0
    steps = 10

!$omp parallel
!$omp private( a, b, result, thid )

    !
    ! Set the parameters per thread
```

```
!
thid = omp_get_thread_num()
a = 1.0 * thid
b = 2.0 * thid
call setab( a, b )

call integrate_trapezoid( f, xmin, xmax, steps, result )

write(*,*) 'Result: a= ', a, ' b = ', b, &
    ' -- result: ', result

!$omp end parallel

end program integrate_function
```

Internal Routines With the Fortran 2008 standard, it has become a standard feature to pass *internal routines* as actual arguments. This introduces a new solution, which is also thread-safe. Use this feature to provide a convenient interface to integrate the example function. As the constants a and b reside in the calling program or subroutine, the internal routine feval that is passed to the actual integration routine can use them directly. In turn, feval calls the function f, passed as an argument, that implements the mathematical function. This gives a general routine that adapts the interface of f to that required by the integration routine:

```
subroutine integrate_function( f, xmin, xmax, a, b, result )

    use integration_library

    implicit none

    interface
        real function f(x, a, b)
            real, intent(in) :: x, a, b
        end function f
    end interface

    real, intent(in)  :: a, b, xmin, xmax
    real, intent(out) ::  result

    integer :: steps

    steps = 10

    call integrate_trapezoid( feval, xmin, xmax, steps, &
                              result )
```

```
contains
real function feval( x )

    real, intent(in) :: x

    feval = f(x, a, b)

end function feval
end subroutine integrate_function
```

5.3 Passing Extra Arguments

As an alternative to the previous approaches, have a look at what you can do with extra arguments. The integration routine does not use them directly because they are only needed by the function. The challenge is to pass them along.

Array of Parameters The simplest solution is to pass an array of parameters:

```
subroutine integrate_trapezoid( f, params, xmin, xmax, &
                                steps, result )
    . . .
    interface
       real function f(x, params)
           real, intent(in)               :: x
           real, dimension(:), intent(in) :: params
       end function f
    end interface

    real, dimension(:) :: params
    . . .
end subroutine
```

The function f can be implemented in a straightforward way:

```
real function f( x, params )
    real, intent(in)               :: x
    real, dimension(:), intent(in) :: params

    f = exp(-params(1)*x) * cos(params(2)*x)

end function f
```

However, if the set of parameters does not only consist of reals, this solution is awkward [65]. In other situations than this numerical integration problem, you might be dealing with character strings or linked lists. Therefore, an alternative needs to allow more general data types.

Use the `transfer()` Function   In FORTRAN 77, there were very few facilities that could help, but with Fortran 90/95 you can use the `transfer()` function to convert arbitrary data into an array of reals and back:

```
type function_parameters
    real :: a
    real :: b
end type function_parameters

type(function_parameters) :: params

! Defines the type for the transfer function
real, dimension(1)          :: real_array
...
call integration_trapezoid( f, transfer(params,real_array), &
    xmin, xmax, steps, result )
...
```

While this works, it is not a very elegant solution: it puts the burden of converting the data on the user, even though you can hide it in an (internal) routine[4]:

```
program integrate

type function_parameters
    real :: a, b
end type function_parameters

type(function_parameters) :: params
...
call integration_trapezoid_ab( f, params, xmin, xmax, &
    steps, result )
...

contains
!
! This code can go into an include file if needed, to hide the
! details from sight
!
subroutine integration_trapezoid_ab( f, params, xmin, xmax, &
                steps, result )
    ...
    type(function_parameters) :: params

    ! Defines the type for the transfer function
    real, dimension(1)          :: real_array
```

---

[4] You might call this and the solution with the internal routine the *Façade pattern* [54].

```
    call integration_trapezoid(          &
        f, transfer(params,real_array), &
        xmin, xmax, steps, result )
end subroutine
end program integrate
```

Type-Bound Procedures   With Fortran 2003, you have more possibilities to
solve this issue in an elegant way ([65], see also Chapter 11):

```
module integration_library

    implicit none

    type, abstract :: user_function
        ! No data - merely a placeholder
    contains
        procedure(function_evaluation), deferred, &
            pass(params) :: eval
    end type user_function

    abstract interface
        real function function_evaluation(x, params)
            import              :: user_function
            real                :: x
            class(user_function) :: params
        end function function_evaluation
    end interface

contains

subroutine integrate_trapezoid( &
            params, xmin, xmax, steps, result )

    class(user_function)     :: params
    real, intent(in)         :: xmin, xmax
    integer, intent(in)      :: steps
    real, intent(out)        :: result

    integer                  :: i
    real                     :: x
    real                     :: deltx

    if ( steps <= 0 ) then
        result = 0.0
        return
    endif

    deltx = (xmax - xmin) / steps
```

```
result = ( params%eval(xmin) + params%eval(xmax) )/ 2.0

do i = 2,steps
    x        = xmin + (i - 1) * deltx
    result = result + params%eval(x)
enddo

result = result * deltx
end subroutine integrate_trapezoid
end module integration_library
```

The preceding module is shown in the following example. Note that the implementation of function f is now a part of the type user_function:

```
module functions
    use integration_library

    implicit none

    type, extends(user_function) :: my_function
        real :: a
        real :: b
    contains
        procedure, pass(params) :: eval => f
    end type my_function

contains
real function f( x, params )

    real, intent(in)    :: x
    class(my_function) :: params

    f = exp(-params%a*x) * cos(params%b*x)

end function f

end module functions
```

Rather than pass the name of the function, you now pass the *derived type* that contains the function you want to integrate:

```
program test_integrate

    use integration_library
    use functions

    implicit none

    type(my_function) :: params
```

```
    real              :: xmin, xmax, result
    integer           :: steps

    params%a = 1.0
    params%b = 2.0

    xmin    = 1.0
    xmax    = 10.0
    steps   = 10

    call integrate_trapezoid( params, xmin, xmax, steps, &
                              result )

    write(*,*) 'Result: ', result

end program test_integrate
```

The abstract derived type user_function provides the common type that the integration library uses for passing the function and its data. You need to define a specific implementation of that type in order to actually do the computation.

The only thing that "feels" awkward about this solution is that each function to integrate requires its own type. You might say: the solution is data-centered instead of function-centered.

Procedure Pointers As in the previous example, if instead of a type-bound procedure you use a procedure pointer, you can change the function that needs to be evaluated – without introducing a new type of each function. For this, you move the procedure component to the "data" section and add the pointer attribute:

```
module integration_library

    implicit none

    type, abstract :: function_parameters
        procedure(eval), pointer, pass(params) :: feval
    end type function_parameters

    abstract interface
        real function eval(x, params)
            import :: function_parameters
            class(function_parameters) :: params
        end function eval
    end interface

contains
```

```
subroutine integrate_trapezoid( &
            params, xmin, xmax, steps, result )

    interface
        real function f( x, params )
            import function_parameters
            real, intent(in)           :: x
            class(function_parameters) :: params
        end function f
    end interface

    class(function_parameters) :: params

    ... (identical to the previous implementation) ...

end subroutine integrate_trapezoid

end module integration_library
```

Now, you can vary the function that is to be integrated without introducing a new type for each function:

```
module functions
    use integration_library

    implicit none

    type, extends(function_parameters) :: my_parameters
        real :: a
    end type my_parameters

contains
real function f( x, params )

    real, intent(in)     :: x
    class(my_parameters) :: params

    f = exp(-params%a*x) * cos(params%b*x)

end function f

!
! Function g() does not use parameter b,
! but otherwise it has the same data requirements, hence
! reuse type "my_parameters".
!
real function g( x, params )
```

```fortran
    real, intent(in)      :: x
    class(my_parameters) :: params

    g = params%a * x

  end function g

end module functions

program test_integrate

  use integration_library
  use functions

  implicit none

  type(my_parameters) :: params
  real                 :: xmin, xmax, result
  integer              :: steps

  params%a    =  1.0
  params%b    =  2.0

  xmin        = 1.0
  xmax        = 10.0
  steps       = 10

  params%feval => f    ! First function

  call integrate_trapezoid( &
          params, xmin, xmax, steps, result )
  write(*,*) 'Result f: ', result

  params%feval => g    ! Second function

  call integrate_trapezoid( &
          params, xmin, xmax, steps, result )
  write(*,*) 'Result g: ', result

end program test_integrate
```

5.4 Control Structures

So far we have concentrated on passing arbitrary data to a subprogram that is itself called from another subprogram that should be general and, therefore, should be independent of these data types. However, the only thing this general integration subprogram needs to know is the value of the function.

This observation leads to a completely different approach – passing the value instead of the function:

```fortran
module integration_library

    implicit none

    type integration_parameters
        private
        integer :: state = -1          ! Not-initialized
        integer :: steps
        integer :: i
        real    :: x, xmin, xmax, deltx
        real    :: result, sum
    end type integration_parameters

    !
    ! Parameters describing actions
    !
    integer, parameter :: get_value = 1
    integer, parameter :: completed = 2
    integer, parameter :: failure   = 3

contains

subroutine set_parameters( data, xmin, xmax, steps )
    type(integration_parameters) :: data
    real, intent(in)             :: xmin, xmax
    integer, intent(in)          :: steps

    if ( steps <= 0 ) then
        return
    endif

    data%xmin   = xmin
    data%xmax   = xmax
    data%steps  = steps

    data%state  = 1
    data%sum    = 0.0
    data%i      = 0
    data%deltx  = (xmax - xmin) / steps

end subroutine set_parameters

subroutine integrate_trapezoid( & data, value, result, action, x )

    type(integration_parameters) :: data
```

```fortran
    real, intent(in)                :: value
    real, intent(out)               :: result
    integer, intent(out)            :: action
    real, intent(out)               :: x

    result  = 0.0
    if ( data%state == -1 ) then
        action = failure
        return
    endif


    !
    ! We split the computation into steps
    !
    select case ( data%state )
        case ( 1 )
            x             = data%xmin
            action      = get_value
            data%state = 2
        case ( 2 )
            data%result = 0.5 * value
            x             = data%xmax
            action      = get_value
            data%state  = 3
        case ( 3 )
            data%result = data%result + 0.5 * value
            x             = data%xmin + data%deltx
            data%i      = 1
            action      = get_value
            data%state  = 4
        case ( 4 )
            data%result = data%result + value
            if ( data%i < data%steps-1 ) then
                data%i      = data%i    + 1
                x             = data%xmin + data%i * data%deltx
                action      = get_value
                data%state  = 4
            else
                result      = data%result * data%deltx
                action      = completed
            endif
        case default
            write(*,*) 'Programming error - unknown state: ', &
                data%state
            stop
    end select

end subroutine integrate_trapezoid
end module integration_library
```

This routine should be used as part of a dedicated control structure, as the following illustrates:

```fortran
module functions

    implicit none

contains

real function f( x, a, b )
    real, intent(in) :: x, a, b

    f = exp(-a*x) * cos(b*x)

end function f
end module functions

program test_integrate

    use integration_library
    use functions

    implicit none

    real    :: xmin, xmax, result, value, x
    real    :: a, b
    integer :: steps
    integer :: action

    type(integration_parameters) :: data

    a     = 1.0
    b     = 2.0

    xmin  = 1.0
    xmax  = 10.0
    steps = 10

    call set_parameters( data, xmin, xmax, steps )

    do
        call integrate_trapezoid( &
                data, value, result, action, x )

        select case ( action )
            case ( get_value )
                value = f(x,a,b)

            case ( completed )
                exit
```

```
            case ( failure )
                write(*,*) 'Error: invalid arguments'

            case default
                write(*,*) &
                    'Programming error: unknown action - ', &
                    action
        end select
    enddo

    write(*,*) 'Computed: ', result

end program test_integrate
```

You have turned the integration procedure into a *finite state machine*. By looping until reaching the final state, you get the final result. The code that takes care of this procedure is completely independent of the evaluation of the function. Furthermore, because the user code (in the main program) controls the steps, this approach allows you to bail out – should the function not be well-behaved over the whole integration interval – without requiring the general library to provide such a feature (or any other useful features). Also, if you need several routines in applying a particular programming/computing facility, this design can be much more flexible than the other ones seen.

A major drawback, however, is that the code for the general integration procedure has become much more complicated: you need to save the local variables between calls and you need to split up the work into steps that require only a single function value.

Another drawback is that you need to program a control structure instead of simply a call to a subroutine, although that can be hidden via an internal routine:

```
program test_integrate

    use functions

    implicit none

    real    :: xmin, xmax, result, value, x
    real    :: a, b
    integer :: steps
    integer :: action

    a    = 1.0
    b    = 2.0

    xmin = 1.0
```

```
    xmax  = 10.0
    steps = 10

    call integrate_trapezoid_ab( f, xmin, xmax, steps, result )

    write(*,*) 'Computed: ', result

contains
!
! The code below can be put into an INCLUDE file, for any
! function f that uses two parameters, a and b
!
! The parameters a and b come from the encompassing program
! unit
!
subroutine integrate_trapezoid_ab( &
                f, xmin, xmax, steps, result )

    use integration_library

    ... identical to previous example ...

end subroutine integrate_trapezoid
end program test_integrate
```

Using this approach, sometimes known as *reverse communication*, is tedious here, but it can be quite useful and natural in other situations. For instance, Section 7.4 discusses reading a file with a structure that requires complicated support code.

OpenMP You can use multiprocessing techniques as well to solve this *environment problem*. It may seem a bit strange, as multiprocessing is usually meant to enhance the performance of a program, but these techniques provide exactly the two simultaneous computational environments you need.

You need to have two threads, one that does the integration and the other that evaluates the function at a given coordinate x. This is accomplished in OpenMP via the *section* directive. The following main program uses this:

```
program test_integrate
    use integration
    use functions

    implicit none

    real    :: x, a, xbegin, xend, result
    integer :: steps
    logical :: next
```

```
type(integration_status) :: status

a      =  1.0
xbegin =  0.0
xend   = 10.0
steps  = 10

! All can be shared!

call start_integration( status )

!
! The first section is to integrate the function,
! the other is to evaluate the function
!

!$omp parallel sections

!$omp section
   call integrate_trapezoid( &
           status, xbegin, xend, steps, result )

!$omp section
   do
       call get_next( status, x, next )
       if ( .not. next ) exit
       call set_value( status, f(x,a) )
   enddo

!$omp end parallel sections

write(*,*) 'Result: ', result

end program test_integrate
```

The difficulty with this approach is the synchronization between the two threads, but that is all hidden in the implementation of the integrate and get_next routines:

```
subroutine get_next( status, x, next )
   type(integration_status) :: status
   real                     :: x
   logical                  :: next

   !
   ! Synchronize the memory
   !
```

```
    !$omp flush
    if ( status%done ) then
        next = .false.
    else
        do while ( .not. status%next )
            !$omp flush
        enddo

        !
        ! This is one of the places where the threads may
        ! get in each others' ways, so use a critical
        ! section
        !
        !$omp critical
        x             = status%xvalue
        status%next  = .false.
        status%ready = .false.
        !$omp end critical

        next = .true.
    endif
end subroutine get_next
```

and similarly for the `integrate_trapezoid` routine.

5.5 Dealing with Different Precisions

We have considered only the matter of passing arbitrary data to a function. A second aspect of a generic interface is whether to perform the computations in single or double precision. Currently, Fortran does not allow you to define one subroutine or function and specify the precision later. You are forced to define a specific routine for all the precisions you are interested in.

Fortran 90 introduced the **kind** atttribute, which makes it possible to at least concentrate the precision in one single location:

```
integer, parameter :: wp = kind(1.0)
real(wp)           :: x
```

defines a parameter **wp** (the *working precision*) that has a value corresponding to single precision - the **kind** of the literal constant 1.0.

You can use this facility and the **include** statement to define the routines with a "generic" kind:

```
module single
    implicit none
```

```
    ! Single precision constant
    integer, parameter :: wp = kind(1.0)

    include "generic.f90"
end module single

module double
    implicit none

    ! Double precision constant
    integer, parameter :: wp = kind(1.0d0)

    include "generic.f90"
end module double

module unite
    use single
    use double
end module unite
```

The include file "generic.f90" contains all the code that is independent of the kind:

```
interface print_kind
    module procedure print_kind_wp
end interface
private :: print_kind_wp

contains
subroutine print_kind_wp( x )
    real(kind=wp), intent(in) :: x

    write(*,*) 'Kind:', kind(x)
end subroutine print_kind_wp
```

The following program shows that it works:

```
program test_kinds

    use unite

    call print_kind( 1.0   )
    call print_kind( 1.0d0 )

end program test_kinds
```

Note that because the two versions of the routine `print_kind_wp` are in different modules, the generic interface `print_kind` needs not refer to unique

Table 5.1. Overview of the Characteristics of the Discussed Solutions

Solution	Type-safe	Thread-safe	Ease of Use[b]	Flexibility[b]	Standard
Filled-in parameters	yes	yes	moderate	no	F77
Function with entry	yes	no[a]	moderate	no	F77
COMMON-block	no	no[a]	moderate	moderate	F77
Module variables	yes	no[a]	moderate	moderate	F90
Internal routine	yes	yes	easy	yes	F2008[c]
REAL array	no	yes	hard	moderate	F77
Transfer function	no	yes	moderate	moderate	F90
Class with procedure pointer	yes	yes	easy	yes	F2003
Type-bound procedure	yes	yes	easy	yes	F2003
Reverse communication	yes	yes	difficult	very flexible	F77
OpenMP solution[d]	yes	yes	moderate	moderate	–

[a] Each of these solutions can be made thread-safe, but it requires the use of an array instead of a scalar variable.
[b] These qualifications are, of course, subjective.
[c] Some compilers offer the required feature as an extension to an older standard.
[d] OpenMP is a separate standard. It can be used, however, in combination with FORTRAN 77 and later.

names. This makes it much easier to write these interface blocks. It even makes it possible to put them in the include file.

5.6 Overview

Designing a suitable interface to a generic programming facility, such as a library of numerical integration methods, is a challenge. The features of modern Fortran do allow for a wide range of solutions, even if you have to work with an implementation over which you have no control.

For the interface problem previously discussed, the characteristics of each solution are found in Table 5.1.

6.

Interfacing to C: *SQLite* As an Example

Quite often the public interface of a library that you are interested in is written in a different programming language than the one you use. You will need an interface library that bridges the gap between both languages. This is the case with SQLite, a lightweight database management system [44]. It is written in C and there is a host of libraries to communicate with SQLite in all manner of languages.

For Fortran, there is the *fsqlite* library that I developed. It was inspired by the work of Al Danial [27], but focused on FORTRAN 77, that was mainly an example of how you could interface to the SQLite library. I wanted a generic solution instead.

The design decisions and the implementation of *fsqlite* illustrate a more general question: how to combine Fortran and other programming languages? Each time you need to consider:

- Low-level aspects of the combination:
  - How do the basic types of the two languages relate to each other?
  - What are the naming and calling conventions?
- High-level aspects relating to the actual library: What is a good "model" for the interface? Should you simply write wrapping routines that merely translate the routine interfaces or should you build a higher-level interface, molding the original interface into something that is a better fit for the library's use?

This chapter will cover both types of issues in the context of interfacing with C (an intermediate layer in C is often a convenient way to communicate with any other language) and of the interface to SQLite.

6.1 Matching Data Types

The basic data types of Fortran are: integer, logical, single, and double precision with real and complex numbers and character strings. C has more or less the same types (as they are dictated by computer hardware and tradition, more than language design), but there are important differences:

- In C, there are no logicals, instead integer values are used. However, nor are there complex numbers (although the C99 standard does define them).

76

A common approach is to mimic complex variables via an array of two real numbers or as a structure with two numbers.

■ In C, double precision reals (double) are the default, rather than single precision as in Fortran. Presumably, that has some historical reasons and does not reflect a typical need for high-precision computations in C programs. In the case of SQLite it means, however, that you do not store single precision reals in the database, only double precision.

■ Fortran does not have unsigned integers. While they can be emulated, handling such data types is a bit awkward. As long as you only need to pass the data, plain integers will suffice.

■ The most complicated aspects of matching data types are how to match character strings and arrays. Character strings in C are actually arrays of single characters where the end of the string is indicated by a NUL character (achar(0) in Fortran). Single characters are different from character strings. In Fortran, a character variable "knows" its length and there is no special convention to indicate that end of the string – strings are padded with spaces. This difference means you have to convert a string from the Fortran convention to the C convention and back, plus there is some loss of information. If trailing blanks are significant, you must adopt a separate mechanism in Fortran; for example, storing the significant length for each string. In C, you must take considerable care not to exceed the space that is allocated for the strings. There is no protection against overflowing the bounds, which could happen if you copy a string that is too long or forget to add the NUL character.

Arrays of any basic data type have their own set of complications. In C, arrays are essentially one-dimensional. Two-dimensional arrays can be emulated by an array of pointers (statically defined two-dimensional arrays behave as a shorthand notation). Here is a pattern you frequently find:

```
int    i;
int **array2d;

/* Create an array[20][10]
*/
array2d = (int **) malloc( 20 * sizeof(int *) );
*array2d = (int *) malloc( 20 * 10 * sizeof(int) ) ;

for ( i = 1; i < 20; i ++ ) {
    array2d[i] = array2d[0] + 10 * i;
}
```

The block of memory is divided into 20 pieces, each ten integers long. However, each piece could be arbitrarily long:

```
for ( i = 0; i < 20; i ++ ) {
    array2d[i] = (int *) malloc( (i+1) * sizeof(int) );
}
```

and will create a set of one-dimensional arrays each with a different length.

Fortran does not allow that sort of pattern, at least not with the same notation as regular two-dimensional arrays. Instead, in Fortran arrays are, at least conceptually, contiguous blocks of memory whose elements can be indexed with one, two, or more indices. If you need to pass a two-dimensional array to C, then use code like this to create the array of pointers that C requires.

```
/* The two-dimensional Fortran array f_array(dim1,dim2) appears
   as a one-dimensional array on the C side
   Extra complication: dimensions in C are reversed wrt Fortran
*/
void pass_2d_array( int *f_array, int *dim1, int *dim2 ) {

    int    i;
    int **c_array;

    /* Create a c_array[dim2][dim1]
    */
    c_array = (int **) malloc( (*dim2) * sizeof(int *) );

    for ( i = 0; i < (*dim2); i ++ ) {
        c_array[i] = f_array + (*dim1) * i;
    }
    . . .
}
```

In the previous C code, you can access Fortran array element f_array(4,5) as c_array[4][3].[1]

With the advent of Fortran 2003, a lot has changed in the way you can interface to C. Using the iso_c_binding intrinsic module, you can specify much more of the interface on the Fortran side (see Section 6.4). For instance, you can specify *kinds* for all basic data types so that they match the C data types. A type integer(c_long) in Fortran corresponds to a long int in C, whereas previously you had to take into account that C does not make guarantees about the actual size of a long int. The C standard only guarantees:

short int <= int <= long int

On 32-bits platforms, a long int is typically 32 bits long and on a 64-bits platform it is 64 bits, while an int is still 32 bits.

---

[1] In C indices, start at 0, meaning you need to offset the indices by −1 and the order of the indices is reversed.

6.2 Passing Arguments Between C and Fortran Routines

Basically speaking, Fortran (up to Fortran 2003) passes all arguments by reference and C passes all arguments by value (even with arrays and pointers, the address is passed as the value and by dereferencing that address you can manipulate the memory contents). In Fortran 2003, you can select the method of passing primarily to make interfacing to C easier, but it has some merits within a Fortran-only context too ([65], Section 14.6).

The result of this difference in argument passing is that you need to have an intermediate routine in C to accommodate for the mismatch. Here is an example from the *fsqlite* library. The routine `sqlite3_column_count_c` is used to get the number of database columns that will be returned in a query. On the Fortran side, it has this interface:

```
interface
    subroutine sqlite3_column_count_c( handle, count )
        integer, dimension(*) :: handle
        integer               :: count
    end subroutine sqlite3_column_count_c
end interface
```

The first argument is actually a pointer to an opaque structure of type `sqlite3_stmt`, defined by the SQLite library. On the Fortran side, it is mapped to a one-dimensional integer array of length 2, to accommodate for both 32-bits and 64-bits platforms. The interface predates the Fortran 2003 standard, otherwise the type `type(c_ptr)` would have been the method of choice.

On the C side, you get the start address of this array, but as it actually represents a pointer, you need two-level indirection (the double asterisk):[2]

```
void FTNCALL sqlite3_column_count_c_(
        sqlite3_stmt **stmt,
        int          *count ) {
    *count = sqlite3_column_count( *stmt ) ;
    return ;
}
```

The plain integer argument count on the Fortran side turns into a *pointer* to an `int` value. As you need to return a value via that argument, this is quite appropriate.

---

[2] The macro FTNCALL is used to get the calling convention correct and the extra underscore has to do with naming conventions (see the next section).

In Fortran 2003, you can solve this in a different way (note the value attribute for the stmt argument):

```
interface
    function sqlite3_column_count( stmt ) bind(C)
        use, intrinsic     :: iso_c_binding
        type(c_ptr), value :: stmt
        integer(c_int)     :: sqlite3_column_count
    end function sqlite3_column_count
end interface
```

You use the *intrinsic* module iso_c_binding to fully describe the interface on the Fortran side. This makes it possible to call the C function sqlite3_column_count directly, instead of via an intermediate C function that translates between the C and Fortran data types and function names. (The original intermediate C function behaves as a subroutine, but that is merely a choice.)

6.3 Naming and Calling Conventions

The next hurdles in combining Fortran and C concern the internal name of the routine you will call and the *calling convention*. For the first one, consider what should happen to a Fortran routine called MyRoutine:

```
subroutine MyRoutine
    ...
end subroutine MyRoutine
```

As Fortran does not distinguish between lowercase and uppercase in variable names and routine names, the name as presented to the linker is translated to either lowercase or uppercase, depending on the compiler.

To distinguish it from names in the system libraries, an underscore may be attached. The end result is that the name MyRoutine, which you use in the Fortran code, becomes MYROUTINE or myroutine_ (or some other variation). Routines defined in a module commonly get the name of the module prepended, so that the result might be mymodule_mp_myroutine_. It is these names that you should use in the C code, unless you use the Fortran 2003 naming feature.

The second issue, the calling convention, is more obscure. It touches upon low-level features of passing arguments and managing the memory involved (the stack). First, to pass a character string, most Fortran compilers insert an argument holding the length of the string that is not visible on the Fortran side, but is visible on the C side. The routine `sqlite3_do_c` looks like this on the Fortran side:

```
integer function sqlite3_do_c( handle, command, errmsg )
    integer, dimension(*) :: handle
    character(len=*)      :: command
    character(len=*)      :: errmsg
end function sqlite3_do_c
```

On the C side, the two hidden arguments are visible:

```
int FTNCALL sqlite3_do_c_(
      sqlite3 **db, char *command, char *errmsg,
      int len_command, int len_errmsg) {
   ...
}
```

With some compilers, hidden arguments are placed right after the string argument, while with other compilers hidden arguments are placed after all the regular arguments. The latter method seems to be the most common.

Finally, on Windows, there are two ways of cleaning up the stack after returning from a subroutine or function: the "cdecl" method where the caller is responsible and the "stdcall" method where the callee takes care of it. This second method appears to be deprecated, but is still used by many libraries. It is important that the proper method is used, otherwise the stack gets corrupted and the program will crash.

While all other aspects of C-Fortran interfacing can be handled in regular C or Fortran code, the matter of this calling convention has to be dealt with using Fortran compiler directives or non-standard C keywords:

```
#ifdef WIN32
#define FTNCALL __stdcall
#endif
```

or (for the *Intel Fortran* compiler – the *gfortran* compiler has a very similar method):

```
!dec$ attributes stdcall :: myroutine
```

Interfacing C and Fortran has become much easier in this case too with the `iso_c_binding` module of Fortran 2003. The preceding C routine can be replaced by a Fortran routine, but it is easier to leave the C version (see Section 6.5 for the code). The hidden arguments, however, can now be made explicit:

```
interface
    integer function sqlite3_do_c( handle, command, &
                        errmsg, len_errmsg ) bind(C)
        use, intrinsic                  :: iso_c_binding
```

```
        type(c_ptr), value                       :: handle
        character(kind=c_char), dimension(*) :: command
        character(kind=c_char), dimension(*) :: errmsg
        integer(kind=c_int), value               :: len_errmsg
    end function sqlite3_do_c
end interface
```

The Fortran routine fsqlite_do, the public routine you are supposed to use, converts the command string to a string in the C convention with a trailing NUL character, the result of trim(string)//achar(0).

When you pass the character strings to a routine that has the C binding attribute, the strings become, just as in C, arrays of single characters. This is a special rule in the standard. It boils down to an implicit conversion of the type:

```
character(len=*) :: string
```

```
character(len=1), dimension(*) :: string
```

As a consequence, there are no hidden length arguments anymore. You do need to pass the (maximum) length of the string that will store an error message, but that is an ordinary argument, visible on both the C and the Fortran sides.

As the names of the C functions match the names on the Fortran side, that is, they are all lowercase, there is no need to use the *binding label* in the bind clause. For a C function that has uppercase characters, like Sqlite3DoC, you would use:

```
interface
    function sqlite3_do_c( handle, command, &
                errmsg, len_errmsg ) &
                bind(C, name = 'Sqlite3DoC')

        . . .

    end function sqlite3_do_c
end interface
```

You can call this function by the name sqlite3_do_c in Fortran while on the C side it is called Sqlite3DoC.

6.4 Dealing with Derived Types

The aspects discussed so far all assume that you use only Fortran 77 features, basic types like single and double precision reals and arrays of fixed or assumed size. What about derived types, Fortran 90 pointers and allocatable arrays, or even Fortran 2003 polymorphic variables?

Because Fortran pointers are actually a very different concept than C pointers and the allocation of arrays in any language must be done in a consistent way, there are a number of restrictions.[3] The most important are:

- The components of a derived type cannot have the pointer or allocatable attributes, or be a derived type that in turn has such components.
- There cannot be any type-bound procedures.

To deal with pointers and allocatable arrays, you can use routines such as c_loc() to get the C address of a Fortran variable (including pointers and allocatables) or c_f_pointer() to convert a C address (C pointer) to a Fortran pointer.

Here is a simple example. The C struct

```
typedef struct {
    int number;
    char name[10];
    float *array;
} mystruct;
```

can be represented in Fortran as:

```
use iso_binding_c
type, bind(C) :: mystruct
    integer(c_int)                    :: number
    character(c_char), dimension(10)  :: name
    type(c_ptr)                       :: array
end type mystruct
```

The component **array** is not recognizable as an array of reals on the Fortran side, so you will have to take special care, as illustrated in the following.

Here are several fragments of a library written by Daniel Kraft to interface with the *MySQL* database management system ([57], the layout has been adjusted to the style used in this book). It uses the iso_c_binding module to completely define this interface in Fortran. Data are stored in dedicated derived types, such as:

```
type myfortran_row
  integer                 :: num_fields
  integer, allocatable :: lengths(:)
  type(c_ptr)             :: c_row
end type myfortran_row
```

---

[3] Work is being done on an extension of the interfacing facilities that will relieve many of these restrictions [12].

The various MySQL routines have interfaces like these:

```
interface
    function c_fetch_row (res) bind(C, name='mysql_fetch_row')
        use, intrinsic      :: iso_c_binding
        type(c_ptr), value :: res
        type(c_ptr)         :: c_fetch_row
    end function c_fetch_row
end interface
```

To get the results of a query, row by row, into a Fortran program, the function myfortran_fetch_row is used: The C function c_fetch_row returns the data in the row as a long string of characters and the C function c_fetch_lengths returns the lengths of the fields within this long string. To manage these C data structures, several intrinsic functions from the iso_c_binding module are used:

```
! Fetch a row.  Returns false if no more rows available.
logical function myfortran_fetch_row( res, row )
    type(myfortran_result), intent(inout) :: res
    type(myfortran_row), intent(out)       :: row

    integer(c_int), pointer                :: lenptr(:)
    type(c_ptr)                            :: lengths

    !
    ! Fetch the row data itself.
    !
    row%c_row           = c_fetch_row( res%res )
    myfortran_fetch_row = c_associated( row%c_row )

    if (.not. myfortran_fetch_row) return

    !
    ! Fetch number of fields.
    !
    row%num_fields = c_num_fields( res%res )

    !
    ! Get field lengths.
    !
    allocate( row%lengths(row%num_fields) )

    lengths = c_fetch_lengths( res%res )
    call c_f_pointer( lengths, lenptr, shape(row%lengths) )

    row%lengths = lenptr

end function myfortran_fetch_row
```

Once the row data has been retrieved, another function takes care of extracting the correct data for a particular field, which again requires a routine from the iso_c_binding module:

```
! Get a field from a row.
function myfortran_get_field( row, ind )
    type(myfortran_row), intent(in) :: row
    integer, intent(in)             :: ind
    character(len=row%lengths(ind)) :: myfortran_get_field

    type(c_ptr), pointer :: cstrs(:)
    character(kind=c_char), pointer :: cstr(:)
    integer :: i

    call c_f_pointer( row%c_row, cstrs, shape (row%lengths) )
    call c_f_pointer( cstrs(ind), cstr, (/row%lengths(ind)/) )

    do i = 1, row%lengths(ind)
        myfortran_get_field(i:i) = cstr(i)
    end do
end function myfortran_get_field
```

6.5 Interfacing to SQLite

SQLite is a well-known open source database management system developed by Richard Hipp [44]. It actually consists of a single C library as it works without a server. A simple but typical scenario for working with SQLite is:

- Open the database (an ordinary file or a block of memory).
- Run one or more SQL statements to create a new table and fill it with data or to select existing data from an existing set of tables.
- Close the file.

The goal of the *fsqlite* library is to work with SQLite without having to know anything about SQL, although for more complicated queries you would need to construct suitable SQL statements. More specifically, *fsqlite* provides high-level routines to:

- Connect to the database
- Create tables and query the structure of the tables
- Select data from the tables
- Enter new data or delete existing data
- Start and stop transactions

The connection to the database is represented by a C pointer to an opaque data structure. Executing SQL statements is at the heart of the library and these statements are represented by a pointer to another opaque structure. For the library to be useable from Fortran, you need to deal with these pointers.

As previously explained, the library *fsqlite* stores these pointers in a small array of integers – long enough to hold C pointers on 32-bits and 64-bits machines. On the Fortran side, the arrays are kept in derived types:

```fortran
type sqlite_database
    integer, dimension(2)    :: db_handle
    integer                  :: error
    character(len=80)        :: errmsg
end type sqlite_database
```

Many of the routines in the *fsqlite* library simply run a single SQL statement, but the only information returned is whether all went well or there was some error condition. To communicate this to the Fortran side, the type sqlite_database also holds the error code and the error message (if any). The Fortran routine sqlite3_do takes care of this:

```fortran
subroutine sqlite3_do( db, command )
   type(sqlite_database) :: db
   character(len=*)       :: command

   interface
      integer function sqlite3_do_c( handle, command, errmsg )
         integer, dimension(*) :: handle
         character(len=*)      :: command
         character(len=*)      :: errmsg
      end function sqlite3_do_c
   end interface

   ! +1 for the NUL character
   character(len=len(command)+1) :: commandc
   integer                       :: k

   commandc = command
   call stringtoc( commandc )

   db%errmsg = ' '
   db%error  = sqlite3_do_c( db%db_handle, commandc, db%errmsg )

end subroutine sqlite3_do
```

Its C counterpart (sqlite3_do_c_, slightly simplified):

```c
int FTNCALL sqlite3_do_c_(
      sqlite3 **db,
      char *command,
      char *errmsg,
      int   len_command,
      int   len_errmsg ) {
   int   rc ;
```

```
    char *msg ;

    rc = sqlite3_exec(*db, command, callback, 0, &msg ) ;
    if ( msg != NULL )
    {
        strncpy( errmsg, msg, len_errmsg ) ;
    }
    return rc ;
}
```

The SQL statement that you must run is contained in the string argument. This string is first converted into a string compatible with C. For this purpose, use a local string variable with a length one larger than that of the incoming string, so that there is always room for the NUL character at the end.

As you can see, the C side does not get passed the derived type. Instead, only pass the individual fields of the sqlite_database type.

This routine suffices for all SQL statements where no information is returned or passed on beyond an error code. It suffices, for instance, to create a new table when the SQL statement to do so has been constructed:

```
subroutine sqlite3_create_table( &
            db, tablename, columns, primary )
    type(sqlite_database)                :: db
    character(len=*)                     :: tablename
    type(sqlite_column), dimension(:)    :: columns
    character(len=*), optional           :: primary

    character(len=20+80*size(columns))   :: command
    character(len=40)                    :: primary_
    integer                              :: i, ncols

    primary_ = ' '
    if ( present(primary) ) then
        primary_ = primary
    endif

    ncols = size(columns)
    write( command, '(100a)' ) &
        'create table ', tablename, ' (', &
        ( trim(columns(i)%name), ' ', &
          trim(typename(columns(i), primary_)), ', ', &
            i = 1,ncols-1 ), &
        trim(columns(ncols)%name), ' ', &
        trim(typename(columns(ncols),primary_)), ')'

    call sqlite3_do( db, command )

end subroutine sqlite3_create_table
```

The description of what columns the table should contain is stored in an array of type sqlite_column. This derived type is used throughout to deal with how the SQL language, as implemented in SQLite, handles data types. Several auxiliary routines are available to fill the fields of this data type and to extract information, as shown in this fragment:

```
type(sqlite_database)              :: db
type(sqlite_column), dimension(4) :: col

call sqlite3_open( 'somedata.db', db )

call sqlite3_column_props( col(1), 'station', sqlite_char, 10 )
call sqlite3_column_props( col(2), 'date', sqlite_char, 10 )
call sqlite3_column_props( col(3), 'salinity', sqlite_real )
call sqlite3_column_props( col(4), 'temperature', sqlite_real )

call sqlite3_create_table( db, 'measurements', col )
```

To get data from the database or store new data, you also use the sqlite_column type, but here you need to be careful: SQLite uses a *binding* technique to communicate the values back and forth – rather than via arguments, which would be awkward as the types and the number of data will vary per query or per table. Therefore, it stores the *addresses* of the variables that (will) hold the data. These variables may not be local variables in a subroutine, as these cease to exist as soon as you return from the subroutine. Instead, use the fields in the sqlite_column type (extracted from the sqlite3_insert routine):

```
!
! Prepare the insert statement for this table
! (The question marks indicate the bound variables)
!
write( command, '(100a)' ) 'insert into ', trim(tablename), &
    ' values(', ('?,', i = 1,size(columns)-1), '?)'

call stringtoc( command )
prepared_columns => columns
call sqlite3_prepare( db, command, stmt, prepared_columns )

!
! Bind the values
!
do i = 1,size(columns)
    select case (columns(i)%type_set)
    case (sqlite_int)
        rc = sqlite3_bind_int_c( &
                stmt%stmt_handle, i, columns(i)%int_value )
    case (sqlite_double)
        rc = sqlite3_bind_double_c( &
                stmt%stmt_handle, i, columns(i)%double_value )
```

```
      case (sqlite_char)
         rc = sqlite3_bind_text_c( &
                  stmt%stmt_handle, i, &
                  trim(columns(i)%char_value) )
      end select
      if ( rc .ne. 0 ) then
         db%error = rc
         call sqlite3_errmsg_c( db%db_handle, db%errmsg )
         call stringtof( db%errmsg )
      endif
enddo

!
! Actually perform the insert command
!
call sqlite3_step( stmt, rc )
call sqlite3_finalize( stmt )
```

(Using the *result* of the trim() function is safe, as the corresponding SQLite routine, sqlite3_bind_text(), is called with the flag SQLITE_TRANSIENT, to indicate that it should create a copy of the string.)

Retrieving the data is done in a completely analogous way. The following program illustrates the interface. It first creates a database with one table and fills it with data from a CSV file, consisting of the name of a monitoring station and three measured values. Then, it queries the database to get averages per station, sorted alphabetically:

```
program csvtable
    use sqlite

    implicit none

    type(sqlite_database)                    :: db
    type(sqlite_statement)                   :: stmt
    type(sqlite_column), dimension(:), pointer :: col

    integer                                  :: lun = 10
    integer                                  :: i
    integer                                  :: j
    integer                                  :: ierr
    character(len=40), dimension(4)          :: name
    real                                     :: salin
    real                                     :: temp
    character(len=40)                        :: station
    character(len=40)                        :: date
    logical                                  :: finished

    character(len=40), pointer, dimension(:,:) :: result
```

```fortran
character(len=80)                                     :: errmsg

!
! Read the CSV file and feed the data into the database
!
open( lun, file = 'somedata.csv' )
read( lun, * ) name

call sqlite3_open( 'somedata.db', db )

allocate( col(4) )
call sqlite3_column_props(col(1), name(1), sqlite_char, 10)
call sqlite3_column_props(col(2), name(2), sqlite_char, 10)
call sqlite3_column_props(col(3), name(3), sqlite_real)
call sqlite3_column_props(col(4), name(4), sqlite_real)
call sqlite3_create_table( db, 'measurements', col )

!
! Insert the values into the table. For better performance,
! make sure (via begin/commit) that the changes are committed
! only once.
!
call sqlite3_begin( db )
do
    read( lun, *, iostat=ierr ) &
        station, date, salin, temp

    if ( ierr .ne. 0 ) exit

    call sqlite3_set_column( col(1), station )
    call sqlite3_set_column( col(2), date   )
    call sqlite3_set_column( col(3), salin  )
    call sqlite3_set_column( col(4), temp   )

    call sqlite3_insert( db, 'measurements', col )

enddo

close( lun )

call sqlite3_commit( db )

!
! We want a simple report, the mean of salinity and
    temperature
! sorted by the station
!
```

```
deallocate( col )
allocate( col(3) )

call sqlite3_column_query( col(1), 'station', sqlite_char )
call sqlite3_column_query( col(2), name(3), sqlite_real, &
        function='avg' )
call sqlite3_column_query( col(3), name(4), sqlite_real, &
        function='avg' )

call sqlite3_prepare_select( db, 'measurements', col, &
        stmt, 'group by station order by station' )

write( *, '(3a20)' ) &
    'Station', 'Mean salinity', 'Mean temperature'
do
    call sqlite3_next_row( stmt, col, finished )

    if ( finished ) exit

    call sqlite3_get_column( col(1), station )
    call sqlite3_get_column( col(2), salin  )
    call sqlite3_get_column( col(3), temp   )

    write( *, '(a20,2f20.3)' ) station, salin, temp
enddo

call sqlite3_close( db )

end program
```

The program lets the *fsqlite* library take care of constructing the various SQL statements. Only the extra clause to the `sqlite3_prepare_select` routine exposes a part of an SQL statement. The results of the query are then retrieved row by row.

7.

Graphics, GUIs, and the Internet

Interaction with the user via graphical presentation or graphical interfaces is an extremely important aspect of computing. It is also an area that depends heavily on the available hardware and the operating system. While much effort has been put into the various operating environments to hide the hardware aspect, programming a graphical user-interface (GUI) on MS Windows is completely different from doing so on Linux or Mac OS X.

Hardly any programming language defines how you can display results graphically or how to build a graphical user-interface. The common approach is to use a library that hides – if possible or desirable – the specifics of the operating system, so that a portable program results. Some libraries, however, have been designed to take advantage of exactly one operating system, so that the program fits seamlessly in that environment, at the cost of not being portable anymore. At the same time, you should not underestimate the effort and skills required for designing and building a useful and usable GUI [3].

For a Fortran programmer, the situation is a bit complicated: most GUI libraries are written with C, C++, and similar languages in mind. Furthermore, a GUI for a long-running computation should have different properties than one for filling in a database form. This chapter examines a variety of solutions.

7.1 Plotting the Results

The first type of graphical interaction to examine is the presentation of the results of a computation. The responses from the user are simple: leaf through the collection of plots – in many cases sequentially – and maybe change a display parameter here and there. Anything more falls in the category of GUIs. This is essentially a one-way interaction, therefore, all you need is a library of routines to draw various objects on the screen or in a file on disk, like a PostScript or PDF file, for later processing.

There exists a broad variety of such libraries [18], [25], many with Fortran bindings and both commercial and open source software. From this collection, I describe *PLplot* in more detail. I chose this library as I have been involved in its development and maintenance for several years now and as a consequence

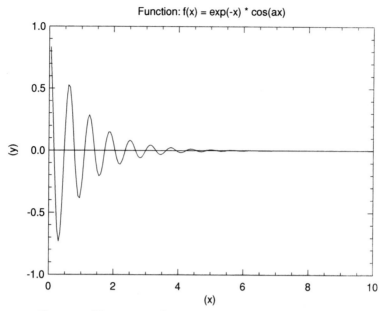

Figure 7.1. Plotting a graph via PLplot

know its usage and capabilities. You can choose any library that better suits your purposes, but the principles will be similar.

PLplot is a library, or rather a collection of libraries, for plotting technical and scientific data, such that the source code is independent of the platform. It offers a wide range of output formats (both on screen and in files on disk) as well as interfaces to a variety of languages (C, Java, Octave, and Tcl to name a few). It has an interface to Fortran in both FORTRAN 77 and Fortran 90 style.

The style of programming is illustrated with a small example. The program reads a parameter a for the function f: $f(x) = \exp(-x) \cos ax$ and then draws a graph of that function. To do this, it uses the following PLplot routines:

- `plparseopts` analyzes the command-line arguments and one or more parameters.
- `plinit` initializes the library, asks for the output device if that is not set (via the command-line arguments or the routine `pldev`), and brings up a graphical window.
- `plenv` and `pllab` are used to draw a simple axis system with labels.
- `plline` draws a continuous line through the data points.
- `plend` finalizes the library (for example, in interactive mode it waits for the user to click in the window, while in batch mode it completes the output files).

The source code for the program follows[1]

```fortran
program plotgraph
    use plplot

    implicit none

    real(kind=plflt)                      :: param
    real(kind=plflt), dimension(201) :: x, y
    real(kind=plflt)                      :: xmin, ymin, xmax, ymax
    integer                               :: justify, axis
    integer                               :: i

    ! Ask for the parameter "a"
    write(*,*) 'Value for the parameter "a":'
    read(*,*) param

    ! Parse the command-line arguments
    call plparseopts(PL_PARSE_FULL)

    ! Initialize the library
    call plinit

    ! Set up the viewport with default axes
    xmin =  0.0_plflt
    xmax = 10.0_plflt
    ymin = -1.0_plflt
    ymax =  1.0_plflt

    justify = 0
    axis    = 0
    call plenv( xmin, xmax, ymin, ymax, justify, axis )
    call pllab( '(x)', '(y)', &
             'Function: f(x) = exp(-x) * cos(ax)' )

    ! Compute the values and draw the graph
    do i = 1,size(x)
        x(i) = (i-1) * 0.05_plflt
        y(i) = func( param, x(i) )
    enddo

    call plline( x, y )

    call plend
contains
```

---

[1] The real kind *plflt* is used to make the program independent of the specific reals the PLplot library expects – it can be either single or double precision, depending on the build options.

```
   real function func( param, x )
      real(kind=plflt) :: param, x

      func = exp(-x) * cos(param*x)

   end function func

   end program plotgraph
```

By selecting the right device, you can get the picture on screen or store it in a PNG file.

Libraries such as PLplot generally offer both low-level routines for plotting graphical primitives, like lines and circles, and high-level routines that take care of many details – plotting a time axis or a complete shaded surface in three dimensions. Some also offer GUI capabilities [*DISLIN* and *Interacter*, for instance, and both commercial products, see also [29] for several others].

An alternative approach is to separate the program that does the graphical presentation and the program that provides the data for that presentation. This gives you a number of benefits:

- The computational program can be developed independently of the presentation program.
- The presentation program in turn could be an off-the-shelf product like *gnuplot* or a MATLAB script.
- If the computations take a long time, simply store the results in a file and present them later. There is no need to try and show intermediate results.

The two programs can actually run together, so for the user, it is irrelevant which program does what. The following Tcl/Tk program presents a very simple interface where the user enters a value for the parameter a and presses the button. It feeds this value to the computational program that then produces a table of values to plot (see Figure 7.2):

```
# plotgui.tcl --
#     Very simple GUI:
#     - Get one value
#     - Run the computational program
#     - Display the result
#

#
# Load a plotting package
#
package require Plotchart
```

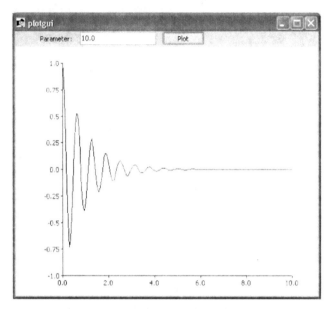

Figure 7.2. Plotting a graph via a simple GUI in Tcl/Tk

```
#
# Create the user-interface elements
#
::ttk::frame   .toprow
::ttk::button  .toprow.b -text Plot \
                    -command {putValue} -width 10
::ttk::label   .toprow.l -text Parameter:
::ttk::entry   .toprow.e -textvariable parameter

canvas .c -width 500 -height 400 -bg white

#
# Arrange them in the main window (.)
grid   .toprow.l .toprow.e .toprow.b -padx 5 -sticky w
grid   .toprow
grid   .c -  -

#
# Auxiliary procedures
#
proc putValue {} {
    global parameter
    global program
    global plot
```

```
        puts $program $parameter
        flush $program

        #
        # Clean up the graph
        #
        $plot plot data {} {}
        .c delete data
}

proc readData {channel} {
    global plot

    if { ![eof $channel] } {

        gets $channel line

        scan $line "%f %f" x y
        $plot plot data $x $y

    } else {
        close $channel
    }
}

#
# Set up the plot and start the program
#
set parameter 1.0

set plot [::Plotchart::createXYPlot .c {0.0 10.0 2.0} \
            {-1.0 1.0 0.25}]

set program [open "|runprogram" r+]
fileevent $program readable [list readData $program]

#
# The event loop starts automatically ...
# We can just wait now
```

The Fortran program that is run is called "runprogram" or "runprogram.exe", depending on the platform. It is run via a so-called pipe, therefore, the Tcl program can send data to the Fortran program and vice versa. The details are hidden in the Tcl open command and the pipe symbol (|) that precedes the name of the program. Because such communication is *event-driven*, use the fileevent command to set up an event handler for this communication. The *Plotchart* package is a Tcl-only package for plotting xy-graphs and other common types of charts [52].

The source code for "runprogram" is straightforward:

```
program runprogram
    use iso_fortran_env

    implicit none

    real    :: param, x, y
    integer :: i

    do
        read(*,*) param

        do i = 0,200
            x = i * 0.05
            y = func( param, x )

            write(*,*) x, y
        enddo

        flush( output_unit )

    enddo
contains

real function func( param, x )
    real :: param, x

    func = exp(-x) * cos(param*x)

end function func
end program runprogram
```

The only special feature is the use of the `flush` statement to ensure that the data are immediately sent to the Tcl program, rather than kept in a buffer until that is full.

With this architecture, the responsibilities are completely separated:

- The presentation program merely expects the computational program to read the parameter and to produce the table.
- The computational program can be changed or completely replaced independently of the presentation program (and vice versa).

7.2 Graphical User-Interfaces

From the programmer's point of view, graphical user-interfaces differ in one important aspect from textual interfaces: There is no predefined order in which the user makes choices. With a textual interface, the program can present a list of possibilities and the user selects one. Based on that choice, the program does some processing and presents the next list of choices, or perhaps a question, to get the value of a parameter. The program, however, dictates the order.

With GUIs, the user sees all possibilities within one screen. He or she can decide to fill in all the entry fields in any order, leave out a few, then press one of a range of buttons, or select a menu item. This has distinct consequences for the architecture of a GUI program. The decision structure at the heart of a textual interface is not present anymore. Instead, the various parts of a GUI program need to respond to *events* such as when the user presses the button "Run", so the program gathers all information typed in the window and runs the computation. In the Tcl/Tk example from the previous section, this is handled by associating the command putValue with the push button labeled "Run." The value that the user entered is kept in a global variable parameter, as the entry widget[2] and that variable are connected:

```
entry   .toprow.e -textvariable parameter
```

In other GUI systems, you may have to read out the contents of the window explicitly before running the computation.

Another type of event is when the keyboard focus is set or lost in an entry widget. You can use this to check if the value that the user typed is acceptable. For example, is it a proper number?

The structure of the program, therefore, will look like this:

- An implicit or explicit event loop, where the program receives the events that describe the user's actions. From the event loop, the routines associated with the events are called.

  In many systems, the interface for these routines is fixed – you cannot pass an arbitrary list of arguments and, therefore, you need access to some global data structure.[3]

- A global data structure that is filled and read by the routines associated with the events.

- A set of routines that are responsible for the appropriate actions based on the event. These routines have to be registered so that the event loop can dispatch each event to such a routine.

With some toolkits for building GUIs, routines for handling events receive all events for a particular window and, therefore, they have to handle events for all widgets inside that window. With other toolkits, routines may be associated with a particular widget or even a particular type of event for the widget. The Software Development Kit (SDK) on MicroSoft Windows, meant for

---

[2] The term *widget* is commonly used for elements of a GUI window. It refers to that element and the way it reacts to various events (mouse clicks, for instance). Another term is *control*.

[3] This is another example of the interface or environment problem, discussed in Chapter 5.

developing C programs, is an example of the first category. The AWT toolkit found in Java is an example of the second.

The Tk toolkit, part of Tcl/Tk[4], takes care of many details automatically and, therefore, offers a high-level interface. Typically, there are only a few events of interest for the programmer, and you bind a routine to the combination of widget and event.

That said, there are roughly four methods to add a GUI to a (computational) program:

- The program and its computations are extended with a GUI library so that it brings up the windows and handles all events.
- The original program is turned into a library. A more or less separate GUI program is written, which calls the routines from the computational library to do the computations.
- The GUI is a completely separate program that merely writes the input files for the computational program.
- The GUI interacts with the computational program in a similar manner as the Tcl/Tk program in the previous section.

An example of the first approach is found in the *Xeffort* library [33].[5] This library, developed by Jugoslav Dujic, allows you to build user-interfaces directly in Fortran. It assumes a particular development environment: MS Windows and the *Intel Fortran* compiler. Here are a few fragments from the *XGraph* example to illustrate the style of programming:

```
!PURPOSE: Initialization function called by XFT library
!         on app start.
LOGICAL FUNCTION XInit(szCmdLine,nCmdShow)
!DEC$ATTRIBUTES DECORATE, ALIAS: "XINIT":: Xinit

USE View
USE FuncDlg

IMPLICIT NONE

CHARACTER(*), INTENT(IN)::    szCmdLine
INTEGER, INTENT(IN)::         nCmdShow

LOGICAL::         bSt
INTEGER::         iSt, iX, iY
```

---

[4] For the Tk toolkit bindings exist for a large number of other programming languages such as Perl and Python.

[5] At the time of this writing, Jerry Delisle is developing Fortran bindings for the *GTK+* toolkit to provide a platform-independent solution [30].

```
INCLUDE 'Resource.fd'

!Loading menu resource
xMenu = XLoadMenu(IDR_MENU_MAIN)

bSt = XLoadAccelerators(IDR_ACCELTABLE)
!Creation of App & frame window
bSt = XCreateSDIApp(xMenu, "XGraph", IDI_ICON_MAIN, &
        iExStyle=WS_EX_CONTROLPARENT+WS_EX_APPWINDOW)

!Handle sizing of the main window
bSt = XSetHandler(XW_FRAME, WM_SIZE, XW_FRAME_OnSize)
bSt = XSetHandler(XW_FRAME, WM_CLOSE, XW_FRAME_OnClose)

!Menu item handlers
bSt = XSetCommand(XW_FRAME, IDM_HELP_ABOUT, XFrame_OnAbout)
bSt = XSetCommand(XW_FRAME, IDM_FILE_CLOSE, XFrame_OnExit)
bSt = XSetCommand(XW_FRAME, IDM_VIEW_GRID, &
        XW_FRAME_OnViewGrid)
bSt = XSetCommand(XW_FRAME, IDM_COPY_WMF, XW_FRAME_OnCopyWmf)
bSt = XSetCommand(XW_FRAME, IDM_COPY_BMP, XW_FRAME_OnCopyBmp)
bSt = XSetCommand(XW_FRAME, IDM_FILE_SAVEAS, &
        XW_FRAME_OnFileSaveas)

!Create dialog for entering function properties
CALL XFuncDlg_Create()
!Create view window for image rendering
CALL XView_Create()

!Force refresh of the window/scrollbar
bSt = XGetClientRect(XW_FRAME, iX, iY)
bSt = XW_FRAME_OnSize(XW_FRAME, iX, iY, 0)

XInit = .TRUE.

END FUNCTION XInit
```

Here is the function to react to the user resizing the window:

```
!=========================================================
!Called whenever the window is resized. It demonstrates
!two types of behavior:
! - when the size is "locked", the virtual image size
!   remains unchanged. Scrollbars appear whenever necessary
! - otherwise, the image is scaled to match the client
!   area dimensions.
LOGICAL FUNCTION XW_FRAME_OnSize( &
        xWnd, iWidth, iHeight, nFlag)
```

```
USE View
USE FuncDlg

TYPE(X_WINDOW)::          xWnd
INTEGER, INTENT(IN)::     iWidth, iHeight
INTEGER, INTENT(IN)::     nFlag

LOGICAL::                 bSt
INTEGER::                 iX, iY, jWidth, jHeight

!Move the FuncDlg window
bSt = XGetWindowPos(xFuncDlg, iX, iY, iWidth=jWidth, &
         iHeight=jHeight)
bSt = XSetWindowPos(xFuncDlg, 0, 0, iWidth, jHeight)
!Move the View window just below the FuncDlg window
bSt = XSetWindowPos(xView, 0, jHeight, iWidth, &
         iHeight-jHeight)
CALL XUpdateWindow(xView)

XW_FRAME_OnSize = .FALSE.

END FUNCTION XW_FRAME_OnSize
```

The resulting user-interface is shown in Figure 7.3. The programming model is therefore:

- Create individual subroutines like XW_FRAME_OnSize for handling particular events in a window.
- Register these routines so that they can be automatically invoked when the event occurs.

The second approach, using the program as a library, is illustrated by the *Ftcl* library that I developed myself [55]. This library enables you to use Fortran routines as new Tcl commands. The method to do so is to create a routine with a predefined interface and to register it as a new command:

```
module functions
    implicit none
contains

! compute_func --
!     Compute the function:
!         f(x) = exp(-x) * cos(ax)
!
! Arguments:
!     cmdname          Name of the Tcl command
!     noargs           Number of arguments
!
subroutine compute_func( cmdname, noargs )
```

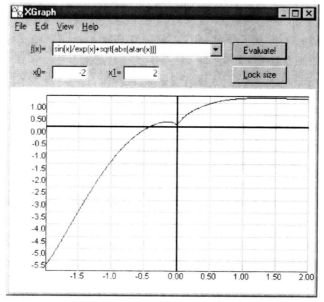

Figure 7.3. Example of a graphical user-interface using the Xeffort library

```fortran
    character(len=*) :: cmdname
    integer          :: noargs

    real             :: param
    real             :: x
    real             :: result

    if ( noargs .ne. 2 ) then
        call ftcl_set_error( &
                "Usage: " // trim(cmdname) // " param x" )
        return
    else
        call ftcl_get_arg( 1, param )
        call ftcl_get_arg( 2, x )

        result = exp(-x) * cos(param * x)

        call ftcl_put_result( result )
    endif
end subroutine compute_func
end module functions

! package_init --
!     Register the commands and the package itself
```

```
!
! Arguments:
!    error              Zero if all is okay, otherwise an error
!                       occurred while initializing
!
subroutine package_init( error )
    use functions

    implicit none
    integer :: error

    error = 0

    call ftcl_make_command( compute_func, "func" )

    call ftcl_provide_package( "functions", "1.0", error )

end subroutine package_init
```

The Fortran subroutine compute_func is callable from Tcl via the command func. The routine ftcl_make_command takes care of the details. Note that the routine package_init is kept out of a module, as it needs to be called from a C function.

Then, the GUI is programmed using Tcl/Tk:[6]

```
...
package require functions
...
::ttk::button .toprow.b -text Plot -command {drawGraph} \
                -width 10

...

proc drawGraph {} {
    global parameter
    global plot

    #
    # Clean up the graph
    #
    $plot plot data {} {}
    .c delete data
```

---

[6] While using two different programming languages makes it is easy to separate the GUI from the computations, this separation, is of course, possible within one language, too. It takes more discipline, however, to maintain the separation of concerns.

Table 7.1. Characteristics of Various Methods for Adding a GUI to a Program

Method	Advantages
Integrated GUI and computations	One programming language GUI and computational program naturally evolve together
GUI with computational library	One or two programming languages, choose the most suitable ones Clear separation of responsibilities
Separate programs and cooperating programs	Complete freedom in choosing the development environment for the GUI Clear separation of responsibilities

Method	Disadvantages
Integrated GUI and computations	Suitable Fortran toolkit required Intertwined of responsibilities
GUI with computational library	Interfacing to Fortran required if the GUI toolkit does not support Fortran directly
Separate programs and Cooperating programs	Independent programs can lead to disparate development

```
for {set i 0} {$i <= 200} {incr i} {
    set x [expr {$i * 0.05}]
    set y [func $parameter $x]
    $plot plot data $x $y
}
}
...
```

Instead of starting an external program as in Section 7.1, call the routine drawGraph in response to pressing the button. This routine calls the Fortran routine via func once for each data point.

The advantages and disadvantages of the various approaches are summarized in Table 7.1.

7.3 The Internet

While creating a complete Internet site that is rich in content is no sinecure, the technical principle is remarkably simple. A server program handles the incoming requests for information. It passes these requests to the right component, which, in turn, produces an HTML file that the server sends back to the client.

Although this book will not consider what the server is all about, it will look at a single method that an Internet server can use to interact with the component – the so-called common gateway interface or CGI. This is the only method that is independent of the chosen server software. With other methods, the program that implements the actual service is called as a library and the interaction with the server relies on a set of routines that are specific to the server.

CGI is a relatively simple, uniform protocol. The server starts the program as a separate process, sending it information about the request either via "standard input" (read(*,*)) or via an environment variable. The program itself then writes the output with a suitable header to the "standard output" (write(*,*)).

The technical complications are limited:

- You need to get the parameters that are part of the user's request from the information supplied by the server. The details depend on which method was used in the HTML file that led to the new request, "GET" or "POST".[7]
- The output should have a header that tells the server (and the receiving client) what kind of output is sent – plain text, HTML text, and so on.

More important, however, are the complications that arise from the modus operandi:

- A CGI program starts and stops independently with each request. Therefore, there is no state information other than that stored in the parameters belonging to the request.
- There may be many requests at once, so that the program is started several times. This means you will have to devise a way to store data in independent files, if you need external files.

Suppose that you want to show the new results in a long-running computation. You have to store what results the user saw last somewhere, if you want to show results they have not seen. This "somewhere" may be a file on disk, but you will have to store the user's identity and what computation he or she wants to see as well. Then, this all information must be somehow retrieved.

The following illustrates the basics of CGI using a simple service. Suppose you want to design a website that presents a table of function values. The function is that of Section 7.1. The user types in the single parameter and sends a request to the server for the table. Here is the initial HTML page:

```
<html>
<head><title>Table of function values</title>
<body>
Parameter: <input type="text" name="param" value="0.0">
<input type="submit">
</body>
</html>
```

---

[7] The CGI module in the *Flibs* library [57] takes care of these details.

The CGI program will produce this same page but extended with the table (or a graph of the function, using PLplot to create a GIF file). This way the user can change the parameter value and ask for a new table without having to navigate back.

When the user clicks on the Submit button, the URL connected to the button is sent back along with the parameter value. On the server side, the CGI program is called. Using the CGI module from the Flibs library, you can write the code like this:

```
program cgi_example

    use cgi_protocol

    implicit none

    ! Initialization is important!
    type(dict_struct), pointer :: dict => null()
    integer                    :: i
    integer                    :: luout
    integer                    :: steps
    real                       :: xmin
    real                       :: xmax
    real                       :: param
    real                       :: x, y
    character(len=20)          :: param_string

    !
    ! Get the CGI information
    ! and write the start of the HTML file (plus the
    ! start of the table)
    ! (Note: we include the text entry and submit button,
    ! so the user can easily select a new value)
    !
    call cgi_begin( output_html, dict, luout )

    call cgi_get( dict, "param", param )
    call cgi_get( dict, "param", param_string )

    write( luout, '(a)' ) '<html>'
    write( luout, '(a)' ) &
        '<head><title>Table of function values</title></head>'
    write( luout, '(a)' ) '<body>'

    write( luout, '(a,a,a)' ) &
        'Parameter: <input type="text" name="param" value="', &
        trim(param_string), '"> <input type="submit">'
```

```fortran
write( luout, '(a)' ) '<table>'
write( luout, '(a)' ) '<tr>'
write( luout, '(3a)' ) &
    '    <td>x</td><td>f(x) = exp(-x) * cos(ax)</td>'
write( luout, '(a)' ) '</tr>'

!
! Produce the table of function values
!
xmin  =   0.0
xmax  =  10.0
steps = 201

do i = 1,steps
    x = (i-1) * 0.05

    y = func(param, x)

    write( luout, '(a)' ) '<tr>'
    write( luout, '(a,f10.4,a,f10.4,a)' ) &
        '    <td>', x, '</td><td>', y, '</td>'
    write( luout, '(a)' ) '</tr>'
enddo

write( luout, '(a)' ) '</table>'
write( luout, '(a)' ) '</body>'
write( luout, '(a)' ) '</html>'

!
! We are done
!
call cgi_end

contains

real function func( param, x )
    real :: param, x

    func = exp(-x) * cos(param*x)

end function func

end program cgi_example
```

The parameters from the request (a single one in this example) are analyzed by the routine cgi_begin and stored in a so-called dictionary. This contains the names of the parameters and their values. Using the routine cgi_get you can then get the value by name, almost all details are hidden in the module.

When the actual output of the program is written to the output file ("word"), the final routine can finish the output, so that it is a valid CGI response.

In a more elaborate web application, you may end up with many such programs or just a few that can write many different HTML pages. The same principle applies though: The various runs must be independent of each other and only by external administration can you keep some form of state information. Well-known techniques for doing so are cookies, but hidden variables in the HTML page may help as well. These topics are beyond the scope of this book [15].

7.4 Dealing with XML Files

With the Internet, one particular file format has become very popular: XML files. The attraction of XML files is that their regular structure makes it possible to develop generic libraries for parsing the contents and verifying that they comply to the expected structure. This makes them very suitable for conveying, configuration information.

Furthermore, the structure is hierarchical, making it easy to group the information in ways that are most suitable for the purpose. This hierarchy is used extensively in *docbook* [81], a set of conventions to structure the text and layout of books, including software manuals (the PLplot library, discussed in the beginning of this chapter, is documented using docbook).

A simple example of an XML file is:

```
<?xml version="1.0"?>
<bibliography>
    <book reference="GulliversTravels">
        <author>Jonathan Swift</author>
        <year>...</year>
        <title>Gulliver's travels</title>
    </book>
    <book reference="Iliad">
        <author>Homer</author>
        <year>unknown</year>
        <title>Iliad</title>
    </book>
    <book reference="Odyssey">
        <author>Homer</author>
        <year>unknown</year>
        <title>Odyssey</title>
    </book>
    ...
</bibliography>
```

The overall *element* "bibliography," encloses a list of zero or more books and other literature references, or everything contained between the "book" tags.

The tag `<book reference=...>` is the start of a reference, while the tag `</book>` is the end of it. All information about the book is contained between these two tags via new tags.

A tag, as in the example of "book", can also contain one or more *attributes*:

```
<book reference="GulliversTravels">
```

These are always interpreted as key-value pairs with a character string as the value.

Parsing the XML file is one thing, but handling the contents is quite another. There are several general strategies, each with its own merits. You can simply read the file and process the contents as you go along. For example, you may want to reformat the preceding bibliography to a more suitable form (HTML with CSS markup, for instance). This is known as the SAX approach.

Another strategy, "document object model" or DOM, is to store the contents in a tree structure, so that you can search for the right elements: load the XML file into memory and print all references to Jonathan Swift or sort the entries in alphabetical order.

Often, it is more convenient to create a data structure that corresponds directly to the structure of the XML file:

```fortran
type book_reference
    character(len=20)   :: key
    character(len=80)   :: author
    character(len=200)  :: title
    integer             :: year
end type book_reference

type(book_reference), dimension(:), allocatable :: bibliography
```

Once you have read the XML file into this structure, you can use the information directly:

```fortran
call load_bibliography( bibliography, xmlfile )
call sort_author_and_year( bibliography )
call pretty_print( bibliography )
```

There are a number of libraries that enable you to read XML files [18]. One is *xml-fortran*. The associated *xmlreader* utility takes a description of the XML file's structure and generates a complete module to read XML files with this structure and store the information automatically. For the preceding bibliography file, the description may look like the following:

```xml
<?xml version="1.0"?>
<template>
    <options strict="yes" rootname="bibliography"/>
    <typedef name="book_t">
```

```
        <component name="reference" type="word" length="40"/>
        <component name="author" type="line" length="40"/>
        <component name="year" type="word" length="10"/>
        <component name="title" type="line" length="80"/>
    </typedef>
    <variable name="book" type="book_t" dimension="1"/>
</template>
```

The type "word" represents items that should consist of a single word only, whereas the "line" represents items that contain arbitrary text contained on a single line.

Reading a bibliography file is done using the generated routine read_xml_file_bibliography:

```
program print_bib

    use xml_data_bibliography

    !
    ! Read in the entire file (leave out optional arguments)
    !
    call read_xml_file_bibliography( "example_bib.xml" )

    !
    ! Print the contents
    !
    do i = 1,size(book)
        write(*,'(a20,a,a)') &
            book(i)%author, ' - ', trim(book(i)%title)
    enddo
end program print_bib
```

The library also supports the SAX approach:[8]

```
module bibliography_scan
    implicit none

    !
    ! Work arrays for storing the information from the XML file
    !
    character(len=20), dimension(2,100) :: attribs
    character(len=80), dimension(100)   :: data
```

---

[8] Other methods store the contents in a general tree or handle the entires file tag by tag. In that case, the routine *xmlparse* is used to get the tag and the data that belong to it. The library does not support searching the tree via "XPath" queries [23].

```fortran
    !
    ! Variables for storing the information that is
    ! to be printed
    !
    character(len=20) :: author
    logical           :: store = .false.

contains
subroutine startfunc( tag, attribs, error )
    character(len=*)                     :: tag



    character(len=*), dimension(:,:) :: attribs
    logical                          :: error

    ! Dummy - has no function in this case
end subroutine startfunc
subroutine endfunc( tag, error )
    character(len=*)                 :: tag
    logical                          :: error

    ! Dummy - has no function in this case
end subroutine endfunc

subroutine datafunc( tag, data, error )
    character(len=*)                 :: tag
    character(len=*), dimension(:)   :: data
    logical                          :: error

    if ( tag == "author" .and. &
         index( data(1), "Swift") > 0 ) then
        author = data(1)
        store  = .true.
    endif
    if ( tag == "title" .and. store ) then
        write(*,'(a20,a,a)') author, ' - ', trim(data(1))
        store = .false.
    endif
end subroutine datafunc
end module bibliography_scan

program select_bib
    use xmlparse
    use bibliography_scan

    implicit none
```

```
integer :: lunrep
logical :: error

!
! Read in the entire file (leave out optional arguments)
!
lunrep = 10
open( lunrep, file = "select_bib.log" )
call xml_process( "example_bib.xml", attribs, data, &
        startfunc, datafunc, endfunc, lunrep, error )

end program select_bib
```

What happens within the xml_process() routine – part of the *xml-fortran* library – is that the XML file is scanned. At the start and end of an element, the three user-supplied subroutines are called. This allows for instant processing instead of first storing the entire file in memory. A disadvantage is, however, that some information must be kept between calls to these user routines. Therefore, programming these routines can be a bit complex.

8.

Unit Testing

The subject of this chapter is a simple framework for automating one particular aspect of testing: unit tests. Unit tests focus on "small" parts of a program, typically single subroutines or functions. The idea is these tests give confidence in the correct operation of routines. As the code for these tests should be considered part of the program, you can repeatedly run them during development and maintenance of the whole system. Some development methods take this to the extreme. Test-driven development (TDD), for instance, prescribes that the tests be written first, before you start implementing the actual code.[1]

This is just one way to develop a program, but thinking about the ways you can test a particular routine helps to define its functionality. Most importantly, however, such unit tests become part of the program. Therefore, testing at that level is not an afterthought, implemented in ad hoc one-off programs.

8.1 Testing Frameworks

Junit is a well-known framework for unit tests in a Java programming environment [37]. It has been seminal for a whole range of similar frameworks for all manner, of programming languages. Junit depends on explicit support from several language features that Fortran does not have, such as special annotations and the possibility to programmatically get a list of routine (method) names from a library. Nevertheless, it is quite possible to implement a unit testing framework in Fortran as well. There are several:

- Funit, by Kleb et al. [50], implemented in Fortran and Ruby
- pfunit, by Womack and Clune [84], a framework, implemented in Fortran
- FRUIT, by Chen [21], implemented in Fortran and Ruby
- *Ftnunit*, by me [56] (implemented in Fortran)

As I know the framework I developed myself best, this chapter only discusses Ftnunit. The framework offers a set of routines to run the tests and a set of routines to check the actual results against the expected results (assertions).

- Write a number of subroutines that exercise parts of the code and check the results using the *assertion* routines.
- These routines get called in a separate subroutine, which does nothing but call the various test subroutines.
- The framework takes care of the administrative tasks.

---

[1] According to [4], Kent Beck is credited for inventing or developing this technique.

8.2 Tridiagonal Matrices As an Example

The following subroutine illustrates the framework from the perspective of a user.

```
module tridiag

    implicit none

contains

subroutine solve( a, b, c, d, x )
    real, dimension(:) :: a, b, c, d, x

    integer :: i
    integer :: n
    real    :: factor

    n = size(a)
    do i = 2,n
        factor = a(i) / b(i-1)
        b(i)   = b(i) - factor * c(i-1)
        d(i)   = d(i) - factor * d(i-1)
    enddo

    x(n) = d(n) / b(n)
    do i = n-1,1,-1
        x(i) = (d(i) - c(i) * x(i+1)) / b(i)
    enddo
end subroutine solve
end module tridiag
```

It is a straightforward implementation of Gauss elimination for a tridiagonal matrix. The matrix is represented by three separate arrays (a, b, and c) and the right-hand side by array d. The system of linear equations reads:

$$a_i x_{i-1} + b_i x_i + c_i x_{i+1} = d_i \tag{8.1}$$

Examples of tests for this routine are:

- Use a diagonal matrix with constant coefficients, such as 3.0 and a right-hand side with a constant value of 1.0. The expected result is a vector with all elements close to $\frac{1}{3}$. It is a trivial system, but the algorithm does not take that into account.
- Use a (diagonally dominant) matrix with diagonals $a = 1$, $b = 2$, and $c = 1$. The right-hand side is chosen so that the exact solution is a vector $1, \frac{1}{2}, \frac{1}{3}, ..., \frac{1}{n}$. By varying the size of the matrix, you can check the accuracy of the implementation.

The first case is implemented as follows:

```fortran
subroutine test_trivial

    integer, parameter :: rows = 10
    real, dimension(rows) :: a, b, c, d, x, y

    a = 0.0
    b = 3.0 ! Using 3 because of numerical rounding issues
    c = 0.0
    d = 1.0

    y = 1.0/3.0 ! Expected solution

    call solve( a, b, c, d, x )
    call assert_comparable( x, y, margin, &
            "Solution is uniformly 1/3" )
end subroutine test_trivial
```

The second case is implemented as follows:

```fortran
subroutine test_diagonal_dom2

    integer, parameter    :: rows = 10
    real, dimension(rows) :: a, b, c, d, x, y
    integer               :: i

    a = -1.0
    b = 2.0
    c = -1.0
    y = (/ (1.0/i ,i=1,rows) /) ! Expected solution

    d(2:rows-1) = a(2:rows-1) * y(1:rows-2) + &
                  b(2:rows-1) * y(2:rows-1) + &
                  c(2:rows-1) * y(3:rows)
    d(1)        = b(1) * y(1) + c(1) * y(2)
    d(rows)     = a(rows)     * y(rows-1)   + &
                  b(rows)     * y(rows)

    call solve( a, b, c, d, x )

    call assert_comparable( x, y, margin, &
            "Solution is 1/k (10 rows)" )
end subroutine test_diagonal_dom2
```

In these routines, you use the assertion routine assert_comparable to check that the solution contained in array x is close enough to $\frac{1}{3}$ or the sequence of fractions $\frac{1}{k}$. The argument margin indicates the *relative* error that is acceptable.

The assertion routine prints a message if there are elements in the two arrays that do not match and records the fact that this assertion failed.

To run the test routines, you put these routines (and several others) in a separate routine and call them indirectly via the routine test, which is part of the framework:

```
subroutine test_all

    call test( test_trivial,        &
            "Solve trivial system a=0, b=3, c=0, d=1" )
    call test( test_basic,          &
            "Solve basic system a=0, b=6, c=-5, d=1" )
    call test( test_diagonal_dom1,  &
            "Solve diagonally dominant system - n=3")
    call test( test_diagonal_dom2,  &
            "Solve diagonally dominant system - n=10")
    call test( test_diagonal_dom3,  &
            "Solve diagonally dominant system - n=100")

end subroutine test_all
```

Now run this routine test_all via the framework at a convenient spot in the program. Typically, this is run at the start for the following reasons:

```
program solve_tridiagonal_systems
    use ftnunit
    use tridiag        ! The actual implementation
    use test_tridiag   ! The tests

    implicit none

    call runtests_init
    call runtests( test_all )
    call runtests_final

    !
    ! If not in testing mode, then proceed with the ordinary
    ! processing ...
    !
    ...
end program solve_tridiagonal_systems
```

The routines runtests_init, runtests, and runtests_final are all part of the framework. If the program is *not* run in test mode (see the following), they do nothing and the program simply continues with its ordinary processing. Otherwise, the tests are run and when the last one is done, the program stops.

The output from the tests looks like this:

```
Test: Solve trivial system a=0, b=3, c=0, d=1

Test: Solve basic system a=0, b=6, c=-5, d=1

Test: Solve diagonally dominant system - n=3

Test: Solve diagonally dominant system - n=10

Test: Solve diagonally dominant system - n=100
      One or more values different: "Solution is 1/k (100 rows)" -
                                                  assertion failed
     Index        First         Second
        22     0.45454E-01    0.45454E-01
        23     0.43478E-01    0.43478E-01
        24     0.41666E-01    0.41666E-01
        25     0.39999E-01    0.39999E-01
        26     0.38461E-01    0.38461E-01
        27     0.37036E-01    0.37037E-01
        28     0.35714E-01    0.35714E-01
        29     0.34482E-01    0.34482E-01
        30     0.33333E-01    0.33333E-01
        31     0.32258E-01    0.32258E-01
        32     0.31249E-01    0.31250E-01
        33     0.30302E-01    0.30303E-01

        ...
        82     0.12195E-01    0.12195E-01
        83     0.12048E-01    0.12048E-01
        84     0.11904E-01    0.11904E-01
        85     0.11764E-01    0.11764E-01
        86     0.11627E-01    0.11627E-01
 Number of differences:                 50
 Number of failed assertions:                   1
 Number of runs needed to complete the tests:   1
```

Only the last test fails, because of small differences between the expected solution and the solution that was found. Apparently, the size of the matrix matters, because for smaller matrices there was no problem.

8.3 Design and Implementation

One of the design goals of the Ftnunit framework is to make it possible to have the code for testing close to the actual program code. Experiences with another framework that I developed show how separating the test code from the actual program makes the test code hard to maintain.

Another goal is to use Fortran as much as possible, and as a consequence you can keep the test code inside the program. The test code is only run if a

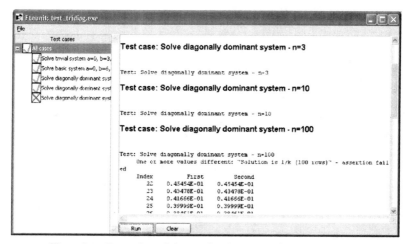

Figure 8.1. Screenshot of the graphical user interface

particular file called ftnunit.run is present in the working directory. If the test code is run, the program stops automatically in the routine runtests_final. This is the reason the test routines should appear early in the program.

Some non-Fortran programming is convenient. If the program under test is suddenly stops because of a runtime error, or because it encounters an error condition that causes it to stop explicitly, the remaining tests should still run. This is achieved in several steps:

- Each time a test is run, a file ftnunit.lst records its start and when successful (that is, the program continues) also its completion.
- The program under test runs via a shell script or a batch file that continues running the program as long as that particular file exists.
- When the last test is run, the file is deleted automatically.

In addition to this *batch mode*, there is a straightforward graphical user interface (Figure 8.1). It first runs the selected program in *list mode* so that it prints the descriptions of the tests (but does not run the routines). The GUI then builds up the list of test cases, so that you can either run them all at once or only a small selection. If, in a test case, an assertion fails or the program stops with a runtime error, this is recorded with an icon forming a red cross.

To accommodate for the problem of large datasets being necessary for a particular test – such as a complicated initial condition that is required for testing a solver for partial differential equations – the framework also offers some storage and retrieval routines. Here you can create and store the data, save them with a descriptive text in a file, and retrieve them in any number of tests.

8.4 Concluding Remarks

While this cannot be enforced in a general framework, it is important that each test routine works independently of any other. This sometimes leads to duplication of code, but an interdependency means that failure in one test obscures the correct execution of the other.

In the example, the test routines are an integral part of the actual program, but this is not the only possible setup. You can put the test routines in a separate program as well. That program should, however, be an integral part of the whole project.

The output from the framework consists of a plain text report (the titles of the test cases and any assertions that failed) and of an HTML file with the same information. You can use the latter type of output to show the report in an Internet browser. For instance, on Windows the following suffices, thanks to the association of the file extension ".html" to the default browser:

```
call system( "ftnunit.html" )
```

Unit testing can be combined with measuring the *test coverage*, recording what parts of the code are run. Tools exist to preprocess the source code, so that the coverage is automatically recorded or it can be left to the compiler via a suitable option (see Appendix A). Test coverage can be used to set up the individual tests, especially if several decisions are involved in the tested code. For numerical programs, the size of the problem to be solved may need to be taken into account.

9.

Code Reviews

There is extensive literature on reviewing code and design documents as a means to check that the software is performing as it should and that the implementation is maintainable and understandable. Some development methodologies, such as Extreme Programming [16], prescribe continuous reviews by peers [40]. In all forms, code reviews are about finding defects in the code, but they are not intended to criticize the programmer.

While the procedural (and psychological) aspects of code reviews are widely described, some practical aspects are not. For example, what should you be looking for in the code? It is not enough to check that the code adheres to the programming standard of the project it belongs to. Such a standard may not exist, be incomplete, or be focused on layout, not on questionable constructs that are a liability (see Appendix B).

What do you want to achieve with code reviews? First, you want to verify that the code is doing its job and that the code is of good enough quality:

- It is readable by others than the author.
- It is maintainable – adding new functionality or correcting bugs should not amount to hard labor.
- It is testable – do you understand what goes in and what comes out?

Secondly, the code should be portable. This means it should be possible to build the program and run it on a different operating system, and also with different compilers and versions of that same compiler. Many compilers offer options to check against the language standard. Therefore, use it to see if you accidentally used some compiler-specific feature.

From these considerations, here are four "principles" and a number of practical guidelines:

- Be explicit.
- Don't stray.
- Avoid traps.
- Use clean code.

9.1 Be Explicit

The source code is the most important product from which you can judge if software works, therefore, you must rely on that source code to give you all the information you need.

Use Explicit Declarations of Variables and Constants   While Fortran of old is perfectly happy to use undeclared variables and determine their types from a few simple rules, it is also easy to make mistakes that go undetected for a long time. Consider this code fragment:

```
integer :: i
real, dimension(10) :: x
...
do i = 1,10
    x(i) = 2.0 * i + 1
enddo
```

The typos (the use of a lower-case "L" instead of a digit "1") would be caught by the compiler if explicit declarations were enforced. Therefore, **always use implicit none**.

Some compilers have an option to force an error if an undeclared variable is used, but then you rely on something outside the source code and it is not a portable feature. Also, some compilers allow you to change the meaning of a default real or integer. This can make reals double precision by default or turn integers into 8-byte integers. Again, this makes the program rely on features not visible in the code.

Another example is the use of literal numbers in the source code:

```
rate = rate * 1.15740740740741e-5
```

The number will probably not be recognized as 1/86400, where 86400 is the number of seconds in a day. The computation is intended to convert the "rate" from day^{-1} to s^{-1}. Instead, declare a parameter to make this conversion explicitly:

```
! Convert from 1/day to 1/s
real, parameter :: per_day = 1.0/(24.0*3600.0)
```

While you are at it, use an explicit kind:

```
integer, parameter :: wp = kind(1.0) ! Working precision
!
! An alternative that is even more precise:
! Working precision
!integer, parameter :: wp = selected_real_kind(6,37)

! Convert from 1/day to 1/s
real(wp), parameter :: per_day = 1.0_wp /(24.0_wp * 3600.0_wp)
```

The reason for this, although it may seem rather pedantic, is that it will be much simpler to change the precision of the program by just replacing the definition of the parameter **wp**:

```
! Working precision is double precision
integer, parameter :: wp = kind(1.0d0)
```

Use Preconditions A subroutine may expect its arguments to conform to particular conditions. For example, if it reads a file, that file must already exist, however, check these conditions inside the routine. In a code fragment like:

```
inquire( file = 'myfile.inp', exist = exists )
if ( exists ) then
    call read_file( ... )
endif
```

the condition should be moved into the subroutine itself. Now you have a distributed responsibility: the calling code must make sure that the routine is not inadvertently called, whereas the routine itself must also make sure that the file can be properly read.

A related issue arises with composite conditions:

```
if ( allocated(array) .and. array(1) > 0 ) then
    ...
endif
```

If the array is not allocated, then the second part does not need to be evaluated. However, there is no guarantee that the program will never do that because Fortran does not guarantee short-circuiting.[1]

Therefore, the preceding should be written as:

```
if ( allocated(array) ) then
    if ( array(1) > 0 ) then
        ...
    endif
endif
```

Variables that Need to Retain Their Values Between Calls Fortran has several rules to determine if a local variable retains its value between calls. But, why rely on your understanding of such rules? Use the **save** attribute or statement wherever you want a variable to behave that way. (Even worse, some compilers keep all the local variables in static memory because it is more efficient on that particular platform. However, this means your program may work on that platform but not on others if you forget the **save** attribute). And, of course, be explicit about what variables you want to save: do not use the **save** statement without any names.

Visibility of the Interface to a Subroutine or Function Modern Fortran programs usually use assumed-shape arrays, optional arguments, or derived types and other features. In these cases, it is very important that the compiler

---

[1] Short-circuiting can lead to inefficient machine code, especially when the condition has multiple logical connectors. The given example could actually fail at run-time without short-circuiting as it may access an element of an unallocated array.

"knows" about the interface for the subroutines and functions. This requirement is automatically fulfilled if you use modules for all your routines. Organize the modules in a comprehensive way. For example, routines that manipulate the contents of the same derived type should go in one module.

Availability of Variables and Routines If you use variables and routines in a module, then, by default, they will be available for any program unit that uses the module. This may or may not be what you want: a program could inadvertently use a variable reserved for the inner workings of your module and cause bugs that are difficult to find. Therefore, use the private statement to hide any data and routines and only make those items public that should be public. The same goes for the content of a derived type.

The Default Case in a Select Block and the Else Case in an If Block
Quite often, you will think a particular condition may not occur, like in a select case block only certain cases will ever need to be handled. It does not hurt to insert code that makes this explicit:

```
select case (case_var)
    ... legitimate cases ...

    case default
        write(*,*) 'Programming error: case should not occur: ', &
            case_var
end select
```

A similar thing occurs with nested if blocks or if/elseif constructions: if you are certain a particular alternative should not occur, then say so.

Appropriate Error Messages Error messages should be to the point, accurately indicate what is wrong, and – if possible – present what can be done about it. Using code like this:

```
if ( n > nmax ) then
    write(*,*) 'Invalid number of items'
    stop
endif
```

is wrong and plainly unhelpful. There is nothing wrong with the number of items, it is merely larger than the maximum is allowed. (I have encountered such code in practice. Only by examining the source code was it finally clear what was wrong.) Use dynamically allocated memory – possibly a bit more work, but more robust – so that the error condition cannot occur anymore.

If that is not practical, replace the error message with something more informative (maybe include the location in the source too):

```
if ( n > nmax ) then
    write(*,*) 'Error: More items (',n, ') than can be handled.'
    write(*,*) '        Parameter nmax (now: ',nmax, &
        ') must be increased to at least ', n
    stop
endif
```

This alternative gives a clear indication of what is wrong and what can be done about it. In summary:

- Use implicit none, parameters instead of literal constants, and parameters to specify the numerical kind.
- Explicitly check the input arguments: do they satisfy the preconditions of the routine? Put these checks inside the routine.
- Watch out for composite logical conditions: do not rely on short-circuiting.
- Use save for local variables that should retain their value.
- Use modules for all of your code.
- Use private and public to control access.
- Provide error messages that inform the user about what to do.

Of course, there are always good reasons why it is impossible or undesirable to conform to these guidelines. For instance, routines called by a program in another language should not be in a module. But, if you have such reasons, be explicit about them!

9.2 Don't Stray

Many projects use a programming standard and guidelines for coding besides the standard of the programming language itself. Published examples include Boukabara and van Delst [19] and Kleb and others [49]. An even more extensive set of guidelines is the book by Clerman and Spector [24], which presents how the various features of modern Fortran can be used in a clear style.

They represent the practical experience people have built up using the language. This may include typical solutions for common programming tasks – the idiom – and choices for the layout of the code such as indentation. Don't go against the grain. Even if the standard or the idiom prescribed by the project is silly, use it anyway:

- If you modify a program's code, use the same layout and programming style. Code that looks like a hotchpotch of styles is not very appealing. If it is already bad, advise to clean it up first.

- Conform to the agreed standard. If you think the standard needs to be changed, discuss it separately from work on the code.[2]

This also means the programmer should have a good understanding of the language: What features are acceptable and what features are a possibly common but nevertheless non-portable extension? The programmer should also be aware of things that are explicitly left to the discretion of the language implementation.

Here are a few examples:

- Declarations of the type `real*4` or `real(4)` are not portable and should be removed. `real*4` is a common extension, but it has never been part of a Fortran standard. `real(4)` hints at a common misunderstanding of the kind mechanism: Compilers are free to use any positive integer number to select the precision and range of the integer and real types. This is not necessarily identical to the number of bytes these types occupy in memory.
- Unformatted files are not portable between platforms: The record structure may differ, although there exists a popular structure that is (almost) universal. Besides the record structure, the ordering of the bytes that make up a single number may differ, as well as the interpretation of these bytes. Again, a ubiquitous ordering and interpretation exist, but they are not universal.
- Direct-access files pose a peculiar issue: The unit of length is one byte with some compilers and one word with others (4 bytes on a 32-bits platform). Use the `file_storage_size` parameter in the intrinsic module `iso_fortran_env` to find out what the unit is (in *bits*).
- Tab characters have no place in Fortran source code (with the possible exception of literal strings). They are not part of the Fortran character set. Simply do not use them. In the editor, they may expand to the right number of positions, but on a printout the resulting indentation can be horrible.
- A code fragment like:

```
if ( x > 0 ) then
    valid = .true.
else
    valid = .false.
endif
```

indicates the programmer does not quite understand logical expressions. Here is a simpler equivalent:

```
valid = x > 0
```

A code fragment such as:

```
if ( x > 0 ) then
    valid = .true.
endif
```

---

[2] Few things seem to be so provocative as posing a standard to programmers [42], [6].

is a completely different matter – the variable `valid` is being updated under some condition. You can do that with:

```
valid = valid .or. x > 0
```

but it is very easy to make a mistake.

■ Code like:

```
if ( string(1:5) == 'start' ) then
```

raises a few questions:

– Is "start" meant to be a prefix? If so, then this code is fine, although the fixed substring index is worrisome. It is easy to miscount, especially with long prefixes. It would be less error-prone to use something along these lines:

```
if ( index( string, 'start' ) == 1 ) then
```

– Is the string meant to contain nothing more than the word "start"? Then,

```
if ( string == 'start' ) then
```

is more appropriate. The original construction indicates yet another misunderstanding: In Fortran, strings are padded with blanks (spaces) before such a comparison. There is no need for taking the substring.

■ Watch out for uninitialized variables. In Fortran, variables do not get a default value. Some compilers can detect particular classes of uninitialized variables, others can generate code where each variable and array is initialized with a special value so that you can detect initialization problems at runtime. (Note that the program will probably be slower because of this.) However, such options are no substitute for proper initialization, making the initialization explicitly visible in the source code.[3]

■ If you initialize a variable via a `data` statement or initialization expression like:

```
integer :: count = 0
```

the initialization is done once, and once only. This is in contrast to C-like languages where the preceding line is shorthand for:

```
integer :: count
...
count = 0
```

■ There is a rather subtle gotcha involving data in modules and COMMON blocks: If no active subroutine or function refers to the module (via `use`) or the

---

[3] Some compilers can find uninitialized variables if both optimization and warnings are turned on [48]. For instance, *gfortran* -Wall -Wextra -O2 will give more information.

COMMON block, the data they contain are discarded – or at least the Fortran standard says so. In practice, few, if any, implementations really do that, but it is something to keep in mind.

■ Beware of micro-optimizations:

```
do i = 1, n
    if ( x(i) .ne. 1.0 ) y(i) = x(i) * y(i)
enddo
```

There is no reason to do something like this:

- The program will be slightly slower, unless you have a very smart compiler, because in every iteration the condition has to be checked.
- The time saved by not multiplying the trivial factor is marginal.
- The code is more difficult to read.
- You do not gain accuracy.

■ A somewhat surprising feature of Fortran is that lower bounds for array indices are not passed on to subroutines or functions, not even with intrinsic functions. The following program illustrates this:

```
program chkidx
    real, dimension(-3:3) :: x
    x    = 0.0
    x(0) = 1.0
    write(*,*) 'Maximum at: ', maxloc(x)
end program chkidx
```

The printed index is 4, not 0. If you think about why, it is quite a reasonable feature. If lower bounds were passed on, then every subroutine and function would have to take care of it, with loops like:

```
do i = 1, n
    y(i) = x(i) * y(i)
enddo
```

These would have to be consistently written as:

```
do i = 1, lbound(x),ubound(x)
    y(i) = x(i) * y(i)
enddo
```

As lower bounds other than 1 are fairly rare, it would put a large burden on the programmer for a small gain.

9.3 Avoid Traps

In any programming language, there are perfectly legal and well-defined constructs or idioms to avoid. Fortran is no exception.

Adequate Error Handling

With respect to errors that may occur, opening and reading a file in Fortran is pretty easy.

- Method 1: you do not explicitly handle errors, therefore, the program will take care of it itself with drastic yet clear measures (it stops and prints an error message, possibly with details of where it occurred).
- Method 2: you use the keywords `err=`, `end=` or `iostat=`.

If you choose the second method, you have the opportunity to recover from the error. But you also have the opportunity to ignore it:

```
open( 10, file = 'non-existing-file.inp', status = 'old', &
    iostat = ierr )

! Happily go on -- ignore ierr
```

Comparing Reals

Common wisdom says you should not compare reals for (strict) equality or inequality, because of the finite precision.[4] Instead, you should use some margin or a "fuzzy" comparison [51]. Actually, this rule can be relaxed in one way: if the mathematical real number can be represented exactly. With a value like -999.0, which is sometimes used to indicate missing values and is exactly representable, the code will work as expected.

```
real, parameter :: missing = -999.0
if ( x == missing ) then
```

On the other hand, checking if a variable is greater than some threshold is just as dangerous as checking if it is equal to that value. Consider a thermostat, for instance. If the temperature is below a threshold, the heating turns on, but if it is above another threshold, it turns off. A precise check $T < T_{min}$ or $T > T_{max}$ may lead to subtle differences when the heating turns on or off, depending on the precise values of the temperature. A slightly different order in the evaluations due to a different optimization option might cause the moment to shift.

A peculiar problem occurs with special numbers, like "not a number" (NaN). Look at this fragment:

```
if ( x < 0.0 ) then
    write(*,*) 'Variable x should be positive'
else
    write(*,*) 'All is well'
endif
```

---

[4] The compiler you use may have an option to warn about such comparisons.

If the value of x is NaN – for instance, the result of sqrt(-1.0) – then, the condition is false. NaNs are unordered, so they are not even equal to themselves. The previous code would *not* give the intended warning. Inverting the condition solves the problem, but be very careful that the result is correct:

```
if ( x >= 0.0 ) then
    write(*,*) 'All is well'
else
    write(*,*) 'Variable x should be positive'
endif
```

[Fortran 2003 defines a number of inquiry functions, such as ieee_is_nan(), that are meant to make handling special numbers easier [65].]

Mixed Precision   When dealing with real constants, take care to use the right precision:

```
real(kind=kind(1.0d0)), parameter ::
    pi = 3.14159265358979932384626433
```

This is how the code may look if you specify the parameter pi with a large number of decimals, but the actual value is default precision. On most computers only 6 or 7 decimals are retained.

The same caution holds for expressions where real or complex numbers of different precision are used. The result may have the desired precision, but the accuracy is that of the item of the lowest precision.

Surprises with Negative Numbers   Fortran defines two functions for dealing with the mathematical modulo operation: mod and modulo. They differ in the way negative arguments are treated. Be sure to choose the right one.

However, negative numbers can cause more surprises. Suppose you use the minimum function to delimit a term so it may not exceed some maximum value:

```
x = min( x, xmax )
```

If your purpose is to make sure that the *magnitude* of the number x does not exceed xmax, then the preceding will not work for negative x. You would have to use:

```
x = max( min( x, xmax ), -xmax )
```

or similar expressions.

Automatic Arrays   One construction in Fortran that may lead to problems is the automatic array. As long as the arrays are small, they fit into the memory set apart for these constructions, usually the stack. If the arrays are too large, however, stack overflows occur and your program simply stops in midair. It is a compiler-dependent problem, but if you deal with potentially large arrays, consider using allocated arrays instead. Here is an example:

```
n = 1
do i = 1,8
    n = n * 10
    call auto_array( n )
enddo
...
contains
subroutine auto_array( n )
    integer :: n
    integer, dimension(n) :: array
    array = n
    write(*,*) array(1)
end subroutine
```

The array is defined as an automatic array with increasing size, and in many implementations it is taken from the stack. Running the program will, at some point, lead to a stack overflow as the array simply does not fit anymore. An alternative is to explicitly allocate the array:

```
subroutine allocated_array( n )
    integer :: n
    integer, dimension(:), allocatable :: array
    allocate( array(n) )
    array = n
    write(*,*) array(1)
end subroutine
```

While this array may become too large as well, the program can at least catch that (via the `stat=` keyword). When leaving the routine, the array is automatically deallocated.

Similar issues exist with array sections: The statement

```
write( 20 ) value(i,:)
```

uses an array section that can be implemented by the compiler as a temporary array. Whether or not this leads to a stack overflow depends on the size of that temporary array, but it is a risk. Here a simple alternative is to use an implied do loop:

```
write( 20 ) (value(i,j), j = 1,size(value,2))
```

Not Just Numbers While it is nonsensical to add one meter to one second, for a computer program these are simply numbers so it does the computation without any protest. There are several libraries [70] that can help with the correct handling of units. If you have not used them during development of the code, then check the various computations manually for this aspect.

The problem occurs not only with physical units: if your program deals with different currencies, for example, you need to do very similar checks.

9.4 Clean Code

The last category consists of a lack of attention to design, readability, and other aspects that are important for the program in the long run.

If your program, however large, is put in a single file on disk, building it (compiling and linking) is almost trivial. However, source files of 100,000 code lines are not easy to work with and printing is a waste of paper, if you only need to look at a few hundred lines. Two related routines may be thousands of lines apart. Therefore, a conscientious organization of the code in files, directories, and subdirectories is just as important as getting the program to work.

Within the code, if you decide to use both uppercase and lowercase letters (such as all keywords are capitalized), do so consistently. It does not matter to the compiler, but it does to the human eye.

Then, there is the complexity of the code itself to consider:

- If a routine has a lot of tasks, is it necessary to do all of them in that one routine? Can you split it up or add an extra level of routines? This will make the structure clearer.
- Routines with a lot of tasks tend to require long argument lists and many lines of code. Understanding them and verifying that the correct arguments are passed is tedious and error-prone work.
- Common subexpressions that are often repeated have a number of draw-backs:
  - Unless the compiler recognizes them, they need to be computed every time.
  - More importantly, if you make a mistake or if the subexpression changes for another reason, you must change it in several places. It is easy to forget one.
  - The code is more difficult to read, so you must recognize that parts of the expressions are the same.

  Store the result in an extra variable and use that instead, or if the expressions are similar, but not identical (differing in one or two variables), it may help to use small functions.
- Sometimes not just subexpressions are repeated, but whole groups of state-ments. Here a function or a subroutine is probably a better solution, as it highlights the role of that group of statements and allows you to concentrate the code in one place, making it easier to consistently correct any bugs or implement an improvement or an extension.

■ Here are a few fragments of code that could be made simpler (all of these fragments are derived from actual code):

```
if ( a+b+c > 0.0 ) then
    x = a + b + c
else
    x = 0.0
endif

if ( x > y ) then
    x = y
endif
```

which can be simplified to:

```
x = max( a+b+c, 0.0 )

x = max( x, y )
```

This longer fragment:

```
if ( have_file ) then
    call read_data( data1, data2, ... )
else
    data1 = 0
    data2 = 0
    ...
endif
```

has the problem that the routine read_data is initializing more variables than the else block. You either always call the routine and first initialize all of these variables inside the routine or initialize the variables and then call the routine:

```
! First alternative
!
call read_data( have_file, data1, data2, ... )
...
!
subroutine read_data( have_file, data1, data2,... )
    ...
    data1 = 0
    data2 = 0
    ...

    ! Read the data
    if ( have_file ) then
        ...
    endif
end subroutine
```

```
!
! Second alternative
!
data1 = 0
data2 = 0
...
if ( have_file ) then
    call read_data( data1, data2, ... )
endif
```

The advantage over the given code is that initialization is taking place first, so its role is more prominently displayed.

■ Functions (as opposed to subroutines) should not have side effects, which means they should return the same value whenever the same arguments are passed and preferably the arguments or anything else is changed. This way they stay close to the mathematical concept and there is less surprise when using them.

Another reason for functions without side effects is that in a multithreaded program, it becomes almost impossible to keep the program correct. In general, a function with side effects poses restrictions on its use:

```
a = 1.0
x = f(a) - f(1.0)
...
real function f( y )
    real :: y
    real, save :: count = 0.0
    f = y + count
    count = count + 1.0
end function
```

The previous code might produce -1 but also 1, depending on the order in which the function is actually called. One piece of useful advice here: make the function pure, this way the compiler will complain if there are any side effects [48].

10.

Robust Implementation of Several Simple Algorithms

Computer programs sometimes exhibit unexpected behavior. They may function correctly for years and then, suddenly, they fail. Computer programs that solve numerical problems are no exception. The unexpected behavior, perhaps a division by zero, is often the consequence of input that does not conform to the hidden assumptions and restrictions of the program. For example, a Gauss elimination procedure to solve systems of linear equations requires the matrix to be non-singular. If the matrix is *numerically* singular or ill-conditioned, the mathematical problem of solving the system is still well-defined, but the numerical counterpart may have a hard time delivering a decent approximation to the exact solution. The conclusion that the matrix is ill-conditioned is only drawn while solving the system.

Sometimes there is a mismatch between the specification and the actual implementation. The part of the program that reads the data accepts input that conforms to the specification, but there are a few tacit assumptions, like line-endings for a text file containing the coefficients of the matrix for the Gauss elimination program.[1]

Subtle bugs may lurk in an otherwise well-written and well-behaved program. Can you avoid them altogether? The unsatisfying answer is probably not, but that does not mean you cannot make an effort to understand the source of these bugs. That is the intention of this chapter – to examine three simple mathematical algorithms and their implementation in Fortran.

The idea is that a straightforward implementation contains all manners of hidden assumptions about the problem that needs solving. Careful examination reveals these assumptions, and then you can take measures to prevent them from causing failures in a practical situation – either by carefully documenting the conditions on the input or by explicitly taking care of them in the code.

---

[1] Problems can occur when the last line in the input file does not end in a proper end-of-line or when the line endings are not in accordance with those of the platform the program is running on.

Ultimately, the implementation should be **robust**:

- Unacceptable input is recognized (if possible).
- If the program can find an adequate answer, it will do so, otherwise, it will indicate why it cannot find it.

In particular, this means no crash and no incorrect answer.

10.1 Related Approaches

Good programming practices that should lead to robust programs are described in many publications, such as in *Safer C*, by Hatton [42] and in *Code Complete*, by McConnell [58]. However, these books present few detailed numerical examples as to how robustness in this area is achieved. Metcalf et al. [65] touch upon the subject when they illustrate the floating-point features new to the Fortran 2003 standard.

The problems that floating-point arithmetic presents to the reliable implementation of numerical algorithms are usually handled in two different ways:

- Use of arbitrary-precision arithmetic
- Use of interval arithmetic

The first approach, as exemplified by Karamcheti and others [47], attempts to overcome the limitations by using arithmetic methods that allow much higher precision than the precision offered by ordinary single and double precision. There is quite a significant impact on the performance, but the alternative of unreliable results is probably worse.

Karamcheti and others apply this method to geometrical computations to obtain so-called exact geometrical computation. The imprecision of floating-point numbers may cause false conclusions about whether two lines in space are parallel or not. Their special library, which can apply more accurate arithmetic at a number of levels of precision, greatly alleviates these and other problems.

In the second approach, the goal is to compute the margins within which the true answer lies [1]. The major criticism is that quite often the intervals become so large that the answer is practically useless. Most implementations cannot account for the dependencies between numbers, but the manual for SUN's Forte Fortran compiler [45] describes an implementation where this is taken care of.

The CADNA library [74] uses a somewhat different method: It computes three different values for each operation using different rounding modes. These modes are chosen randomly. As the library requires only limited changes to the original source code, it is particularly suitable for investigating possible numerical instabilities in existing programs.

In this chapter, you will reason mostly about the visible part of the implementation, the source code. The actual program that is derived from this may have some unexpected and different properties. Corden and Kreizer [26] explain in some detail how these differences arise as a consequence of various compiler options. Some of these consequences are actually visible in the results of the sample programs given here.

10.2 Linear Interpolation

The first algorithm to consider is linear interpolation. The mathematics is simple enough: given an interval $[a,b]$ and the values of a function f at the endpoints a and b to be estimated at a point x within that interval, estimate the value at x to be:

$$f(x) \approx f(a) + \frac{(x-a)}{(b-a)}(f(b) - f(a)) \qquad (10.1)$$

In practice, you have several such intervals. This leads to a straightforward implementation like:

```
module interpolation_methods
    implicit none

contains

real function interpolate( x, y, xp )

    real, dimension(:), intent(in) :: x, y
    real, intent(in)               :: xp

    integer                        :: i, idx

    !
    ! Search for the interval that contains xp
    !
    idx = size(x) - 1

    do i = 2,size(x)-1
       if ( xp < x(i) ) then
          idx = i - 1
          exit
       endif
    enddo

    !
    ! Estimate the function value
    !
    interpolate = y(idx) + (xp-x(idx)) * (y(idx+1)-y(idx)) / &
                  (x(idx+1)-x(idx))

end function interpolate

end module interpolation_methods
```

The implementation presumes a number of things about the input, but it is not clear what happens with a number of edge cases. The following examines them:

- Input arrays x and y should be filled with data for the x-coordinate in ascending order. If not, the do loop will turn up an arbitrary starting point and the result is equally arbitrary.
- The size of array y must be at least that of x – otherwise, at some data point xp, you will be using elements out of the valid range.
- The implementation tacitly assumes that linear *extrapolation* is required if the coordinate xp is lower than x(1) or greater than x(size(x)). Whether this is a useful approach will depend on the application. Alternatives are: return either x(1) or x(size(x)) or return an indication that xp was outside the given range.
- The number of data points, size(x), is assumed to be at least two. If not, the implementation will violate the array bounds.
- If two values in the array x are the same, the implementation is a model of discontinuity in the function. However, this does not work for xp exactly equal to these values for x: a division by zero results.
  This is unlikely to occur in practice.[2] Nonetheless, one might want to control – just as in the case of extrapolation – what the program returns at the jump: the value left, the value right or the average. At the very least, the documentation should be clear about this.
- As a last point of criticism, the implementation may fail with an overflow error if the values of x and y are large enough:

$$x = \{1, 10^{30}\}, y = \{1, 10^{30}\}, xp = 10^{20}. \qquad (10.2)$$

The last statement in the program would then involve the computation of $(10^{20} - 1) \times (10^{30} - 1)$, which is a result that exceeds the range for single-precision floating-point numbers.

If you change it to:

```
factor      = (xp - x(idx)) / (x(idx+1) - x(idx))
interpolate = y(idx) + factor * (y(idx+1) -  y(idx))
```

all operations involve numbers that are within range, if the exact result is within range.

You can improve the implementation in two ways: by documenting in detail the assumptions (thereby, making the user responsible) or by checking the conditions on the input and allowing the user some control over the details.

---

[2] While I was working on this chapter, I came across a bug report for one of the software products of my company that related to just this type of bug, a division by zero because two x-values were inadvertently equal.

Checking the "sortedness" of the array x for each invocation of the interpolation routine is overdoing it. It is more efficient to create a self-contained "object" that requires such checking only when it is created. The routine to create this object can also check the sizes of the arrays x and y and store options with respect to extrapolation and jumps. The interpolation object holds a copy of the two arrays, as you do not want data to change without repeated checking. Here is the improved implementation:

```
! robust_interp.f90 --
!     Robust version of interpolation
!
module interpolation

    implicit none

    type interpolation_data
        logical                          :: useable = .false.
        integer                          :: extrapolation
        real, dimension(:), allocatable :: x, y
    end type interpolation_data

    integer, parameter :: extrapolation_none     = 0
    integer, parameter :: extrapolation_constant = 1
    integer, parameter :: extrapolation_linear   = 2

contains

function interpolation_object( x, y, extrapolation )
    type(interpolation_data)      :: interpolation_object
    real, dimension(:), intent(in) :: x, y
    integer, intent(in)            :: extrapolation

    integer                        :: i, ierr, n
    logical                        :: success

    interpolation_object%useable = .false.

    if ( allocated(interpolation_object%x) ) then
        deallocate(interpolation_object%x )
    endif
    if ( allocated(interpolation_object%y) ) then
        deallocate(interpolation_object%y )
    endif

    !
    ! Set the extrapolation method
    !
```

```
interpolation_object%extrapolation = extrapolation_none
if ( extrapolation == extrapolation_constant .or. &
     extrapolation == extrapolation_linear          ) then
    interpolation_object%extrapolation = extrapolation
endif

!
! Enough data? If not, simply return
!
if ( size(x) < 2 .or. size(y) < size(x) ) then
    return
endif

!
! Data sorted?
!
success = .true.

do i = 2,size(x)
    if ( x(i) < x(i-1) ) then
        success = .false.
        exit
    endif
enddo

if ( .not. success ) then
    return
endif

!
! Copy the data
!
n = size(x)
allocate( interpolation_object%x(n), &
          interpolation_object%y(n), stat = ierr )

if ( ierr /= 0 ) then
    return
endif

!
! We allow array y to be larger than x,
! so take care of that
!
interpolation_object%x(1:n) = x(1:n)
interpolation_object%y(1:n) = y(1:n)

interpolation_object%useable = .true.
```

```
end function interpolation_object
subroutine interpolate( object, xp, estimate, success )

    type(interpolation_data)       :: object
    real, intent(in)               :: xp
    real, intent(out)              :: estimate
    logical, intent(out)           :: success

    integer                        :: i, idx, nd
    real                           :: dx, factor

    estimate = 0.0
    success  = .false.

    if ( .not. object%useable ) then
        return
    endif


    !
    ! Check extrapolation
    !
    nd = size(object%x)

    if ( object%extrapolation == extrapolation_none ) then
        if ( xp < object%x(1)  ) return
        if ( xp > object%x(nd) ) return
    endif
    if ( object%extrapolation == extrapolation_constant ) then
        if ( xp < object%x(1) ) then
            estimate = object%x(1)
            success  = .true.
            return
        endif
        if ( xp > object%x(nd) ) then
            estimate = object%x(nd)
            success  = .true.
            return
        endif
    endif


    !
    ! Search for the interval that contains xp
    ! (Linear extrapolation is taken care of
    ! automatically)
    !
    idx = nd - 1
```

```
do i = 2,nd - 1
    if ( xp < object%x(i) ) then
        idx = i - 1
        exit
    endif
enddo

dx = object%x(idx+1) - object%x(idx)

if ( dx /= 0.0 ) then
    factor   = (xp - object%x(idx)) / dx
    estimate = object%y(idx) + &
        factor * (object%y(idx+1) - object%y(idx))
else
    !
    ! In case of jumps, we simply take the average
    !
    estimate = 0.5 * (object%y(idx+1) + object%y(idx))
endif

success = .true.

end subroutine interpolate

end module interpolation
```

The following program shows how it can be used:

```
program test_interpolation
    use interpolation

    implicit none

    real, dimension(6) :: &
            x = (/ 0.0, 1.0, 10.0, 10.0, 20.0, 20.0 /)
    real, dimension(6) :: &
            y = (/ 0.0, 2.0, 20.0, 20.0, 10.0, 10.0 /)

    type(interpolation_data) :: interp

    integer            :: i
    real               :: xp, result
    logical            :: success

    interp = interpolation_object( x, y, &
                extrapolation_constant )

    do i = 1,25
```

Table 10.1. Results of Two Implementations of Linear Interpolation. Extrapolation Option: Constant

X Value	Straightforward Interpolation	Robust Interpolation	Remark
−3.000	−6.000	0.000	Extrapolation
−2.000	−4.000	0.000	Extrapolation
−1.000	−2.000	0.000	Extrapolation
0.000	0.000	0.000	
1.000	2.000	2.000	
2.000	4.000	4.000	
8.000	16.00	16.00	
9.000	18.00	18.00	
10.00	20.00	20.00	
11.00	19.00	19.00	
12.00	18.00	18.00	
13.00	17.00	17.00	
18.00	12.00	12.00	
19.00	11.00	11.00	
20.00	NaN	10.00	Double point
21.00	NaN	20.00	Extrapolation

```
      xp = -4.0 + 1.0 * i
      call interpolate( interp, xp, result, success )
      write(*,'(2g12.4,5x,l)') xp, result, success
   enddo
end program
```

Using this implementation is a bit more complicated, unfortunately, but it gives the user more flexibility: a choice for extrapolation and an indication whether or not an estimate is possible. The results for the two implementations are given in Table 10.1.

10.3 Basic Statistics

Another well-known programming problem is the determination of the mean and standard deviation of a series of data. Consider this problem in the following context: You have a file with the data, one value per line, and there may be missing data as well, indicated with a question mark. You will produce the mean, the standard deviation, the number of data, and the number of missing data (to indicate the quality of the series). At first sight, this is a straightforward exercise:

```
! basic_stat.f90 --
!     Basic statistical parameters - straightforward version
!
program basic_stat
```

```fortran
implicit none
real    :: value, sum, sumsq, stdev, vmean
integer :: i, j, nodata, nomissing, ierr

open( 10, file = 'basic_stat.data', status = 'old', &
    iostat = ierr )

if ( ierr /= 0 ) then
    write(*,*) 'Error opening file with input data &
        &- basic_stat.data'
    write(*,*) 'Check that it exists'
    stop
endif


!
! One value per line, ? means a missing value ...
! (As a ? can not be read into a number, we treat
! each line that causes a read error as a missing value)
!
sum       = 0.0
sumsq     = 0.0
nodata    = 0
nomissing = 0

do
    read( 10, *, iostat = ierr ) value

    if ( ierr < 0 ) then
        !
        ! End of file
        !
        exit
    elseif ( ierr > 0 ) then
        !
        ! Missing value
        !
        nomissing = nomissing + 1
        cycle
    endif

    sum   = sum    + value
    sumsq = sumsq  + value ** 2
    nodata = nodata + 1
enddo

close( 10 )

!
```

```
! Report our findings
!
write(*,*) 'Outcome:'
write(*,*) '    Number of valid data:   ', nodata
write(*,*) '    Number of missing data:', nomissing
write(*,*) ' '

if ( nodata > 0 ) then
    vmean = sum / nodata
    write(*,*) '    Mean value:                ', vmean

    if ( nodata > 1 ) then
        stdev  = &
            sqrt( (sumsq - sum**2/nodata) / (nodata-1) )
        write(*,*) '    Standard deviation:    ', stdev
    else
        write(*,*) &
            '    Standard deviation:    too few data'
    endif
else
    write(*,*) '    Mean value:                too few data'
endif
end program basic_stat
```

Note that you use the mathematical identity:

$$\sigma^2 = \frac{1}{n-1}\sum_{i=1}^{n}(x_i - \mu)^2 = \frac{1}{n-1}(\sum_{i=1}^{n} x_i - n\mu^2) \qquad (10.3)$$

to avoid having to store the individual data and to loop over the data twice.

The preceding implementation can be split into two parts, each with its own robustness issues. Reading the data from file is one part, computing the statistical parameters is the second part.

The statement

```
read( 10, *, iostat = ierr) value
```

reads a number using Fortran's list-directed input features. While this is very flexible, it does assume that input conforms to the rules. More specifically, the input is supposed to consist of valid numbers, separated by spaces, commas, or new lines. After each read statement, the file pointer advances to the next line, if there is any, thereby skipping and ignoring whatever comes after the last read item. If the input encountered does not match the expected type, the variable ierr is set to a positive value. If the end of the file is encountered, it is set to a negative value.

This raises some questions about the details of the file format:

- List-directed input will skip an empty line. Should that have been interpreted by the previous program as a missing value?
- If the line contains more than one value, it is accepted, but the other values are silently ignored. Is that acceptable behavior?
- What happens if the line contains an invalid number, such as "1.0?"? Is this interpreted as a missing value or is it reported separately?
- More subtle problems:
  - What happens if the line endings in the file do not match those of the platform? (Perhaps you have a UNIX/Linux file on Windows or vice versa.)
  - Sometimes files on Windows do not terminate the last line with an end-of-file sequence. Is that acceptable? Can the list-directed read statement handle that in a clear way?
  - Fortran's list-directed input does not accept tab characters. As they are often not visible when viewing the file, they can be difficult to detect.

The remedy to the issues mentioned here is not simple. It is not, however, the fault of Fortran's list-directed input features, rather you have underspecified what acceptable input should be. The specification must pay attention to what is *not* acceptable, too.

You can implement reading the data in such a way that you can detect most of the issues already mentioned, by reading a line of text from the file and analyzing that in detail. This is done in the second version of the program. But, first pay attention to the computational part.

The second part of the program is the actual computation of the statistical parameters. The formulae are simple, but they present a few important problems. First of all, the computation of the variance is numerically unstable. It is easy to see: The program computes two sums and then uses the difference as the final result. If the variation is small, then you subtract two large quantities and significant rounding errors occur. A dramatic example is an input consisting of nine times 0.1:[3]

```
Outcome:
    Number of valid data:           9
    Number of missing data:         0

    Mean value:          0.10000001
    Standard deviation:              NaN
```

Not only is the mean value slightly different than 0.1, a result of the finite precision, the standard deviation, which should have been 0, is in fact computed from the square root of a small negative number, $-1.93715111.10^{-9}$.

---

[3] I used the *gfortran* compiler under Windows XP with default options to compute this result.

Alternatives to this formula exist that do not exhibit numerical instability, but they are more complicated. A simple workaround for the problem is to modify the values that are being summed:

```
sum    = sum    + (value - offset)
sumsq  = sumsq  + (value - offset) ** 2
```

where `offset` is one of the non-missing values in the series of data. As the values in the two sums capture only the *variation* in the numbers, the roundoff errors are smaller.

Secondly, when the input value are either very large ($> 10^{30}$) or very small ($< 10^{-30}$), overflow or underflow may occur – the square of such extreme numbers cannot be represented with standard single-precision floating-point numbers. There are several methods to avoid this particular issue:

- Use a type of floating-point numbers that allows a wider range, like double precision. This merely expands the range of numbers you can deal with.
- Use scaling to force the numbers into a more convenient range.

Whether it is worth introducing such measures, depends on the expected data and the emphasis you must put on the robustness aspects. The simplest way to deal with the problem is to warn about numbers outside a particular safe range. This is exactly what is done in the following revised version:

```
! robust_stat.f90 --
!     Basic statistical parameters - robust version
!
program robust_stat

    character(len=80) :: line
    real              :: value, sum, sumsq, var
    integer           :: i, j, nodata, nomissing
    integer           :: noerrors, noempty, nolines, ierr
    logical           :: first_value = .true.

    open( 10, file = 'robust_stat.data', status = 'old', &
        iostat = ierr )

    if ( ierr /= 0 ) then
        write(*,*) 'Error opening file with input data - &
            &robust_stat.data'
        write(*,*) 'Check that it exists'
        stop
    endif


    !
    ! One value per line, ? means a missing value ...
```

```fortran
! (Any other value that can not be read is regarded to
! be an error, ! empty lines are reported but
! not counted)
!
sum       = 0.0
sumsq     = 0.0
nodata    = 0
nomissing = 0
nolines   = 0
noerrors  = 0

do
    read( 10, '(a)', iostat = ierr ) line

    if ( ierr < 0 ) then
        !
        ! End of file
        !
        exit
    elseif ( ierr > 0 ) then
        !
        ! Some reading error occurred - report it
        !
        write(*,*) 'Error reading line no.', nolines+1
        write(*,*) 'Skipping the rest of the file'
        exit
    else
        !
        ! Get rid of tabs and carriage returns
        !
        call cleanup_line( line )
        !
        ! Analyze the contents:
        ! - Empty line?
        ! - Missing value?
        ! - Not a valid number?
        ! - Valid number
        !
        ! Note: only the first value on the line is used
        ! Anything else is ignored.
        !
        nolines = nolines + 1

        if ( line == ' ' ) then
            noempty = noempty + 1
            cycle
        endif
```

```
      if ( adjustl(line) == '?' ) then
          nomissing = nomissing + 1
          cycle
      endif

      read( line, *, iostat = ierr ) value

      if ( ierr /= 0 ) then
          noerrors = noerrors + 1
          cycle
      endif

      !
      ! If the value is out of range, report it and
      ! skip it
      !
      if ( abs(value) > sqrt(huge(value) .or. &
          ( abs(value) < tiny(value) .and. &
            abs(value) /= 0.0 ) ) then
          write(*,*) 'Value out of range: ', value, &
              ' - ignoring it!'
          nomissing = nomissing + 1
          cycle
      endif

      !
      ! We do have a valid value
      !
      if ( first_value ) then
          first_value = .false.
          offset      = value
      endif

      sum   = sum   + (value - offset)
      sumsq = sumsq + (value - offset) ** 2
      nodata = nodata + 1
  endif
enddo

close( 10 )

!
! Report our findings
!
write(*,*) 'Outcome:'
write(*,*) '    Number of lines read: ', nolines
write(*,*) '    Number of empty lines: ', noempty
```

```fortran
    write(*,*) '    Number of valid data:   ', nodata
    write(*,*) '    Number of missing data:', nomissing
    write(*,*) '    Number of invalid data:', noerrors
    write(*,*) ' '

    if ( nodata > 0 ) then
        vmean = offset + sum / nodata
        write(*,*) '    Mean value:              ', vmean

        if ( nodata > 1 ) then
            stdev  = &
                sqrt( (sumsq - sum**2/nodata) / (nodata-1) )
            write(*,*) '    Standard deviation:    ', stdev
        else
            write(*,*) &
                '    Standard deviation:    too few data'
        endif
    else
        write(*,*) '    Mean value:              too few data'
    endif
contains

subroutine cleanup_line( line )
    character(len=*), intent(inout) :: line

    logical                         :: found
    integer                         :: i, k
    integer, dimension(3)           :: chars = (/9,10,13/)

    found = .true.
    do while ( found )

        found = .false.
        !
        ! Remove any tabs, carriage returns and newlines
        !
        do i = 1,size(chars)
            k = index( line, achar(chars(i)) )
            if ( k > 0 ) then
                found     = .true.
                line(k:k) = ' '
            endif
        enddo
    endif

end subroutine cleanup_line

end program robust_stat
```

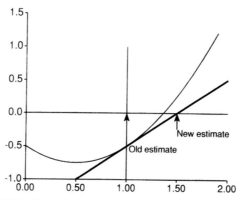

Figure 10.1. Constructing a new estimate with the Newton-Raphson algorithm

10.4 Finding the Roots of an Equation

The Newton-Raphson method is a popular algorithm for finding the roots of an equation. It is fast (quadratic convergence), if it converges, and you need only a single starting point. Geometrically it works by constructing the tangent line through the current estimate and using the zero of that tangent as the next estimate (see Figure 10.1).

The formula for the iteration process is:

$$x_{k+1} = x_k - \frac{f(x_k)}{f'(x_k)} \tag{10.4}$$

Drawbacks are as follows:

- You need the first derivative of the function.
- If the root is a multiple root (the first derivative is zero also), convergence slows down to a linear rate.
- Local extrema (where the derivative has a zero) may cause the estimates to "run away."

The issue of the derivative is solved in a number of ways:

- The user must supply a routine that computes the value of the function as well as its first derivative explicitly.
- Use automatic or symbolic differentation (see Chapter 3).
- Estimate the derivative numerically.

For complicated functions, the first method is rather error-prone. The second method is closest to the mathematical formulation, but it may not be implemented easily in the chosen programming language.

From the point of view of robustness, the third method is the most interesting. The focus is on that method, but the algorithm itself poses a few intriguing riddles, too.

Here again is a straightforward implementation:

```fortran
module newton_raphson

    implicit none

contains

subroutine find_root( f, xinit, tol, maxiter, result, success )

    interface
        real function f(x)
            real, intent(in) :: x
        end function f
    end interface

    real,    intent(in)  :: xinit, tol
    integer, intent(in)  :: maxiter
    real,    intent(out) :: result
    logical, intent(out) :: success

    real             :: eps = 1.0e-4
    real             :: fx1, fx2, fprime, x, xnew
    integer          :: i

    result  = 0.0
    success = .false.

    x = xinit
    do i = 1,max(1,maxiter)
        fx1    = f(x)
        fx2    = f(x+eps)
        fprime = (fx2 - fx1) / eps

        xnew   = x - fx1 / fprime

        if ( abs(xnew-x) <= tol ) then
            success = .true.
            result  = xnew
            exit
        endif

        x = xnew
    enddo

end subroutine find_root

end module
```

Table 10.2. Results of the Straightforward Newton-Raphson Implementation for Several Functions. Relative Tolerance: 10^{-5}.

Function	Start Value	Root Found	Remarks
$\ln x - 1$	0.1	2.7182817	7 iterations
$\ln x - 1$	10	Outside domain (NaN)	x_1 is negative
x^2	10	$3.99.10^{-5}$	Slow convergence – 20 iterations
$x^2 + 1$	10	No convergence	There is no real root
$\sqrt{|x|}$	1.0	Oscillation	Theoretically: $x_{k+1} = -x_k$

Some results of this program are shown in Table 10.2.

Sometimes the process will converge, sometimes it will not, and sometimes the function cannot be properly evaluated. A robust implementation should try to accurately diagnose the situation. More subtle problems exist as well: How do you choose the tolerance? And for that matter, how do you define the tolerance?

Let us examine the simplest case first: a simple root. There is not always a floating-point value for x for which the numerical implementation of $f(x)$ is exactly zero. However, you can find two numbers, x_1 and x_2, such that $f(x_1)$ and $f(x_2)$ have opposite signs, thus bracketing the exact root.

Therefore, the two floating-point numbers on either side of the exact zero that are closest together are in fact the closest approximations you can get. It may not be necessary to go that far, but it is reassuring to know that you can find such a pair. This is *not* the case for multiple roots of even order. They present an entirely different problem.

If you do not need to find this narrow interval, but rather an approximation to within 10^{-4}, what exactly do you need? This is more involved than you might think. It is tempting to think it means:

"We accept any number x that lies in the interval $((1 - \epsilon)r, (1 + \epsilon)r)$, with r the exact root and ϵ the relative tolerance."

This definition is meaningless if the exact root is 0. If the root is small, with respect to 1, say 10^{-6}, and you are interested in numbers ranging from -10 to 10, you may want to accept an interval $(-10^{-4}, 10^{-4})$, instead of $(0.9999 \times 10^{-6}, 1.0001 \times 10^{-6})$.

If the numbers have a "logarithmic" character, meaning you interpret a number based on its order of magnitude, rather than the absolute value, the original relative interpretation is called for.

Leave the decision to the user: if he or she requires a logarithmic interpretation, then the function should actually be formulated as such:

- Rewrite $f(x)$ as $g(y)$, $y = \ln x$.
- Determine the root of g and transform the result.

A useful criterium for convergence that tries to overcome the preceding criticisms:

■ The best estimate x_{k+1} lies in the interval $(x_k - S\delta, x_k + S\delta)$, where S is a *scale factor*, indicating the typical values of x for which the function is relevant and δ is the relative tolerance.
■ The function values at the end points of this interval have opposite signs.
■ If convergence does not happen within a preset number of iterations, assume it will not happen at all.

The first point guarantees that you have a meaningful, small interval under all circumstances, while the second guarantees that you bracket the exact root. The choice of S and δ is left to the user.

The next step is: how to determine the derivative numerically? You will use finite differences to approximate the derivative:

$$f'(x) \approx \frac{f(x + \eta) - f(x)}{\eta} \tag{10.5}$$

This is prone to numerical errors (subtracting two almost equal quantities), but there is no alternative, if we cannot or do not want to use automatic or explicit differentiation. The criterium for selecting the stepsize η in this formula is that the two function values differ significantly enough to avoid rounding errors, but are small enough to avoid effects of the higher-order derivatives.

Unfortunately, it is not trivial to decide what stepsize to use. Take the following example:

$$f(x) = \begin{cases} \dfrac{1 - \cos x}{x} & \text{if } x \neq 0 \\ 0 & \text{if } x = 0 \end{cases} \tag{10.6}$$

The mathematically exact derivative at $x = 0$ is $\frac{1}{2}$. Determining this value via a small program requires selecting a value of $x = 0 + \eta$, where $\cos x$ numerically differs from 1 (see Table 10.3).

The smallest value of η where this theoretically can happen is:[4]

$$\cos(0 + \eta) = \textit{largest value smaller than } 1 = 0.999999940395 \tag{10.7}$$

giving:

$$\eta \approx 3.453 \times 10^{-4} \tag{10.8}$$

Therefore, it makes *no sense* to try and determine the root to an error smaller than that.

---

[4] You can use the *nearest()* function to determine the largest distinguishable value smallest than 1.

Table 10.3. Computed Values for the Function $f(x) = \frac{1-\cos x}{x}$ for Various Implementations

x	Direct Implementation	Via f(x) and g(x)	Mathematical Equivalent
1.0000×10^{-10}	0.0	0.0	5.0000×10^{-11}
1.0000×10^{-8}	4.9982×10^{-9}	0.0	5.0000×10^{-9}
1.0000×10^{-6}	5.0000×10^{-7}	0.0	5.0000×10^{-7}
1.0000×10^{-5}	5.0000×10^{-6}	0.0	5.0000×10^{-6}
1.0000×10^{-4}	5.0000×10^{-5}	0.0	5.0000×10^{-5}
3.0000×10^{-4}	1.5000×10^{-4}	1.9868×10^{-4}	1.5000×10^{-4}
1.0000×10^{-3}	5.0000×10^{-4}	4.7684×10^{-4}	5.0000×10^{-4}
1.0000×10^{-2}	5.0000×10^{-3}	5.0008×10^{-3}	5.0000×10^{-3}
1.0000×10^{-1}	4.9958×10^{-2}	4.9958×10^{-2}	4.9958×10^{-2}
1.0	4.5970×10^{-1}	4.5970×10^{-1}	4.5970×10^{-1}

You can, however, write the function in a mathematically equivalent way as:

$$f(x) = \begin{cases} \dfrac{2\sin^2 \frac{1}{2}x}{x} & \text{if } x \neq 0 \\ 0 & \text{if } x = 0 \end{cases} \tag{10.9}$$

With an implementation of this form, the minimum value of η is much smaller (see Table 10.3).

These estimates are complicated by the fact that many modern computers use extended precision to store intermediate results, as can be seen in Table 10.3. The apparent greater accuracy in the computations is offset by the fact that this extra precision is a rather volatile feature. If you evaluate the function f using the following implementation or if you use compiler options to guarantee floating-point consistency,[5] the results are that in a fairly large range the numerical implementation of the function gives exactly zero:

```
real function f(x)
    real, intent(in) :: x

    if ( x /= 0.0 ) then
        f = (1.0 - g(x)) / x
    else
        f = 0.0
    endif
end function f

real function g(x)
    real, intent(in) :: x

    g = cos(x)
end function g
```

---

[5] *gfortran*, for instance, has the option *-ffloat-store* to store intermediate results as a regular number.

Just as with the tolerance, the value of the stepsize is meaningless, unless you relate it to the *scale* of the function – a value of 1.0×10^{-3} works with this function, but it does not with:

$$h(x) = \begin{cases} \dfrac{1 - \cos(10^4 x)}{x} & \text{if } x \neq 0 \\ 0 & \text{if } x = 0 \end{cases} \qquad (10.10)$$

The first has a scale of 1, which is the order of magnitude for x over which the function values change considerably. The second has a scale of 10^{-4}, therefore, the function varies much more rapidly.

Given these considerations, you should ask the user to supply that scale, because it can be used to define the tolerance interval and the stepsize for numerical differentiation.

Yet another refinement that you need if the implementation is to be robust: not all functions are defined over the entire range of floating-point numbers. For f defined by:

$$f(x) = \ln x - 1 \qquad (10.11)$$

the iteration may produce a negative value of x. For a function like:

$$f(x) = e^x - 1 \qquad (10.12)$$

the problem is that the function value may become too large to be represented as a floating-point number (for example, use a starting value of -10).

Therefore, you need to deal with partial functions as well. One way is to ask the user to return a flag indicating if a domain error occurs or not. Then after determining the next acceptable estimate, you

- Compute the next regular estimate:

$$x_{k+1} = x_k - \frac{f(x)}{f'(x)} \qquad (10.13)$$

- If x_{k+1} is within the domain, accept it.
- If it is not, try:

$$x_{k+1} = x_k - \frac{f(x)}{2 f'(x)} \qquad (10.14)$$

- Repeat the halving until an acceptable value is found.

The initial estimate must, of course, be within the domain of f.

The last point of concern is roots that are not first order. As long as the values in the neighborhood are both positive and negative, you get the same situation as before, only the convergence is not quadratic anymore. The most problematic situation is roots where the function does not change sign. The function $f(x) = \sqrt{|x|}$ leads to an oscillation:

$$x_{k+1} = x_k - f(x_k)/f'(x_k) = -x_k \qquad (10.15)$$

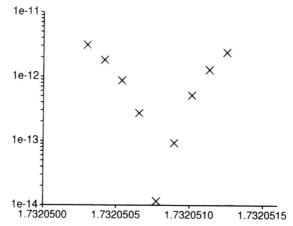

Figure 10.2. Values of the quartic function $f(x) = (x^2 - 3)^2$ around the root $\sqrt{3}$. The floating-point values of x were enumerated using the Fortran 90 nearest() function.

With functions like:

$$f(x) = (x^2 - 3)^2 \qquad (10.16)$$

you have a more subtle problem: Mathematically, you have two double roots, $-\sqrt{3}$ and $+\sqrt{3}$, but the function as implemented in a small program never attains the value zero (see Figure 10.2). The minimum value is attained at the value of sqrt(3.0), but this value can be arbitrarily large. Consider, for instance, the same function with a large constant:

$$f(x) = 10^{10}(x^2 - 3)^2 \qquad (10.17)$$

Furthermore, the values around the precise minimum are 10 times larger.

A solution around this could be to specify a tolerance for the function value: any point where the function reaches a small enough absolute value is regarded as an approximation to its zero.

Piecing it all together, you get the following steps:

1. Determine if the initial guess, x_0, is within the domain of the function. If not, you cannot continue.
2. If the function value is small enough, you stop. However, also see if the exact root is enclosed or not in the tolerance interval.
3. Determine a reasonable stepsize δ for estimating the derivative then take care of the step's direction. If you cannot find a reasonable step, stop the procedure. (A reasonable stepsize is one where the function values changes enough to determine the derivative accurately.)
4. Determine the next iterate. If not within the function's domain, modify the estimate.

5. If you have the maximum number of function evaluations, stop the procedure: no convergence. If you have not reached the maximum yet, go back to step 2.

The implementation uses the number of function evaluations as the cancellation criterium, because evaluating the function is generally the most expensive step.

Here is an implementation:

```fortran
! robust_newton.f90 --
!     Robust version of the Newton-Raphson method
!
module robust_newton

    implicit none

    integer, parameter :: bracketed_root       = 1
    integer, parameter :: small_value_solution = 2
    integer, parameter :: convergence_reached   = 3
    integer, parameter :: invalid_start_value  = -1
    integer, parameter :: no_convergence       = -2
    integer, parameter :: invalid_arguments    = -3

contains

subroutine find_root( f, xinit, scalex, tolx, smallf, &
            maxevals, result, success )

    interface
        subroutine f( x, indomain, value )
            real, intent(in)      :: x
            logical, intent(out)  :: indomain
            real, intent(out)     :: value
        end subroutine f
    end interface

    real, intent(in)      :: xinit, scalex, tolx, smallf
    integer, intent(in)   :: maxevals
    real, intent(out)     :: result
    integer, intent(out)  :: success

    real                  :: eps, epsinit, epsf
    real                  :: fx1, fx2, fxnew, fprime, fscale
    real                  :: x, xnew
    integer               :: i, evals
    logical               :: indomain

    result = 0.0
```

```
success = no_convergence

!
! Sanity check
!
if ( scalex <= 0.0 .or. tolx <= 0.0 .or. &
     smallf <= 0.0                        ) then
    success = invalid_arguments
    return
endif


!
! Starting value for the stepsize
!
epsinit = scalex * sqrt( epsilon(xinit) )
epsf    =  100.0 * epsilon(fx1)


!
! Check the initial value
!
x = xinit

call f( x, indomain, fx1 )
evals = 1

if ( .not. indomain ) then
    success = invalid_start_value
    return
endif

outerloop: &
    do
        !
        ! Is the function value small enough?
        ! Then stop
        !
        if ( abs(fx1) <= smallf ) then
            success = small_value_solution
            result  = x
            exit
        endif


        !
        ! Determine the derivative - be careful about
        ! the domain
        !
        eps = epsinit
```

```fortran
epsloop: &
        do while ( evals < maxevals )
            call f( x+eps, indomain, fx2 )

            evals = evals + 1
            if ( evals >= maxevals ) exit

            if ( .not. indomain ) then
                eps = -eps
                call f( x+eps, indomain, fx2 )

                evals = evals + 1
                if ( evals >= maxevals ) exit outerloop

                if ( .not. indomain ) exit outerloop
            endif

            fscale = (abs(fx2)+abs(fx1))/2.0
            if ( abs(fx2-fx1) < epsf * fscale + smallf ) then
                eps = 2.0 * eps
            else
                exit epsloop
            endif
        enddo &
epsloop

        fprime = (fx2 - fx1) / eps

        !
        ! Determine the next estimate
        !
newxloop: &
        do while ( evals < maxevals )
            xnew  = x - fx1 / fprime

            call f( xnew, indomain, fxnew )
            evals = evals + 1

            if ( .not. indomain ) then
                fx1  = fx1 / 2.0
            else
                exit newxloop
            endif
        enddo &
newxloop

        fx1 = fxnew
```

```
      !
      ! Have we reached convergence?
      !
      if ( evals < maxevals ) then
          if ( abs(xnew-x) <= scalex * tolx ) then
              success = convergence_reached
              if ( abs(fx1) < smallf ) then
                  success = small_value_solution
              endif
              result  = xnew
              exit outerloop
          endif
      else
          exit outerloop
      endif

      x = xnew
   enddo &
outerloop

      !
      ! Simply a small value or a bracketed root?
      !
      call f( x - scalex*tolx, indomain, fx1 )
      evals = evals + 1
      if ( indomain ) then
          call f( x + scalex*tolx, indomain, fx2 )
          evals = evals + 1
          if ( indomain ) then
              if ( fx1 * fx2 <= 0.0 ) then
                  success = bracketed_root
              endif
          endif
      endif

end subroutine find_root

end module
```

It may be difficult to determine whether the x value is within the domain of
the function. In that case, the intrinsic module ieee_arithmetic introduced
in Fortran 2003 is helpful. This module contains the functions ieee_is_nan()
and ieee_is_finite() to check if a number is a valid, ordered number or not,
and whether it is a finite number (see Chapter 9). Instead of demanding the
user to indicate that the value of x is within the function's domain, you can
check that the returned value is still usable:

Table 10.4. Results of the Robust Newton-Raphson Implementation for Several Functions. Relative Tolerance: 10^{-5}, Maximum Number of Evaluations: 20 (except for the parabola, there it was 40). For the Cosine Function, a Scale Factor of 10^{-4} was Used and the Root Found is Approximately $57.5\,\beta \times 10^{-4}$

Function	Start Value	Root Found	Conclusion	Evaluations
$\ln x - 1$	0.1	2.7182817	convergence	15
$\ln x - 1$	10	2.7182817	convergence	12
x^2	10	2.87×10^{-3}	small value solution	30
$x^2 + 1$	10	–	no convergence	22
$\sqrt{|x|}$	1.0	–	no convergence	22
$\cos(10^4 x)$	0.0	0.0184064158	convergence	16

```
use, intrinsic :: ieee_arithmetic, only :: ieee_is_finite
```

```
. . .
fxnew = f( xnew )
indomain = ieee_is_finite( fxnew )
. . .
```

Table 10.4 contains the results for the same set of functions as you started with and one extra function to examine what happens if the scale factor is very different from 1. Some experimenting shows that it is very difficult to reach $\frac{1}{2}\pi \times 10^{-4}$ via the scale factor and a starting value of 0. A different starting value ($2.355 \times 10^{-4} \approx 0.75\pi \times 10^{-4}$) does give approximately $\frac{1}{2}\pi \times 10^{-4}$ as the root.

11.

Object-Oriented Programming

An interesting feature of Fortran 2003 is the possibility to use an object-oriented style of programming. While Akin [2] and Decyk and Gardner [28] have shown that object-oriented programming (OOP) is possible in Fortran 90/95, the lack of inheritance and run-time polymorphism poses some limits on what you can do. Fortran 2003 makes these aspects of OOP readily available. Furthermore, in combination with other facilities you can do more than merely class-based OOP.

One thing to note: Object-oriented programming is a subject that is both vast and confusing at times. Not only does the terminology that is used differ per programming language, but also their semantics, or what the concepts actually mean. Authors differ in what they consider to be the essential concepts of OOP. Rouson and Adalsteinsson [73] compare Fortran 2003 and C++ implementations of several *design patterns* and they provide synonyms for the various concepts in these two languages.

11.1 Extending Types and Type-Bound Procedures

The basic features that allow you to create an object-oriented program are type extension and type-bound procedures. For example, consider points in two-dimensional space. The following elaborates this example in several directions. The starting point is this derived type:

```
type point2d
    real :: x, y
end type point2d
```

You can define operations like adding a vector to this point or scaling with respect to the origin in the classical way using Fortran 90/95:

```
module points2d

    implicit none

    type point2d
        real :: x, y
    end type point2d
```

```
contains
type(point2d) function add_vector( point, vector )
    type(point2d), intent(in) :: point, vector

    add_vector%x = point%x + vector%x
    add_vector%y = point%y + vector%y
end function add_vector

type(point2d) function scale_by_factor( point, factor )
    type(point2d), intent(in) :: point, vector
    real, intent(in)          :: factor

    scale_by_factor%x = factor * point%x
    scale_by_factor%y = factor * point%y
end function scale_by_factor

end module points2d
```

But these procedures (with one modification) can also be **bound to the type**:

```
type point2d
    real :: x, y
contains
    procedure :: add   => add_vector
    procedure :: scale => scale_by_factor
end type point2d
```

The consequence of this binding is that you can use them as follows:

```
! Translate the point over the vector

newpoint = point%add( vector )
```

You may conclude that this is merely a syntactic difference from:

```
! Translate the point over the vector

newpoint = add_vector( point, vector )
```

In a way that is true. Even though the procedure is now bound to the point2d type, you can still call it with the object as an explicit argument.

Because types can, in principle, be *extended*, the signature of the type-bound procedures add_vector and scale_by_factor must be changed to accommodate for these extended types. This is done by making at least the object that is implicitly passed a so-called polymorphic variable, that is, a variable that has a declared type and a *dynamic* type. This type of variable is declared via the class keyword:

```fortran
type(point2d) function add_vector( point, vector )
    class(point2d), intent(in) :: point
    type(point2d), intent(in)  :: vector

    add_vector%x = point%x + vector%x
    add_vector%y = point%y + vector%y
end function add_vector
```

Passing the Object Via Another Argument If the argument containing the object is not the first, you can specify that:

```fortran
type point2d
    real :: x, y
contains
    procedure :: add, pass(vector) => add_vector
end type point2d
```

This has the effect that the left-hand side pnt of pnt%add(vec) is no longer passed as the first argument, but as the argument whose name is "vector":

```fortran
newpnt = pnt%add(vec)
```

It is now equivalent to:

```fortran
newpnt = add( vec, pnt )
```

instead of:

```fortran
newpnt = add( pnt, vec )
```

If you want to suppress this automatic passing of the left-hand side, you can use the nopass keyword instead of pass.

Extending to Three Dimensions You have points in a two-dimensional space, so use this type as the basis for points in 3D space by **extending** the point2d type:

```fortran
type, extends(point2d) :: point3d
    real :: z
contains
    procedure :: add => add_vector3d
end type point3d
```

This new type inherits all the components and type-bound procedures of the type it extends, but you need to revise the procedures (hence the new procedure add_vector3d) to reflect that these are points in 3D space and to accommodate for the restrictions the Fortran standard imposes.

First, interfaces like **add** are overwritten in extended types, but then you need to take care that the **signature** remains essentially the same. The only required change is that the type of the object passed is the extended type. In the preceding case, the signature of the routine add_vector3d becomes:

```
type(point2d) function add_vector3d( point, vector )
    class(point3d), intent(in) :: point    ! Required change!
    type(point2d), intent(in) :: vector
    . . .
end function add_vector3d
```

Note that the returned value and the vector over which the point translates are still type(point2d), not type(point3d). The Fortran standard does not allow you to change that. Instead, you need polymorphic variables.

For the two-dimensional case:

```
class(point2d) function add_vector_2d( point, vector )
    class(point2d), intent(in) :: point
    class(point2d), intent(in) :: vector
    . . .
end function add_vector_2d
```

For the three-dimensional case:

```
class(point2d) function add_vector_3d( point, vector )
    class(point3d), intent(in) :: point

    ! This one still point2d
    class(point2d), intent(in) :: vector
    . . .
end function add_vector_3d
```

This has some consequences for the implementation of the actual routines as well: You cannot simply return a **class** variable. It must be either an allocatable or a pointer, because the type is dynamic. The allocation or the association transfers the type information as well as information on the memory to be used. Therefore, the two-dimensional variant becomes (note the allocation):

```
function add_vector_2d( point, vector )
    class(point2d), intent(in) :: point, vector
    class(point2d), allocatable :: add_vector_2d

    allocate( add_vector_2d )

    add_vector_2d%x = point%x + vector%x
    add_vector_2d%y = point%y + vector%y

end function add_vector_2d
```

The three-dimensional variant has an additional difficulty to cope with. The result must be class(point2d), not class(point3d), so you need to adjust the dynamic type of the result before returning. Here is one solution:

```
function add_vector_3d( point, vector )
    class(point3d), intent(in)  :: point
    class(point2d), intent(in)  :: vector

    class(point2d), allocatable :: add_vector_3d
    class(point3d), allocatable :: add_result

    allocate( add_result )

    add_result%point2d = point%point2d%add(vector)
    add_result%z       = 0.0

    select type (vector)
        class is (point3d)
            add_result%z = point%z + vector%z
    end select

    call move_alloc( add_result, add_vector_3d )

end function add_vector_3d
```

In this example, you allocate a local variable add_result, which has the right basic type, and use the move_alloc intrinsic routine to move the memory **and the type information** into the result variable, using add_vector_3d. To make sure you know the type of the vector argument – known as basic type type(point2d) only – use the select type construction.[1]

The type from which you extended the 3D point is available with all its components and procedures, as an implicit component point2d. Therefore, do the part of the task that has not changed and add the new aspects separately.[2]

Example: Random Walk in Two and Three Dimensions The dynamic type of these polymorphic variables is exploited in a program to simulate a random walk in two or three dimensions. The random walk is constructed by repeatedly selecting a random vector and adding that to the current position of a point to get the new position. If you are using ordinary types, use:

```
do i = 1,nsteps
    call random_vector( vector )
```

---

[1] This may seem awkward, but it is not that different from languages like C++ or Java where you first have to create an object of the right type as well.

[2] In C++ and Java, you would use the *super class* to achieve this effect.

```
    point = point + deltt * vector

    call print( point )
enddo
```

The compact expression point = point + deltt * vector relies on defining operator interfaces, so that the compiler knows what the + and * operations mean for the involved derived types:

```
interface operator(+)
    module procedure add_vector_2d
end interface
```

This does not work for type-bound procedures, such as an interface block:

```
interface operator(+)
    module procedure add_vector_2d
    module procedure add_vector_3d
end interface
```

This would result in a compiler error because the compiler cannot distinguish between these two routines. A variable of type class(point3d) is regarded as class(point2d) as well, due to the fact that one is *extended* from the other.

The proper way to do this is using **generic** interfaces:

```
type point2d
    real :: x, y
contains
    procedure :: add => add_vector
    generic   :: operator(+) => add
end type point2d
```

Using the **generic** keyword, you associate the procedure add with the operation +. In extended types, the actual routine that implements the add procedure is different and, therefore, the + operation has a different meaning for such extended types. But that is, of course, exactly what you want.

In the following program, the variables point and vector are polymorphic and assume the dynamic types of point2d and point3d during the run of the program (not all code, such as the subroutine random_vector, is shown):

```
program random_walk

    use point3d   ! Both 2D and 3D points available

    type(point2d), target  :: point_2d, vector_2d
    type(point3d), target  :: point_3d, vector_3d

    !
    ! A variable of class point2d can point to point_2d but
```

```
    ! also to point_3d
    !
    class(point2d), pointer :: point, vector

    integer         :: nsteps = 100
    integer         :: i
    integer         :: trial
    real            :: deltt  = 0.1

    do trial = 1,2
        ! Select what type of point ...
        if ( trial == 1 ) then
            point  => point_2d
            vector => vector_2d

            write(*,*) 'Two-dimensional walk:'
        else
            point  => point_3d
            vector => vector_3d

            write(*,*) 'Three-dimensional walk:'
        endif

        call point%random_vector

        do i = 1,nsteps
            call vector%random_vector

            point = point + deltt * vector

            call point%print
        enddo
    enddo
end program random_walk
```

Because the variable point is declared to be of class(point2d), it can point to any variable of type either point2d or an extension, like point3d.

The second iteration of the outer loop can use a 3D point. This would, in general, be much harder to achieve with Fortran 90/95. One way, however, is to let a general point type consist of both a point2d pointer component and a point3d pointer component:

```
type :: point_t
    type(point2d), pointer :: p2d => null()
    type(point3d), pointer :: p3d => null()
end type point_t
```

Though in this simple case, it would not be entirely impossible, the code for the routine `random_vector` and others needs to distinguish between the two types. Therefore, only one of the two pointer components is associated and this is used to select the relevant code.

With the runtime polymorphism that Fortran 2003 offers, this selection mechanism is completely transparent. It is the dynamic type of the variable `point` that determines it.

Determining the Dynamic Type As previously discussed, sometimes you need to know the dynamic type of a polymorphic variable to use it in the correct way. For this, Fortran 2003 offers the `select type` construction as well as two intrinsic functions to inquire about (dynamic) types, `same_type_as()` and `extends_type_of()`.

Particle Tracking To further illustrate object-oriented programming in Fortran, extend the 2D point example in a different way. The points will become particles in a hydrodynamic flow field, or an electromagnetic force field, if you prefer that. You need a way to let the particles go with the flow field, but if they represent oil droplets or grains of silt or sand, they will be influenced by gravitational forces in addition to the flow field. The flow field itself may be schematized by a set of analytical functions, an approximation on a rectangular grid or a finite-element mesh. The variety in particle behavior, or the way the flow field is handled, is encapsulated in the precise type of particles and in the type of flow field, but the basic types are:

```
module particle_modelling
    use points2d3d

    implicit none

    type, extends(point2d) :: basic_particle_type
        real :: mass
    contains
        procedure :: force => force_basic_particle
        procedure, pass(particle) &
                :: new_position => position_basic_particle
    end type basic_particle_type

    type :: basic_flow_field_type
    contains
        procedure :: flow_velocity => velocity_basic_flow_field
    end type basic_flow_field_type

contains
```

```
subroutine position_basic_particle( &
          particle, flow_field, deltt )

    class(basic_particle_type),   intent(inout) :: particle
    class(basic_flow_field_type), intent(in)    :: flow_field
    real, intent(in)                            :: deltt

    ! Empty routine
end subroutine position_basic_particle

subroutine force_basic_particle( particle, force_vector )

    class(basic_particle_type), intent(inout) :: particle
    class(point2d), intent(out)               :: force_vector

    ! Empty routine
end subroutine force_basic_particle

subroutine velocity_basic_flow_field( &
          flow_field, position, velocity )

    class(basic_flow_field_type), intent(in) :: flow_field
    class(point2d), intent(in)               :: position
    class(point2d), intent(out)              :: velocity

    ! Empty routine
end subroutine velocity_basic_flow_field
end module particle_modelling
```

In this example, using empty routines emphasizes that you need to fill in the details before you can actually use them. The next section describes a method to formalize this via so-called *abstract interfaces*.

Simulating the behavior over time of a set of particles that are supposed to model oil, now becomes a matter of updating the position in response to the flow field, and to the processes that act on the oil, such as sticking to the bottom:[3]

```
subroutine position_oil_particle( particle, flow_field, deltt )
    class(oil_particle), target :: particle
    real                        :: deltt
    class(basic_flow_field_type) :: flow_field

    class(point2d), pointer      :: position
```

---

[3] This is a rather naive implementation, as it assumes that the flow field does not change over time and that the flow velocity does not change appreciably over the distance a particle travels within one time step.

```
    class(point2d)                :: flow_velocity
    class(point2d)                :: random_displacement

    real                          :: r

    !
    ! The particle may get stuck to the bottom ...
    !
    call random_number( r )
    if ( r > 0.99 ) then
        particle%stuck = .true.
    endif
    !
    ! If it is stuck to the bottom, no further motion
    !
    if ( particle%stuck ) then
        return
    endif


    !
    ! Else let it be transported with the flow. Add a
    ! random displacement due to mixing and turbulence
    !
    position => particle%point2d

    call flow_field%flow_velocity( position, velocity )
    call random_displacement%random_vector

    position = position + deltt * velocity + &
               random_displacement

end subroutine position_oil_particle
```

The simulation itself then computes the tracks of a large number of oil particles over time:

```
type(oil_particle), dimension(100000) :: particle
type(analytical_field)                 :: flow_field
real                                   :: deltt

... initialize the flow field and the particle positions ...

do time = 1,number_times
    do p = 1,size(particle)
        call particle(p)%new_position( flow_field, deltt )
    enddo
enddo
```

The preceding takes a "particle-centric" point of view where the particles are the most important agent, hence the call:

```
call particle(p)%new_position( flow_field, deltt )
```

You may want to change that viewpoint to a "flow-field-centric" one:

```
type(analytical_field)                :: flow_field
type(oil_particle), dimension(100000) :: particle
real                                  :: deltt

do time = 1,number_times
    ... compute the flow field for this time ...

    !
    ! Update the particle positions using the new flow field
    !
    do p = 1,size(particle)
        call flow_field%new_position( particle(p), deltt )
    enddo
enddo
```

This "inversion" is achieved, not by changing the interface of the actual routine, but via the pass() keyword. The definition of the flow field type becomes:

```
type :: basic_flow_field_type
contains
    procedure :: flow_velocity => velocity_basic_flow_field
    procedure, pass(flow_field) :: &
        new_position => position_basic_particle
end type basic_flow_field_type
```

11.2 Interfaces As Contracts

Fortran 2003 does not allow multiple inheritance (in contrast to C++), which is sometimes useful to combine properties. It does not allow you to specify Java-style **interfaces** either, assuring that certain routines with a predefined interface are available. Instead, you can emulate these features by extending types from a basic type.

The idea is to use **abstract types** and **abstract interfaces**. This is a mechanism to specify what is expected of a derived type, in particular what routines are available with what interface without actually defining them. You use the deferred keyword and the abstract interface keyword:

```
type, abstract :: abstract_point
    ! No coordinates, leave that to the extending types
contains
    procedure(add_vector), deferred :: add
end type abstract_point
```

```
!
! Define what the named interface "add_vector" should
! look like
!
abstract interface
    subroutine add_vector( point, vector )
        import abstract_point
        class(abstract_point), intent(inout) :: point
        class(abstract_point), intent(in)    :: vector
    end subroutine add_vector
end interface
```

You cannot declare ordinary variables to be of type(abstract_point) because it is an abstract type. To use it you need to define some type that extends it (note that the procedure add is not given an interface name):

```
type, extends(abstract_point) :: point2d
    real :: x, y
contains
    procedure :: add => add_vector_2d
end type point2d

type(point2d) :: point
```

You can declare a pointer (or allocatable) variable to be of class(abstract_point), but at some point it should be associated with a "concrete" type, such as point2d:

```
class(abstract_point), pointer :: p
type(point2d), target          :: point
type(point2d)                  :: vector

p => point
call p%add_vector( vector )
```

Any type that extends abstract_point must define the add procedure with the correct interface. This guarantees that you can write generic code like the random walk program presented in the previous section. In other words, the abstract type defines a contract [64]. If you want to use facilities that rely on this abstract type, you will have to satisfy this contract. However, then you have access to a generic interface of these facilities.

Another example is a module to sort an array of items. In Fortran 90/95, you need to implement a specific version for each type you want to use, even though this can be done with a minimum of repeated code (replace <module> and <type> by the appropriate actual names):

```
module <module>_sorting

    use <module>, data_type => <type>

    !
    ! Include the generic code
    !
    include "sort_f90_include.f90"

end module <module>_sorting

module <module>_public
    use <module>_sorting, <type> => data_type
end module <module>_public
```

This implementation relies on renaming a derived type and on user-defined operations.

The file "sort_f90_include.f90" is completely oblivious of the particular type to be sorted. The interface statement ensures you can have several sorting routines without a naming conflict, and the sort routine relies on a user-defined comparison operation.

```
private :: sort
interface sort_data
    module procedure sort
end interface

contains

subroutine sort( data )
    implicit none

    type(data_type), dimension(:) :: data

    type(data_type)                :: tmp
    integer                        :: i, j

    do i = 1,size(data)
        do j = i+1,size(data)
            if ( data(j) < data(i) ) then
                tmp     = data(i)
                data(i) = data(j)
                data(j) = tmp
            endif
        enddo
    enddo
end subroutine sort
```

Two modules are required to rename the specific derived type (for instance, address) to the generic name data_type then back to the specific name again.

The one requirement to the derived type is that it provides a comparison operation to determine if one value of that type is smaller than another. For example:

```fortran
module address_module
    type address
        character(len=40) :: name
        character(len=40) :: street
    end type address

    interface operator(<)
        module procedure lower_address
    end interface
contains
logical function lower_address( x, y )
    type(address), intent(in) :: x, y

    if ( x%name /= y%name ) then
        lower_address = x%name < y%name
    else
        lower_address = x%street < y%street
    endif
end function lower_address

end module address_module
```

In Fortran 2003, you make these requirements part of the definition of an abstract type:

```fortran
module sortable_types

    type, abstract :: sortable
        ! No particular data
    contains
        procedure(islower), deferred :: islower
        procedure(assignx), deferred :: assign_data
        generic :: operator(<)      => islower
        generic :: assignment(=)    => assign_data
    end type
    abstract interface
        logical function islower( item1, item2 )
            import sortable
            class(sortable), intent(in) :: item1, item2
        end function islower
    end interface
```

```
    abstract interface
        subroutine assignx( item1, item2 )
            import sortable
            class(sortable), intent(inout) :: item1
            class(sortable), intent(in)    :: item2
        end subroutine assignx
    end interface

contains

subroutine sort( array )
    class(sortable), dimension(:), &
        intent(inout), target    :: array

    class(sortable), allocatable :: tmp
    class(sortable), pointer     :: first_element

    integer                      :: i, j

    !
    ! Allocate the temporary variable such that it has the
    ! proper dynamic type
    !
    allocate( tmp, source = array(1) )

    do i = 1,size(array)
        do j = i+1,size(array)
            if ( array(j) < array(i) ) then
                tmp      = array(i)
                array(i) = array(j)
                array(j) = tmp
            endif
        enddo
    enddo
end subroutine sort

end module sortable_types
```

The only requirement to the types you pass is they extend from the sortable abstract type.

Approximating Multiple Inheritance   The fact that you cannot use multiple inheritance may be considered a hindrance. Suppose you require both sorting and printing for a derived type. Do you need to define an abstract type that combines all the required features and then extend that type? Not necessarily, because you can do it in steps:

```
module printable_sortable_types
    use sortable_types

    implicit none

    type, abstract, extends(sortable) :: printable_sortable
        ! No particular data
    contains
        procedure(print_item), deferred :: print
    end type printable_sortable

    abstract interface
        subroutine print_item( item )
            import printable_sortable
            class(printable_sortable), intent(in) :: item
        end subroutine print_item
    end interface

contains


    ...


end module printable_sortable_types
```

In this way, the properties of the **sortable** type are propagated to a **printable** type. The result is a derived type that combines the properties of both.

11.3 Using a Prototype Approach

So far this chapter emphasized the class-based style of object-oriented programming, meaning objects get their behavior from a centrally defined "class" (the derived type and its type-bound procedures). An alternative approach is that some behavior is made specific for the object. For instance, you have a set of polygons and one of the procedures that are bound to the corresponding polygon type is to determine the surface area. You could decide to specialize that procedure if the polygons happen to be a square or a rectangle:

```
module polygons

    implicit none

    type polygon_type
        real, dimension(:), allocatable   :: x, y
        procedure(compute_value), &
            pointer :: area => area_polygon
    contains
        procedure :: draw => draw_polygon
    end type polygon_type
```

```fortran
      abstract interface
         real function compute_value(polygon)
             import :: polygon_type
             class(polygon_type) :: polygon
         end function compute_value
      end interface

contains

subroutine draw_polygon( polygon )
    class(polygon_type) :: polygon
    ... general drawing method ...
end subroutine draw_polygon

real function area_polygon( polygon )
    type(polygon_type) :: polygon
    ... general method to determine the area ...
end function area_polygon


!
! Alternative for rectangles: simpler method
!
real function area_rectangle( polygon )
    type(polygon_type) :: polygon

    associate( x => polygon%x, y => polygon%y )
        area_rectangle = abs( (x(2)-x(1)) * (y(3) - y(2)) )
    end associate
end function area_rectangle

subroutine new_polygon( polygon, x, y )
    real, dimension(:)                :: x, y
    type(polygon_type), allocatable :: polygon

    allocate( polygon%x(size(x)), polygon%y(size(x)))
    polygon%x = x
    polygon%y = y
end subroutine new_polygon

!
! Alternative method to construct a rectangle
! Override the default method for computing the area!
!
subroutine new_rectangle( rectangle, x1, y1, width, height )
    real                              :: x1, y1, width, height
    type(polygon_type), allocatable :: rectangle
```

```
allocate( rectangle%x(4), rectangle%y(4) )
rectangle%x = (/ x1, x1+width, x1+width, x1 /)
rectangle%y = (/ y1, y1, y1+height, y1+height /)

rectangle%area => area_rectangle

end subroutine new_rectangle

end module polygons
```

Therefore, drawing the polygons makes use of the general drawing procedure while for squares and rectangles the computation of the area is done by the alternative routine pointed to by the *procedure pointer*. A very nice aspect of procedure pointers in Fortran is that they are indistinguishable – to the using code – from type-bound procedures. You can use procedure pointers instead of type-bound procedures, with the same **pass()** property. Only the position of the declaration is different (they come before the **contains** keyword) and the fact that they can be changed dynamically per object.

Therefore, objects can obtain a different behavior but still belong to the same "class". For instance, in ecological modelling systems where the behavior of individuals depends on their age or even the time of year, this flexibility can be gratefully deployed (see the following).

A concise example is shown in Chapter 5. Instead of separate classes for all functions to integrate, you can define a single class that takes a pointer to the specific function, as long as these functions share the set of parameters defined in this class.

There are more alternatives conceivable, such as *delegation*. The object in question can delegate the actual work to a component or to a specific routine if one is defined on a per-object basis:

```
module flow_fields

    use grids

    implicit none

    type flow_field_type
        class(geometry_type) :: grid
    contains
        procedure :: cell_index => get_cell_index
    end type flow_field_type

contains

function get_cell_index( this, x, y )
    type(flow_field_type)           :: this
```

```
    real                        :: x, y
    class(cell_data), allocatable :: get_cell_index

    call this%grid%cell_index( x, y, get_cell_index )
end function get_cell_index
```

Therefore, rather than extend the grid type to form a new flow field type based on the chosen type of grid, use the grid as a component in the `flow_field` type and use the facilities, such as the `geometry_type` type, to implement the geometrical functions that are required.

If an object has both generic and specific implementations of certain functions or tasks, for instance, you may want to track one particular particle in the computation, this can be solved elegantly via:

```
subroutine new_position( particle, flow_field )
    type(particle_type)    :: particle
    type(flow_field_type) :: flow_field

    if ( associated( particle%special_new_position ) ) then
        call particle%special_new_position(flow_field)
    else
        ! General code
    endif
end subroutine new_position
```

You can also move the condition to the initialization of the computation:

```
!
! Initialize the particles
!
do i = 1,number_particles
    if ( ... special particle ... ) then
        particle%new_position => special_new_position
    else
        particle%new_position => general_new_position
    endif
enddo
```

The caller does not need to take the special property into account because it is handled automatically. However, if desired, the caller can use their own version of the special routine to determine the new position:

```
call particle(idx)%set_position_handler( my_new_position )
```

Example: Modeling Fish Behavior   As a strongly simplified (and ecologically unrealistic) example, consider the fate of a number of salmon-like fish. As larvae they have no individual motion and are just transported along with the flow. As adults, however, they need to swim to their food and, later on to their mating grounds. The various stages of their life can be modeled using different routines:

```fortran
module fishes

    use flow_fields
    use food_situations

    type fish_type
        real              :: x, y
        real              :: age
        procedure, pointer :: behave
    end type fish_type
                        ! Grown up at age 1/2
    real, parameter :: age_reach_adulthood = 0.5

                        ! Mating start at age 5
    real, parameter :: age_reach_mating    = 5.0

contains

subroutine behave_juvenile( &
            this, deltt, flow_field, food_situation )
    type(fish_type)          :: this
    real                     :: deltt
    type(flow_field_type)     :: flow_field
    type(food_situation_type) :: food_situation

    !
    ! No motion of their own
    !
    call this%update_position( deltt, flow_field )

    !
    ! Update age
    !
    this%age = this%age + deltt

    if ( this%age >= age_reach_adulthood ) then
        this%behave => behave_adult
    endif
end subroutine behave_juvenile
```

```
subroutine behave_adult( &
             this, deltt, flow_field, food_situation )
    type(fish_type)            :: this
    real                       :: deltt
    type(flow_field_type)      :: flow_field
    type(food_situation_type)  :: food_situation

    !
    ! New position: where is the food?
    !
    call this%update_position( deltt, flow_field )

    call this%swim_to_food( deltt, food_situation )

    !
    ! Update age - time to mate?
    !
    this%age = this%age + deltt

    if ( this%age >= age_reach_mating ) then
        this%behave => behave_migrate
    endif
end subroutine behave_adult

... Similar for behave_migrate

end module fishes
```

In the main program, you need not to worry about the changes in the behavior of the fish. This is all taken care of inside the module:

```
program test_fishes
    use fishes
    implicit none

    integer, parameter                    :: number = 1000
    type(fish_type), dimension(number) :: fish
    type(flow_field_type)                 :: flow
    type(food_situation_type)             :: food

    real                                  :: deltt
    integer                               :: i, time

    !
    ! Initialize the information on fish, flow and food:
    ! fish in a square of 100x100 km
    !
    call random_number( fish%x )
```

```
   call random_number( fish%y )

   fish%x   =  100000.0 * fish%x
   fish%y   =  100000.0 * fish%y
   fish%age =  0.0

   deltt    =  0.1

   do time = 1,100
       do i = 1,size(fish)
           call fish(i)%behave( deltt, flow, food )
       enddo
   enddo
end program test_fishes
```

11.4 Abstract Data Types and Generic Programming

With the introduction of pointers in Fortran 90, it became straightforward to
develop code for manipulating other data structures than arrays. In fact, any
recursively defined *abstract data type*, such as linked lists and binary trees, can
be implemented directly in Fortran 90:[4]

```
type linked_list
    integer :: value
    type(linked_list), pointer :: next
end type linked_list
```

The essential feature is that it allows use of a pointer to a component of a
type that is not (fully) defined yet. The definition should appear in the same
compilation unit.

The main problem to confront is the type of the data to be stored. Fortran 90
does not easily allow different data types to be stored in one linked list or tree.
That means for a list that should contain both arrays of reals and strings, you
need a construction like:

```
type linked_list
    real, dimension(:), pointer :: array
    character(len=80)           :: string ! Not used if array
                                          ! is associated
    type(linked_list), pointer  :: next
end type linked_list
```

This is much like the solution discussed in Section 11.1 for dealing with points
in two- and three-dimensional space.

---

[4] In Fortran 77, the basic data structure is the array. While it is quite possible to use that as a basis for
linked lists, an implementation would be much less flexible than in Fortran 90 or later.

A completely different approach is to transform the data into the type you do store and to keep track of the original type separately:

```
type linked_list
    integer, dimension(:), pointer :: array
    integer :: type_indicator          ! 1 - real array,
                                       ! 2 - character string
    type(linked_list), pointer  :: next
end type linked_list
```

Here is the code with associated routines:

```
subroutine store_real_array( element, array )
    type(linked_list)   :: element
    real, dimension(:)  :: array

    element%type_indicator = 1
    call store_integer_array( &
            element, transfer(array,element%array) )
end subroutine store_real_array

subroutine store_character_string( element, string )
    type(linked_list)   :: element
    character(len=*)    :: string

    element%type_indicator = 2
    call store_integer_array( &
            element, transfer(string,element%array) )
end subroutine store_character_string

! Private routine - here we know the exact size
subroutine store_integer_array( element, data )
    type(linked_list)    :: element
    integer, dimension(:) :: data

    allocate( element%array(size(data) )
    element%array = data
end subroutine store_integer_array
```

```
... Similar routines to retrieve the data in the original form
```

(You use the transfer() function to transform the data from one type into another; in this case, an integer array.)

The code for an abstract data type is easily reused to store the data of any type, if the type is a derived type:

```
module linked_list_points2d
    use points2d, stored_type => point2d
```

```
    private
    public :: linked_list, add, ....

    type linked_list
        type(stored_type)            :: data
        type(linked_list), pointer :: next
    end type linked_list

    !
    ! Define generic names for the functionality
    ! - makes using different types of lists easier
    !
    interface add
        module procedure :: add_element
    end interface

    ... Other interfaces

contains

    ... Subroutines and functions needed

end module linked_list_points2d
```

As there is only a small part that is specific to the data type, you can put the *generic* part of the code in a file that is be included for specific implementations:

```
module linked_list_points2d
    use points2d, stored_type => point2d
    include 'generic_lists.f90'
end module linked_list_points2d

module linked_list_grids
    use grids, stored_type => grid
    include 'generic_lists.f90'
end module linked_list_grids

module linked_lists
    use linked_list_points2d, &
            linked_list_of_2dpoints => linked_list
    use linked_list_grids, &
            linked_list_of_grids   => linked_list
end module linked_lists
```

Both types of lists can be used in the same program without naming conflicts because of the generic names. The original routines live in different modules and are made private. The *using* program only sees the generic names. Via the renaming facility of the use statement, the general name `linked_list` for the derived type is made more specific.

Using polymorphic variables (declared as `class(some_type)`), you can, of course, store data of any type as long as their type extends from the basic type:

```
type linked_list
    class(basic_type), allocatable :: data
    type(linked_list), pointer     :: next
end type linked_list
```

This last restriction is lifted if you use so-called *unlimited polymorphic* variables, declared as `class(*)`. These can be associated with *any* data, at the cost of requiring some extra code to make them useful:

```
real, target :: x = 3.1415926
class(*)      :: pi

pi => x

select type
    type is real
        write(*,*) 'x = ', pi
end select
```

The additional flexibility of polymorpic variables, limited or unlimited, comes at a cost. If you want to guarantee that all data are of the same type, you need to take extra measures:

```
subroutine add_element( element, data )
    type(linked_list) :: element
    class(*)          :: data

    if ( same_type_as( element%data, data ) ) then
        ... add the new element
    else
        write(*,*) 'Wrong type of data!'
    endif
end subroutine add_element
```

11.5 Changing the Behavior of a Type

When you use a module, you can rename the names of variables, data types, and routines to avoid name conflicts. This feature actually allows you to "mix in" functionality without changing the original implementation. In the realm of dynamic languages, such as Python or Tcl, this process is known as adding mixins or filters [67]. There the process is quite transparent, due to the dynamic nature of the languages. Variables do not have a fixed data type, even the implementation of a routine can be changed at runtime. In Fortran, you need to do a bit more work.

Suppose you want to keep track of the state of objects of a particular type, a common enough example is logging the activities of a program via its objects. Then, do the following:

■ Use the module containing the type's definition and rename that type:

```
module new_points2d
    use points2d, point2d_original => point2d, &
                  add_vector_2d_original => add_vector_2d
    ...
end module new_points2d
```

■ Define a *new* type point2d that extends the original one:

```
type, extends(point2d_original) :: point2d
    ...
contains
    procedure :: add_vector => add_vector_2d
end type point2d
```

■ The hard work is to extend all the type-bound procedures that you want to track:

```
subroutine add_vector_2d( point, vector )
    class(point2d)          :: point
    class(point2d_original) :: vector

    write(*,*) 'Calling "add_vector"'

    call point%point2d_original%add_vector( vector )
end subroutine add_vector
```

■ Finally, use the new module instead of the old one. This can be done transparently as modules pass on the functionality they define themselves as well as the functionality they import from others. The only thing to watch out for is that the name of a module is global to the program:

```
module point2d_functionality
    !
    ! This module merely passes on the functionality we
    ! import from the various underlying modules. This
    ! allows us to change the actual modules in one
    ! place only
    !
    ! We have extended the point2d type - so use the
    ! new module
    !
```

```
    ! use points2d
     use new_points2d
  end module point2d_functionality
```

The change in the type's implementation is completely hidden from the using program. You only need to rebuild it, all the other source code remaining the same.

11.6 Design Patterns

While design patterns have been described mostly in the context of programming languages such as C++ and Java, the principles involved are quite universal [35], [28]. Design patterns try to capture the essence of common solutions to a wide range of software problems. Rouson, Xia and Xu [34] compare implementations in Fortran 2003 and C++ of a number of design patterns. Some are quite well-known, others are domain-specific, therefore, they are particularly useful in, for example, physical simulations.

The following considers two examples only, the *Factory* pattern and the *Observer* pattern, to illustrate how design patterns can be applied in a Fortran program [see also [54] and [73]) for some other examples].

The Factory Pattern

One popular design pattern in object-oriented programming is the so-called *factory pattern*. The idea behind this pattern is that a program may need one or more objects of a certain type, but it should not take the responsibility of properly initializing or managing such objects, if it takes more than merely creating it, [9]. Proper initialization or management include tasks like:

- Allocating memory for its components.
- Setting initial values.
- Opening a file and reading its contents if that is part of how the object works.
- The object may be part of a *pool* of objects and then managing the associated resources should be done consistently.

Another use of the factory pattern is to allow the using program to handle a generic object rather than an object of a specific type. Here is an example: The program requests an object that generates a pseudo-random number, either with a uniform or an exponential distribution. The creation function returns a polymorphic object that behaves as either type. It is completely transparent to the program, so extending the set of pseudo-random number generators with generators to support new distributions has no effect on its source code, except perhaps that a new type becomes available:

```
program test_prng_factory
    use prng_factory

    class(prng), pointer :: p
    integer              :: i

    p => prng_create( type_uniform, 1.0, 2.0 )

    do i = 1,10
        write(*,*) p%get()
    enddo

    p => prng_create( type_exponential, 10.0 )

    do i = 1,10
        write(*,*) p%get()
    enddo

end program test_prng_factory
```

The module achieves this effect via a straightforward construction:

```
function prng_create( type, param1, param2 )
    integer                    :: type
    real                       :: param1
    real, optional             :: param2

    class(prng), pointer                  :: prng_create
    type(prng_uniform), pointer           :: uniform
    type(prng_exponential), pointer :: exponential

    select case (type)
        case (type_uniform)
            allocate( uniform )
            prng_create => uniform

            if ( present(param2) ) then
                prng_create%xmin = param1
                prng_create%xmax = param2
            else
                prng_create%xmin = 0.0
                prng_create%xmax = param1
            endif

        case (type_exponential)
            allocate( exponential )
            prng_create => exponential
            prng_create%xmean = param1
```

```
      case default
          nullify( prng_create )
   end select
end function prng_create
```

As long as the interface of the extended types, prng_uniform and prng_exponential, does not add new methods, you can use the full functionality via the base type and never know how it is implemented. (It might not even be a set of extended types, but instead one where a single routine takes care of each type of distribution.)

This method can be used as a basis for a *plugin* architecture, illustrated here using an auxiliary module that hides the (platform-dependent) details of loading a dynamic library (a shared library or a DLL):

```
! Private routine - initialize the factory
!
subroutine initialize_factory

    character(len=20), dimension(2) :: prng_name
    character(len=20), dimension(2) :: libname
    type(dynamic_library)           :: dynlib
    logical                         :: success

    integer                         :: i

    prng_name = &
        (/ 'uniform             ', 'exponential          ' /)
    libname   = &
        (/ 'prng_uniform.dll    ', 'prng_exponential.dll' /)

    do i = 1,size(libname)
        call load_library( dynlib, libname(i), success )
        if ( success ) then
            call get_procedure( dynlib, 'create_prng', &
                    prng_creators(i)%create, success )
            if ( .not. success ) then
                write(*,*) 'Could not load create_prng - ', &
                    libname(i)
            endif
            prng_creators(i)%name = prng_name(i)
        endif
    enddo

end subroutine initialize_factory

! Return an object of the right dynamic type
!
```

```fortran
function prng_create( type, param1, param2 )

    character(len=*)      :: type
    real                  :: param1
    real, optional        :: param2

    class(prng), pointer  :: prng_create
    real                  :: param2opt
    integer               :: i

    if ( .not. initialized ) then
        initialized = .true.
        call initialize_factory
    endif

    param2opt = 0.0
    if ( present(param2) ) then
        param2opt = param2
    endif

    prng_create => null()

    do i = 1,size(prng_creators)
        if ( prng_creators(i)%name == type ) then
            call prng_creators(i)%create( prng_create, &
                    param1, param2opt )
            exit
        endif
    enddo
end function prng_create
```

In this case, the public creation routine first checks if the dynamic libraries have been loaded already and that the pointer to the actual creation routine is available. If not, it loads the libraries. For simplicity, this example uses fixed names for the dynamic libraries, but it is straightforward to read them from some configuration file.

This setup has the very attractive property that you can expand the functionality of the program (for instance, introduce new probability distributions) without changing the code and even without rebuilding it.

The Observer Pattern

A design pattern that is very interesting from the point of view of numerical computation is the *Observer pattern*. This pattern allows you to extend the functionality of a program without having to designhow to extend it. Instead of prescribing where in the computation the user should insert a subroutine call to check the properties of a solution, your program offers a facility to register routines or data objects with type-bound procedures that are invoked whenever a particular event occurs.

For example, when computing the flow of water in a network of pipes an interesting event could be the completion of a single step in the integration over time. Here are some fragments of code that accomplish this:

In the module containing the definitions of the solver, you have the following types, one to serve as a "parent" class for the actual observer objects and the other to hold all the interesting data on the solution:

```
type, abstract :: observer
contains
    procedure(check_result), deferred, pass(obs) :: check
end type observer

type :: observer_list
contains
    class(observer), pointer :: observer
end type observer_list

type solution_data
    type(observer_list), dimension(:), allocatable :: list
    ... ! Fields defining the solution
end type solution_data
```

The type observer_list is introduced because you cannot use *default assignment* to a class variable. The alternative is to require a user-defined assignment routine. Therefore, instead of the observer objects themselves you store a pointer to these objects. Fortran does not have arrays of pointers, but you can use a workaround: an array of a derived type which contains a pointer component.

You can define an abstract interface to the checking routine and an abstract type that serves as a "parent" class for the actual observer objects:

```
abstract interface
    logical function check_result( obs, result_data )
        import :: observer, solution_data
        class(observer)     :: obs
        type(solution_data) :: result_data ! Type, not class
    end function check_result
end interface
```

Descendents of the class observer must define a procedure check with the interface check_result. What is done in this procedure is completely up to the particular implementation.

The solver module contains at least procedures like the following to allow the registration of the specific observer objects and the evaluation of the solution by these procedures:

```fortran
subroutine add_observer( solution, obs )
    type(solution_data)     :: solution
    class(observer), target :: obs

    solution%list = (/ solution%list, observer_list(obs) /)
end subroutine add_observer

subroutine solve( solution, ... )
    type(solution_data) :: solution

    ... ! Preliminaries

    do while ( time < time_end + 0.5*time_step )
        call solution%solve_one_step( ... )

        !
        ! This is the moment in the computation to
        ! see if the solution still obeys our
        ! requirements
        !
        acceptable = .true.
        do i = 1,size(solution%list)
            acceptable = acceptable .and. &
                solution%list(i)%observer%check( solution )
        enddo
        if ( .not. acceptable ) exit

        time = time + time_step

    enddo
    ...
end subroutine solve
```

Via the subroutine add_observer, register *observer* objects that can check the solution according to some specific criteria. The *solution* object (or the associated procedures) contains no details whatsoever of these checks, except that the *observer* object must be of a particular lineage. Therefore, its type must be an extension of observer. (Note the use of the automatic reallocation feature in the subroutine add_observer. This makes extending arrays really easy.)

In the example, you have only one interesting type of event: the completion of a single time step. However, you can easily extend this to any number of event types, each associated with its own type-bound procedure.

The purpose of the *Observer* pattern is to ensure a loose coupling between two parts of a program that need to interact. Ideally, there should be no or very little feedback from the observing data object to the calling solution object (or its `solve` procedure), limiting it to setting a flag.

12.

Parallel Programming

The ubiquity of computers with multiple processors and computers cooperating in some network has made parallel computing a mainstream subject. Up to the Fortran 2008 standard, Fortran did not offer any language constructs for such a programming style. The two approaches that are most popular at the moment are message passing interface [83] (MPI) and open multiprocessing [14] (OpenMP). These two approaches actually complement each other: MPI deals with different processes running on, possibly, different computers that communicate with one another explicitly and OpenMP is a method to run parts of a program in parallel (multiple threads), so there is only a single process running.

Fortran 2008 introduces **coarrays** and supporting statements and intrinsic routines to enable a Fortran program to run multiple copies (called *images*) that interact. Sharing the data between these images is done transparently. It is the task of the compiler to insert the required data communication, not the programmer's.

This chapter discusses these three forms and uses two examples: a program to find the first N prime numbers and a program that numerically solves a partial differential equation using several *domains*. Neither program is meant to be very practical, they merely illustrate the techniques involved.

12.1 Prime Numbers

Here is a straightforward program to determine the first 1000 prime numbers:

```fortran
program primes_plain

    implicit none

    integer, dimension(1000) :: prime
    integer                  :: number_primes
    integer                  :: candidate
    integer                  :: residue
    integer                  :: j
    logical                  :: isprime

    number_primes = 0
    candidate     = 2
```

```
    do while ( number_primes < size(prime) )
        isprime = .true.
        do j = 2,int(sqrt(real(candidate)))
            residue = mod(candidate,j)
            if ( residue == 0 ) then
                isprime = .false.
                exit
            endif
        enddo
        if ( isprime ) then
            number_primes = number_primes + 1
            prime(number_primes) = candidate
        endif

        candidate = candidate + 1
    enddo

    write(*,'(10i5)' ) prime

end program primes_plain
```

As it stands, it is difficult to parallellize: the do while loop represents a formidable obstacle. You cannot split it up in portions as you do not know how many iterations are needed. This depends on the work that is actually done inside the do loop. Moreover, the various iterations depend on each other via the index number_primes into the array of primes found so far.

Using OpenMP, you may split up the inner loop:

```
!$omp parallel do private(residue)
do j = 2,int(sqrt(real(candidate)))
    residue = mod(candidate,j)
    if ( residue == 0 ) then
        isprime = .false.
    endif
enddo
!$omp end parallel do
```

The directive !$omp parallel do instructs the compiler to create a parallel region and to distribute the individual iterations of the inner do loop over the threads that exist within this region. However, you need to be careful with the characteristics of the variables. By default variables are **shared** among the threads so that setting them in one thread may unexpectedly change the results of another thread.

This is the reason for the private(residue) clause: One thread may have found a divisor of the candidate prime number, whereas another thread has also finished the computation and found a non-zero residue. By the time the if-statement is run, the variable `residue` is overwritten, if it was not a private variable.

You do not need to be careful about variable `isprime`. If it is set, then all threads would set it to the same value.

Note also that you cannot leave the loop, because this is a consequence of the way OpenMP works. There is an implicit synchronization at the end of the parallel region and all threads must reach this.

Parallellizing do loops with fixed ranges is a typical use of OpenMP, but, in this case, it will not gain you any performance: starting up the threads and stopping them again present a considerable overhead. The amount of work to be done in each iteration must be large enough to justify this overhead.

By restructuring the program, you take a chunk of integers and examine each in turn. Now the program deals with well-defined and, importantly, independent tasks[1]:

```
program primes_chunks

    implicit none

    integer, dimension(2)    :: range
    integer                  :: number_tasks, number_primes
    integer, dimension(1000) :: prime
    logical                  :: new_results, new_task
    logical                  :: ready

    ready         = .false.
    new_results   = .false.
    new_task      = .false.
    number_tasks  = 0
    number_primes = 0

    range(2)      = 0

    !
    ! Determine the primes: iterate over small ranges of
    ! integers and gather the results.
    !
    do while ( .not. ready )
        range(1) = range(2) + 1
        range(2) = range(2) + 100

        call find_primes
    enddo
```

---

[1] Sanders and others describe this type of parallellization as the *task parallel pattern* [78].

```
      write(*,'(10i5)') prime

contains

   ... Implementation of the subroutine find_primes not shown
   ... Sets "ready" when enough primes have been found

end program primes_chunks
```

OpenMP

When using OpenMP it is important to realize that the sections of code that you want to be run in parallel are run by *all* the threads. Only by additional instructions (compiler directives like !$omp do or if-statements involving the thread number), do you actually divide the work over the various threads.

In this example, you divide the entire domain of candidate prime numbers into intervals of 100 integers and these are each handled by one single thread. Therefore, the main problems to solve are how to hand out these pieces to a thread and how to store the results once they are available.

To make sure that the threads can handle a given interval, you have to put the information in shared variables, so that any thread can pick it up. You need to do something similar for the results. Only one thread at a time is allowed to pick up a task or store the results, so you need to properly protect these variables. You do that via the **critical sections** in the adapted program:

```
program primes_openmp
    use omp_lib

    implicit none

    integer, dimension(2)    :: range
    integer                  :: number_tasks, number_primes
    integer, dimension(1000) :: prime
    logical                  :: new_results, new_task
    logical                  :: ready

    ready        = .false.
    new_results  = .false.
    new_task     = .false.
    number_tasks  = 0
    number_primes = 0

    range(2)     = 0

!$omp parallel
    !
    ! Create tasks
```

```fortran
        !
        do while ( .not. ready )
            if ( omp_get_thread_num() == 0 ) then
                call add_task
            endif

            call get_task
        enddo
!$omp end parallel

    write(*,'(10i5)') prime

contains

    !
    ! Subroutine to post a new task (consisting of a
    ! range of integers in which to look for primes)
    !
    ! Note: make sure there is only one thread at
    ! a time that changes "new_task"
    !
    subroutine add_task

    !$omp critical
        if ( .not. new_task ) then
            range(1) = range(2) + 1
            range(2) = range(2) + 100
            new_task = .true.
        endif
    !$omp end critical

    end subroutine add_task

    !
    ! Subroutine to get a task and search for
    ! primes inside the new range
    !
    subroutine get_task

        integer, dimension(100) :: new_prime
        integer                 :: lower, upper
        logical                 :: isprime, got_task
        integer                 :: np, i, j
        integer                 :: residue, maxindex

        got_task = .false.
        np       = 0
```

```
!$omp critical
    if ( new_task ) then
        lower = range(1)
        upper = range(2)
        new_task = .false.
        got_task = .true.
    endif
!$omp end critical

    if ( got_task ) then
        do i = lower,upper
            isprime = .true.
            do j = 2,int(sqrt(real(i)))
                residue = mod(i,j)
                if ( residue == 0 ) then
                    isprime = .false.
                    exit
                endif
            enddo
            if ( isprime ) then
                np = np + 1
                new_prime(np) = i
            endif
        enddo
    endif

!$omp critical
    if ( got_task ) then
        maxindex = min( size(prime) - number_primes, np )
        prime(number_primes+1:number_primes+maxindex) = &
            new_prime(1:maxindex)
        number_primes = number_primes + maxindex

        ready = number_primes >= size(prime)
    endif
!$omp end critical

end subroutine get_task

end program primes_openmp
```

When you run it, the output of primes is not necessarily sorted. The threads run independently and it is not possible to predict which one will get what chunk of integers or in what order they deliver their results. It may in fact differ for each run. This is inherent to parallel computing.

MPI

An often cited advantage of OpenMP over MPI is that with OpenMP you can work incrementally: Just parallellize those sections you want to speed up one by one. With MPI, you need to carefully reorganize the whole program, as the communication between the individual processes has to be implemented manually. A clear advantage of MPI over OpenMP, however, is that data are not shared accidentally. An MPI program is run as several separate processes that explicitly communicate their data.

Here is an MPI version of the example:

```fortran
program primes_mpi
    use mpi

    implicit none

    integer, parameter :: tag_new_task = 1 ! Get new task
    integer, parameter :: tag_results  = 2 ! Transmit results

    integer                :: rank
    integer                :: main = 0
    integer                :: error

    integer                :: number_images

    integer, dimension(2)  :: range
    integer                :: number_tasks
    integer, dimension(1000) :: prime
    integer                :: number_primes
    integer, dimension(MPI_STATUS_SIZE) :: status
    logical                :: new_results
    logical                :: new_task
    logical                :: ready

    call mpi_init( error )

    call mpi_comm_rank( MPI_COMM_WORLD, rank, error )
    call mpi_comm_size( MPI_COMM_WORLD, number_images, error )

    !
    ! What we do depends on the rank:
    ! Rank 0 is the main program that hands out the chunks
    ! and gathers the results
    ! All others do the work
    !

    if ( rank == 0 ) then
        ready          = .false.
```

```fortran
        new_results   = .false.
        number_tasks  = 0
        number_primes = 0

        ! The main program:
        ! Hand out the chunks and receive the results
        !
        range(2)      = 0

        do while ( .not. ready )
            call handle_communication
        enddo
    else
        !
        ! Worker programs:
        ! Get a task (new range, determine the primes)
        !
        new_task = .false.
        do
            call get_range

            if ( new_task ) then
                call find_primes
                call mpi_send( &
                        prime, number_primes, MPI_INTEGER, &
                        main, tag_results, MPI_COMM_WORLD, &
                        status, error )
            else
                exit
            endif
        enddo
    endif

    !
    ! Print the results
    !
    if ( rank == 0 ) then
        write(*,'(10i5)') prime
    endif

    call mpi_finalize

    stop

contains
    ...
end program
```

The main program sets up the MPI environment and then splits into two parts:

- Via MPI a number of copies of the program are started. They interact with each other via the MPI routines.
- The copy with *rank* 0 gets the task of coordinating the communication (handing out new tasks, receiving the results). This is a design choice, which differs from the OpenMP version, where the master thread takes tasks as well. With this choice, the program is somewhat simpler.
- All other copies wait for a new task, therefore, determine the primes within the given range and then pass back the results.

The routine `handle_communication` sends out the data for the new task and receives the primes that are found by examining the message received. When enough primes are found, all copies are informed that there are no more tasks to be done.

The routine `get_range` that is run by all worker copies sends a request for a new task and waits for the data for that new task by using the blocking versions of the MPI routines. If there is no new task, the copy stops.

Here is the code for these two routines:

```
. . .
contains
!
! Communicate with the worker images
!
subroutine handle_communication
    integer, dimension(MPI_STATUS_SIZE) :: status
    integer                             :: error
    integer                             :: count
    integer, dimension(100)             :: result
    integer                             :: i
    integer                             :: number_store
    integer                             :: end_store

    do
        call mpi_recv( result, size(result), MPI_INTEGER,      &
                MPI_ANY_SOURCE, MPI_ANY_TAG, MPI_COMM_WORLD, &
                status, error )
        !
        ! Send a new task or store the results?
        !
        if ( status(MPI_TAG) == tag_new_task ) then
            range(1) = range(2) + 1
            range(2) = range(2) + 100
            call mpi_send( range, 2, MPI_INTEGER,       &
```

```fortran
                    status(MPI_SOURCE), tag_new_task, &
                    MPI_COMM_WORLD, status, error )
            call mpi_send( range, 2, MPI_INTEGER,        &
                    status(MPI_SOURCE), tag_new_task, &
                    MPI_COMM_WORLD, status, error )
        else
            call mpi_get_count( &
                    status, MPI_INTEGER, count, error )

            number_store = &
                min( size(prime) - number_primes, count )

            end_store = number_prime + number_store
            prime(number_primes+1:end_store) = &
                result(1:number_store)
            number_primes = end_store

            !
            ! Signal the worker programs to stop
            !
            if ( number_primes == size(prime) ) then
                do i = 1,number_images-1
                    range = -1
                    call mpi_send( range, 2, MPI_INTEGER, &
                            i, tag_new_task,                &
                            MPI_COMM_WORLD, status, error )
                enddo
                exit
            endif
        endif
    enddo

end subroutine handle_communication

!
! Get the range - if any
!
subroutine get_range
    integer, dimension(MPI_STATUS_SIZE) :: status
    integer                             :: error

    call mpi_send( 1,     1,             MPI_INTEGER, main, &
            tag_new_task, MPI_COMM_WORLD, status, error )

    call mpi_recv( range, size(range), MPI_INTEGER, main, &
            tag_new_task, MPI_COMM_WORLD, status, error )
```

```
    !
    ! Do we have a task?
    !
    new_task = range(2) > range(1)

end subroutine get_range
...
```

(The routine to find the primes is straightforward as no MPI calls are involved.)

Coarrays

The *coarrays* feature of the Fortran 2008 standard [71] resembles OpenMP in that communication between the threads (or *images* as they are called in the standard) because it is hidden from the programmer. However, it resembles MPI in that the images have their own memory, only the *coarrays* are shared. When handing out the chunks of integers, you need to again make sure that the shared data are updated by only one image at a time.

You have a choice here, just as with OpenMP and MPI, which image (or thread or copy) is responsible for gathering the data. You can dedicate one single image to the task or you can have each image store the data in the result array. The two choices involve different synchronization methods. Here the first option is used:[2]

```
program primes_coarrays
    implicit none

    integer, dimension(2)                       :: range_priv
    integer, dimension(2), codimension[*]       :: range
    integer, dimension(1000)                    :: prime
    integer                                     :: total_primes
    integer, dimension(100), codimension[*]     :: primes_in_task
    integer, codimension[*]                     :: number_in_task
    logical, codimension[*]                     :: new_results
    logical, codimension[*]                     :: new_task
    logical, codimension[*]                     :: ready

    ready           = .false.
    new_results     = .true.   ! Indicates the image has
                               ! results available
    new_task        = .false.  ! Indicates a new task has been
                               ! issued for the image
    number_in_task  = 0        ! Number of primes found in task

    range_priv(2)   = 0
    total_primes    = 0
```

---

[2] The collection of examples at the website contains an implementation of the second option as well.

```
    sync all

    !
    ! Collect the found primes in image 1, create new tasks
    ! for all images
    !
    do while ( .not. ready )
        if ( this_image() == 1 ) then
            call collect_results
            call create_tasks
            sync images(*)
        else
            sync images(1)
        endif

        call get_task
    enddo

    if ( this_image() == 1 ) then
        write(*,*) 'Primes:'
        write(*,'(20i5)') prime
    endif

contains
    ...
end program primes_coarrays
```

In the main program, you define a number of *coarray* variables. These are the variables that are shared among the images. As you will have Image 1 collect all the primes, the result array `prime` is an ordinary array.

After an initial synchronization step via the `sync all` statement, the do loop starts. The pattern should be familiar: Image 1 collects the results, just as with the MPI version and hands out new tasks.

To ensure the data are distributed, it synchronizes with all images via the `sync images(*)` statement. The counterpart of this statement is `sync images(1)`, which is run by all other images. The advantage of `sync images` over `sync all` is that the individual images can start as soon as the synchronization with the first image is completed. They do not have to wait for all others.

The routine `collect_results` checks which images complete their task, and they set the `new_results` variable to indicate that. If an image completes its task, the *coindex* [i] selects the value from Image i. Then, Image 1 copies the data into the `prime` array.

Once enough primes are found, Image 1 signals to all images that the program has completed its job by setting the `ready` variable in all images.

After gathering the new results, Image 1 hands out new tasks for those images that complete their tasks. Again, this is accomplished by examining and setting coarray variables.

The routine get_task can now rely on the coarray variables to have the right values for that image, so no *coindices* are required:

```
. . .
contains
!
! Subroutine to collect the results from all
! images (run by image 1)
!
subroutine collect_results
    integer :: i
    integer :: np
    integer :: maxindex

    do i = 1,num_images()
        sync images(i)
        if ( new_results[i] ) then
            np       = number_in_task[i]

            maxindex = min( size(prime) - total_primes, np )
            prime(total_primes+1:total_primes+maxindex) = &
                primes_in_task(1:maxindex)[i]

            total_primes = total_primes + maxindex
        endif
    enddo

    ready = total_primes >= size(prime)

    if ( ready ) then
        do i = 1,num_images()
            ready[i] = .true.
        enddo
    endif
end subroutine collect_results

!
! Subroutine to post new tasks (consisting of a
! range of integers in which to look for primes)
!
! Loop over the images to see which one wants a
! new task
!
```

```fortran
subroutine create_tasks
    integer :: i

    do i = 1,num_images()
        if ( new_results[i] ) then
            new_results[i] = .false.
            range_priv(1)  = range_priv(2) + 1
            range_priv(2)  = range_priv(2) + 100

            range(:)[i]    = range_priv(:)
            new_task[i]    = .true.
        endif
    enddo

end subroutine create_tasks

!
! Subroutine to get a task and search for
! primes inside the new range
!
subroutine get_task

    integer                :: lower
    integer                :: upper
    logical                :: isprime
    integer                :: np
    integer                :: i
    integer                :: j
    integer                :: residue

    if ( new_task ) then
        np = 0
        new_task = .false.
        lower = range(1)
        upper = range(2)

        !
        ! Determine what primes we have in this range
        !
        do i = lower,upper
            isprime = .true.
            do j = 2,int(sqrt(real(i)))
                residue = mod(i,j)
                if ( residue == 0 ) then
                    isprime = .false.
                    exit
                endif
```

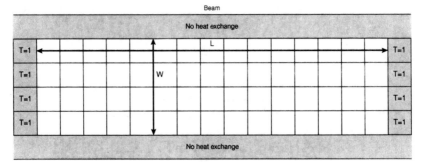

Figure 12.1. Schematic representation of the beam with a square grid overlaid

```
      enddo
      if ( isprime ) then
          np = np + 1
          primes_in_task(np) = i
      endif
      enddo

      number_in_task = np
      new_results    = .true.
   endif

end subroutine get_task

. . .

end program primes_coarrays
```

12.2 Domain Decomposition

The second example demonstrates how parallel computing is used to solve partial differential equations (PDE). Consider as a typical situation the conduction of heat in a beam of metal. The equation you need to solve, together with its boundary conditions is (see Figure 12.1):[3]

$$\frac{\partial T}{\partial t} = a \nabla^2 T \tag{12.1}$$

$$t = 0 : T = 0 \qquad (initial\ condition) \tag{12.2}$$

$$x = 0\ or\ L : T = 1 \qquad (Dirichlet) \tag{12.3}$$

$$y = 0\ or\ B : \frac{\partial T}{\partial y} = 0 \qquad (Neumann) \tag{12.4}$$

---

[3] For simplicity, you will assume a two-dimensional geometry, rather than a three-dimensional one.

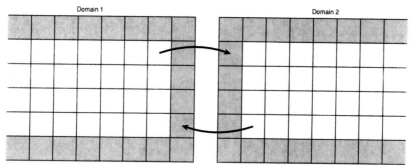

Figure 12.2. Grid split up in two separate domains with an internal boundary

Solving this mathematical problem using finite differences gives a set of *algebraic* equations:

$$T_{ij}^{t+\Delta t} = T_{ij}^t + a\,\Delta t\left(\frac{T_{i-1,j}^t + T_{i+1,j}^t - 2T_{ij}^t}{\Delta x^2} + \frac{T_{i,j-1}^t + T_{i,j+1}^t - 2T_{ij}^t}{\Delta y^2}\right)$$

$$(12.5)$$

where the indices i and j run over the whole interior of the grid.

You can apply parallel programming techniques in a variety of ways. With OpenMP, you can split up the do loops, for instance, the outer one, but that gives a low-level type of parallel computing only. A more interesting method is to split up the beam (or whatever geometry you encounter in practice) into smaller domains (see Figure 12.2). Each domain is now handled by a single thread or image. At the end of each time step, you will communicate the values at the internal boundaries and wait until all threads/images have finished their work before proceeding with the next time.

OpenMP

There is only one process if we use OpenMP, therefore, you be careful to provide all the data for one domain to one thread. You use an array of matrices to store the temperature per domain:

```
type domain_data
    real, dimension(:,:), allocatable :: temperature
    integer                           :: ibound
    integer                           :: icopy
    integer                           :: todomain
end type

type(domain_data), dimension(2), target :: domain
```

The temperature data at the internal boundary must be available for all domains. You store it in a two-dimensional array where the first dimension is the number of grid cells along that boundary and the second dimension is used for the two domains at each side:

```
real, dimension(:,:), pointer      :: temp

. . .

!
! Allocate the array we need to transfer the temperature
! at the interface
!
allocate( temp_interface(20,2) )
temp_interface = 0.0

!$omp parallel private( thid, side, ibound, icopy, &
!$omp                   xmax, ymax, todomain, temp )

do itime = 1,10000
    thid = 1 + omp_get_thread_num()

    temp     => domain(thid)%temperature
    ibound   =  domain(thid)%ibound
    icopy    =  domain(thid)%icopy
    todomain =  domain(thid)%todomain

    ... set Neumann boundary conditions

    !
    ! Copy the temperature at the interface from
    ! the other thread
    !
    temp(:,ibound) = temp_interface(:,thid)

    ... determine temperature at new time

    !
    ! Copy the values to the other thread
    !
    temp_interface(:,todomain) = temp(:,icopy)

    !$omp barrier
  enddo
  !$omp end parallel
```

The entire program follows:

```fortran
program dd_openmp

    use omp_lib

    implicit none

    type domain_data
        real, dimension(:,:), allocatable :: temperature
        integer                           :: ibound
        integer                           :: icopy
        integer                           :: todomain
    end type

    type(domain_data), dimension(2), target :: domain

    real, dimension(:,:), allocatable :: temp_interface
    real, dimension(:,:), pointer     :: temp

    integer                           :: itime
    integer                           :: ibound
    integer                           :: icopy
    integer                           :: todomain
    integer                           :: side
    integer                           :: xmax
    integer                           :: ymax
    integer                           :: thid

    real                              :: deltt
    real                              :: coeff

    !
    ! Allocate the arrays we need
    !
    deltt = 0.1
    coeff = 1.0     ! Contains the thermal conductivity
                    ! and grid cell size

    call omp_set_num_threads( 2 )

    !$omp parallel

    if ( omp_get_thread_num() == 0 ) then
        allocate( domain(1)%temperature(20,20) )
        domain(1)%temperature = 0.0
```

```
    !
    ! Left boundary value
    !
    domain(1)%temperature(:,1) = 1.0
    !
    ! Right interface
    !
    domain(1)%ibound   = size(domain(1)%temperature,2)
    domain(1)%icopy    = domain(1)%ibound - 1
    domain(1)%todomain = 2
else
    allocate( domain(2)%temperature(20,30) )
    domain(2)%temperature = 0.0
    !
    ! Right boundary value
    !
    domain(2)%temperature(:,30) = 1.0
    !
    ! Left interface
    !
    domain(2)%ibound   = 1
    domain(2)%icopy    = domain(2)%ibound + 1
    domain(2)%todomain = 1
endif

!$omp end parallel

!
! Allocate the array we need to transfer the temperature
! at the interface
!
allocate( temp_interface(20,2) )
temp_interface = 0.0

!
! From now on: compute
!
!$omp parallel private( thid, side, ibound, icopy, &
!$omp                   xmax, ymax, todomain )

do itime = 1,10000
    thid = 1 + omp_get_thread_num()

    temp     => domain(thid)%temperature
    ibound   =  domain(thid)%ibound
    icopy    =  domain(thid)%icopy
    todomain =  domain(thid)%todomain
```

```
      !
      ! Set the Neumann boundary conditions
      !
      side = size(temp,1)
      temp(1,:)    = temp(2,:)
      temp(side,:) = temp(side-1,:)

      !
      ! Copy the temperature at the interface from
      ! the other image
      !
      temp(:,ibound) = temp_interface(:,thid)

      !
      ! Determine the new values
      !
      xmax = size(temp,1) - 1
      ymax = size(temp,2) - 1
      temp(2:xmax,2:ymax) = temp(2:xmax,2:ymax) + &
          deltt * coeff * &
            ( temp(1:xmax-1,2:ymax) + temp(3:xmax+1,2:ymax) + &
              temp(2:xmax,1:ymax-1) + temp(2:xmax,3:ymax+1) &
              - 4.0*temp(2:xmax,2:ymax) )

      !
      ! Copy the values to the other image
      !
      temp_interface(:,todomain) = temp(:,icopy)

      !
      ! Make sure all images wait for the next step
      !

      !$omp barrier

      write(*,*) itime, thid, &
          temp(10,10), temp_interface(10,thid)
    enddo
    !$omp end parallel
    stop
end program
```

Some things to note:

- Threads are numbered from zero onwards. To use them as indices in the arrays, thread IDs are incremented by 1.

- The program is designed for running with two threads, one for each domain. You, therefore, explicitly set the number of threads to use although that is not possible with MPI or coarrays as the **environment** in which the copies of the program run determines their number. You need means outside the program itself to prevent excess copies from disturbing the computation, although you can check how many copies are active.
- The !$omp barrier statement synchronizes all threads before continuing with the next step. Just before that, the temperature data are copied to the other domain.
- The administrative variables side, ibound, and so on must be private per thread. This is a drawback of the OpenMP approach as it is very easy to make a mistake.
- The program explicitly stops with the STOP statement after completing the loop. This should not be necessary, but with one compiler I used a problem occurs without it: the program would not finish.

MPI

Using MPI, you end up with a program that is largely similar, but it is the details that are important:

- You explicitly send the data to the other domain, but without waiting for that domain to pick them up. This asynchronous sending is achieved with the MPI_Isend() routine.
- You cannot continue until receiving the data from the other domain, therefore, use the synchronous receive routine MPI_Recv() to wait for the data. This means that you synchronize the two copies automatically because there is no need for an explicit synchronisation.
- Every copy has its own memory space, so simply allocate the two-dimensional array that holds the temperature and the **one-dimensional** array that is used to send and receive the data on the inner boundary.

Leaving out some of the details, here is the do loop to integrate over time:

```
do itime = 1,10000

    ... Set the Neumann boundary conditions

    !
    ! Copy the temperature at the interface from the other image
    !
    temp(:,ibound) = temp_interface(:)

    ... Determine the new values

    !
    ! Copy the values to the other image
    ! - do not wait for an answer
```

```
      !
      temp_interface(:) = temp(:,icopy)
      call mpi_isend( temp_interface, size(temp_interface), &
              MPI_REAL, tag, tag, MPI_COMM_WORLD, &
              handle, error )

      !
      ! Receive them from the other side (use rank as the tag!)
      !
      call mpi_recv( temp_interface, size(temp_interface), &
              MPI_REAL, tag, rank, MPI_COMM_WORLD, &
              status, error )

      !
      ! Make sure all images wait for the next step
      ! - this is implicit in the fact that we have to
      ! receive the data first
      !
      write(*,*) itime, rank, &
          temp(10,10), temp_interface(10)
enddo
```

Coarrays

It should come as no surprise that you need only one coarray variable for this PDE problem: The data at the interface of the two domains. Just as in the OpenMP version, you need to synchronize the images at the end of each time step. And, like in the MPI version, you can use a simple two-dimensional array to store the temperature for a domain.

The array temperature is an ordinary array that stores the temperature for a single domain. It is allocated to a different size on each image, to match the geometry. The **coarray** variable temp_interface that is used to exchange the temperature at the interface of the two domains must, however, have the same dimensions on all images:

```
real, dimension(:,:), allocatable                    :: temp
real, dimension(:), codimension[:], allocatable :: &
          temp_interface
...
if ( this_image() == 1 ) then
    allocate( temp(20,20) )
    temp = 0.0
    !
    ! Left boundary
    !
    temp(:,1) = 1.0
else
```

```
    allocate( temp(20,30) )
    temp = 0.0
    !
    ! Right boundary value
    !
    temp(:,30) = 1.0
endif
```

```
!
! Allocate the one coarray we need to transfer the temperature
! at the interface
!
allocate( temp_interface(20)[*] )
temp_interface = 0.0
```

The do loop by which the evolution of the temperature over time is computed becomes:

```
do itime = 1,10000

    ... Set the Neumann boundary conditions

    !
    ! Copy the temperature at the interface from
    ! the other image
    !
    temp(:,ibound) = temp_interface

    ... Determine the new values

    !
    ! Copy the values to the other image
    !
    temp_interface(:)[toimage] = temp(:,icopy)

    !
    ! Make sure all images wait for the next step
    !
    sync all

    write(*,*) itime, this_image(), &
        temp(10,10), temp_interface(10)
enddo
```

Note that you do not collect the data for each domain into one large array. For a more serious program, you do have to consider such a feature since the results for all domains together form the results you are after.

12.3 Alternatives

OpenMP, MPI, and *coarrays* are but three techniques you can employ to create a parallel program. The following are a few alternatives:

- Using shared memory to communicate between two or more programs on the same computer.
- POSIX or Windows threads instead of OpenMP for a fine-grained and explicit control of the threads in the same program.
- TCP/IP communication between programs on possibly different computers.

Drawbacks of the preceding approaches are that they all rely on platform-specific system libraries and require considering low-level details.

A different aspect of parallel computing that is worth discussing is the way the threads or images cooperate. The first example used a master-workers setup – one thread handing out the tasks and collecting the results. The second example used two threads that synchronize with each other without any playing a special role. Depending on the problem to solve, very different setups are possible [78], [39], for instance:

- *Pipeline architecture*: The data undergo a series of transformations, where each transformation is handled by a different thread. Once the transformation is complete, the result is transferred to the next stage and a new set of data is requested.
- *Tuplespaces*: The threads request a task with certain characteristics from a central repository and hand back new tasks. This type of parallelism is very flexible, because synchronization needs to be done between the thread and the repository only.

The past couple of years using the *graphics card* (GPU) for parallel processing has received much attention. GPUs are attractive because they consist of many hundreds of fast processors. The drawback is that they have only indirect access to the data to be processed and this requires redesigning the entire algorithm. Another drawback is that programming for the GPU requires vendor-specific extensions to the programming language.[4] Besides C and C++, it is possible to use Fortran to program for the GPU, the PGI CUDA Fortran compiler being one compiler that supports this natively [41].

Various research groups have been successful in developing complex programs using this technique for a variety of computational problems. Xian and Takayuki [85], for instance, report on the use of a cluster of GPUs to compute the flow of an incompressible fluid around obstacles.

---

[4] Standardization is being developed in the form of *OpenCL*.

Table 12.1. Characteristics of the Three Parallel Programming Techniques

Method	Support	Incremental Development	Main Issue
OpenMP	Compiler	Yes	Easy to make mistakes in shared/private variables
MPI	External libraries	Limited	Communication of data is responsibility of the programmer
coarrays	Compiler supporting Fortran 2008	Yes	Synchronization must be carefully designed

12.4 Overview

All three methods of creating a program for parallel computing have their pros and cons. From a programming point of view, **coarrays** seem to combine the advantages of OpenMP with those of MPI – data communication is transparent and what data are shared is defined explicitly. From a usage point of view, **coarrays** have the disadvantage that they require a supporting environment to start the separate processes and to control the number of processes. This is not different from MPI, however. Like OpenMP, **coarrays** of only require the compiler to support them. There is no need for an external library.

The major disadvantage of **coarrays** is that the rules are rather complex. They are complex to ensure both efficiency and data consistency. Table 12.1 compares the methods.

As mentioned, besides OpenMP, MPI, and **coarrays** there are several other methods to exploit parallel programming, such as the use of shared memory and multithreading libraries as *pthreads*. They are much more difficult to use, however, and they have not reached much popularity within the Fortran community.

Appendix A

Tools for Development and Maintenance

Nowadays there are myriad tools to select from if you develop and maintain software. Much is open source, but there are also many commercial tools available. The development and maintenance tools include:

- Compilers, linkers, and interactive debuggers
- Build tools to automatically compile the source code in the right order
- Integrated development environments
- Tools for static and dynamic analysis
- Version control systems
- Tools for source code documentation

This appendix describes some uses of these tools, but it does not provide a complete overview.

A.1 The Compiler

Since the Fortran 90 standard, the language has gained features that make it easier for the compiler to perform static and dynamic analysis:

- The `implicit none` statement (or equivalent compiler options) force the compiler to check that every variable is explicitly declared. This reduces the chance that typos inadvertently introduce bugs in the form of stray variables names into the program.
- By putting all routines in modules, you make sure the compiler checks the number and types of the arguments for subroutine and function calls.[1] It also reduces name clashes when linking a large program, which uses many libraries.
- By using assumed-shape arrays instead of assumed-size, the compiler can insert runtime checks for array bounds. Moreover, you do not need to add separate arguments for the size of arrays anymore. This makes the call simpler and less error-prone.

Therefore, the compiler has become a much more powerful tool with respect to static and dynamic analysis.

---

[1] Some compilers, like the *Intel Fortran* compiler, generate interfaces for all routines that are not part of a module. This enhances the compiler's capability to diagnose mismatches in the arguments lists.

A.2 Build Tools

The classic tool that helps build a program efficiently is the UNIX utility *make* that can be found on most, if not all, systems in wide use today. The main attraction of *make* is that it checks if the source code needs to be compiled or not, thus reducing the runtime of the build process. It does so by checking the given dependencies between the object file, the source file, and any other files (such as include files or module files).

Creating and maintaining the input files for *make*, the so-called makefiles, can be tedious and error-prone, as they contain platform dependencies, different compilers with different options or the names and locations of system libraries, to name but a few. This maintenance task is made easier by software that actually generates these makefiles from more abstract and generic descriptions.

This software typically examines the source code (you specify a list of source files to check), determines from that the dependencies, and generates the makefiles. Two examples of these software systems are: *autotools* [20] and *CMake* [5]. Of the two, *autotools* is the oldest and it is well-established. However, it relies on tools typically available under a UNIX-like environment only, and it only generates makefiles. *CMake*, on the other hand, can run on MS Windows, Linux, and Mac OSX and it can generate project files for an integrated development environment such as MS Visual Studio.

Here is a small example of both. The program consists of a source file "prog.f90" living in the directory "main" and a file "lib.f90" living in the directory "lib". For *autotools*, you need files like this "Makefile.am" to describe how to build the program from its components:

```
include $(top_srcdir)/common.am
bin_PROGRAMS = example

example_SOURCES = \
        prog.f90


#
# Extend the macro FMODULES, defined in "common.am" to access
# the directory with the module file.
#
FMODULES += -I$(top_srcdir)/lib

example_LDADD = \
        $(top_srcdir)/lib/liblib.a
```

You then run the **autoreconf** program that delivers a shell script *configure* and templates for the makefiles:

```
autoreconf -ivf
./configure
```

You would distribute the file configure and several other files besides the source code. It is not necessary for a user to have *autotools* installed.

The procedure for *CMake* is similar. To build the program, you have a file "CMakeLists.txt" for the main program and similar files for the library:

```
#
# Add the directory with the module file to the compile options.
#
include_directories(${CMAKE_BINARY_DIR}/lib)

add_executable(example prog.f90)

target_link_libraries(example lib)
```

Then, run *CMake* in a separate directory:

```
cd build-example
cmake ../sources -G "Unix Makefiles"
```

This gives a set of makefiles so that typing make suffices to build the program. Using *MicroSoft Visual Studio 2008*:

```
cd build-example
cmake ../sources -G "Visual Studio 9 2008"
```

gives a solution file that you can load into visual studio.

The drawback is that these makefiles are specific to the system on which they were generated, so you need to distribute the CMakeLists.txt files along with the source code and the user will have to run *CMake* themselves. The advantage is, of course, that *CMake* itself is platform-independent and has excellent support for Fortran.

Table A.1 gives an overview of the files needed in both cases.

A.3 Integrated Development Environments

The purpose of integrated development environments (IDEs) is to offer the user a complete set of tools to edit the source code, build the program, and debug or run it. They also help maintain the information about how to build it (from what sources, what compiler options, and so on).

Having all these tools within one single (graphical) environment is certainly worthwhile, but it does have a few drawbacks. They often work with very specific files that describe how to build the program, which limits you to that IDE. The source file editor integrated into the environment may not be to your liking. Another important drawback, they tend to be platform-specific (only running on a particular operating system and the choice of compilers is limited).

The major advantage of IDEs is that they take care of tedious aspects of building a program: set up the dependencies or determine the order in which

Table A.1. Overview of the Source and Build Files Required for the Sample Program

Directory	File	Description
sources		Main directory
	configure.ac	Main configuration file (autotools)
	common.am	File with compiler options (autotools)
	CMakeLists.txt	Main configuration file (CMake)
	NEWS, ...	Auxiliary text files required by *autotools*
sources/prog		Directory with main program
	prog.f90	Fortran source file
	Makefile.am	How to build the program (autotools)
	CMakeLists.txt	How to build the program (CMake)
sources/lib		Directory with library
	lib.f90	Fortran source file
	Makefile.am	How to build the library (autotools)
	CMakeLists.txt	How to build the library (CMake)

the source files have to be compiled. In this respect, they are akin to the build tools described previously. It is mostly a matter of personal preference which type of supporting software you should use.

A gain-source IDE for Fortran is *Photran*, itself based on *Eclipse* [10], and it can be run on various operating systems. See Figure A.1 for a screenshot. It provides a set of *refactorings*, transformations of source code with the aim to make the program better readable and maintainable, that are specific for Fortran [59].

A.4 Run-Time Checking

Memory leaks are especially an issue for long-running programs as the memory that is no longer reachable typically accumulates. While the compiler can insert runtime checks for array bound violations, keeping track of the allocated and deallocated memory is a completely separate problem.

Most compilers do not do this, unless you specify extra options. The *g95* compiler provides an overview by default [80], but the *valgrind* utility [75] gives more detailed information about where in the program memory was allocated that was not deallocated afterward. It also reports array bound violations. The following sample program contains an easy to spot memory leak and an array bound violation:

```
program test_valgrind

    integer, dimension(:), pointer :: data

    allocate( data(100) )
```

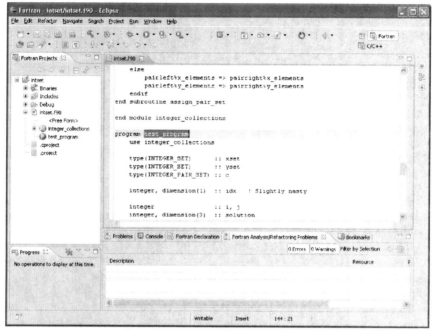

Figure A.1. Eclipse/Photran integrated development environment

```
      data(1) = 1
      data(101) = 2
      nullify( data )
end program test_valgrind
```

Compile this program on Linux (*valgrind* is limited to this platform) with the debug flag on, then run it via *valgrind*:

```
valgrind --leak-check=full program
```

The code reports:

```
==27770== Memcheck, a memory error detector.
==27770== Copyright (C) 2002-2006, and GNU GPL'd, by Julian Seward et al.
==27770== Using LibVEX rev 1658, a library for dynamic binary translation.
==27770== Copyright (C) 2004-2006, and GNU GPL'd, by OpenWorks LLP.
==27770== Using valgrind-3.2.1, a dynamic binary instrumentation framework.
==27770== Copyright (C) 2000-2006, and GNU GPL'd, by Julian Seward et al.
==27770== For more details, rerun with: -v
==27770==
==27770== Invalid write of size 4
==27770==    at 0x400711: MAIN__ (test_valgrind.f90:11)
==27770==    by 0x40073D: main (in /tmp/fort90/test_valgrind)
```

```
==27770==   Address 0x4EF9700 is 0 bytes after a block of size 400 alloc'd
==27770==     at 0x4A05809: malloc (vg_replace_malloc.c:149)
==27770==     by 0x4C6A34C: (within /usr/lib64/libgfortran.so.1.0.0)
==27770==     by 0x4006BE: MAIN__ (test_valgrind.f90:8)
==27770==     by 0x40073D: main (in /tmp/fort90/test_valgrind)
==27770==
==27770== ERROR SUMMARY: 1 errors from 1 contexts (suppressed: 4 from 1)
==27770== malloc/free: in use at exit: 400 bytes in 1 blocks.
==27770== malloc/free: 7 allocs, 6 frees, 26,032 bytes allocated.
==27770== For counts of detected errors, rerun with: -v
==27770== searching for pointers to 1 not-freed blocks.
==27770== checked 85,752 bytes.
==27770==
==27770==
==27770== 400 bytes in 1 blocks are definitely lost in loss record 1 of 1
==27770==     at 0x4A05809: malloc (vg_replace_malloc.c:149)
==27770==     by 0x4C6A34C: (within /usr/lib64/libgfortran.so.1.0.0)
==27770==     by 0x4006BE: MAIN__ (test_valgrind.f90:8)
==27770==     by 0x40073D: main (in /tmp/fort90/test_valgrind)
==27770==
==27770== LEAK SUMMARY:
==27770==    definitely lost: 400 bytes in 1 blocks.
==27770==    possibly lost: 0 bytes in 0 blocks.
==27770==    still reachable: 0 bytes in 0 blocks.
==27770==         suppressed: 0 bytes in 0 blocks.
==27770== Reachable blocks (those to which a pointer was found)
            are not shown.
==27770== To see them, rerun with: --show-reachable=yes
```

As it indicates exactly where the memory was allocated, you have a much lighter task determining a solution for this problem. It also reports where the array bound violation occurs – at least, for explicitly allocated memory.

A.5 Version Control Systems

An indispensable tool in modern software development is the version control system. The basic idea of the system is that you record the changes over time in the source code, documentation, and build files. This enables you to roll back changes that turned out to be unwanted, to experiment with alternatives, or use new features while keeping the mainstream version intact. Most importantly, it allows for cooperation with other programmers.

There is a wide variety of systems available: From the classic CVS or Subversion with a central repository to the newer distributed version control systems, such as *git* or *fossil*, where every developer has a copy of the repository [8], [76]. Up to a point, it is a matter of taste which one to select. Most, if not all, offer commands such as:

- *checkout*: get the (current) version of the source files into a new directory.
- *update*: merge the latest changes into your own source files.

- *commit*: put your changes back into the repository so that your co-developers can get your work. Other benefits of committing regularly, are recording the various stages of development or retrieving a previous version, if necessary.
- *diff*: compare two versions of the source files.
- *branch and merge*: start a parallel development, to test a new feature without interrupting the mainstream, and later bring the changes back into the mainstream.

These are just the basic features you may expect from a version control system.[2]

A.6 Documenting the Source Code

Many programmers have trouble keeping the documentation of their programs updated or even to create some formal documentation at all. This is especially true if you have to write the documentation after the program or library is finished. Tools like *Doxygen* and *ROBODoc* can help to automate the process. They extract the documentation via specially formatted comments from the source code itself. In this way, the source code and the documentation are intimately connected.

ROBODoc [77] is a tool that relies entirely on extracting the information from comments, whereas Doxygen [79] analyzes the source code to extract further details. With the first tool, you have to do more work, but it is essentially agnostic with respect to the programming language and it allows easy customization. Doxygen is capable of extracting most of the structure of the program automatically, but it requires knowledge of the programming language to do this. The consequence is that the structuring concepts of one language have to be mapped on those of the tool. For example, where Fortran has one definition of *module*, C++ has a different concept.

Both tools can be used to create comprehensive documentation, in various formats (HTML, LaTeX, and others), if you supply the right information.

Here is a small example of the code required by ROBODoc:

```
!****h* Utilities/sort_routines
! FUNCTION
!     The sort_routines module provides several routines
!     to sort arrays
!!****
!
module sort_routines
    implicit none

    !****m* sort_routines/sort
```

---

[2] At least one, *fossil* [43], comes with a built-in Internet server, a Wiki, and an issue tracker system, so that you can maintain much more than source code with one tool.

```
! NAME
!    sort - generic name for the sorting routines
! PURPOSE
!    The sort interface allows the programmer
!    to use a single generic name
!****
!
interface sort
    ...
end interface
```

```
contains
    ... actual code ...
end module sort_routines
```

The comment lines starting with "!****h*" and "!****m*" introduce comment blocks that contain the documentation. ROBODoc uses a large number of keywords to identify the role of the text.

A similar example for Doxygen is:

```
!> @file
!! The sort_routines module provides several routines
!! to sort arrays
!<
!
!> @defgroup Sort library
!! The sort_routines module provides several routines
!! to sort arrays
!!
module sort_routines
    implicit none

    !> generic name for the sorting routines
    !! The sort interface allows the programmer to use
    !! a single generic name
    !<
    interface sort
        ...
    end interface
```

```
contains
    ... actual code ...
end module sort_routines
```

Doxygen determines the items to be extracted itself and can also produce call-graphs from the source code. Both programs have a large number of options to customize the output.

A.7 Code Coverage and Static Analysis

A technique that should to be part of the testing procedure is *test coverage*.
This means measuring what part of the code has actually been run. Consider
for example:

```
program test_coverage
    implicit none

    real :: a = 0.0

    call setvalue( a, 1 )

    write(*,*) 'Parameter = ', a

contains
subroutine setvalue( param, type )

    real, intent(inout) :: param
    integer, intent(in) :: type

    if ( type == 0 ) then
        param = param * exp(-param)
    endif

end subroutine setvalue
end program test_coverage
```

The statement in the subroutine setvalue that assigns a new value to its first
argument is not run. With the given start value of variable a, its effect would
be undetectable, meaning a test on the output will not reveal if the assignment
has run. By measuring the test coverage, you get insight into this fact. Here
is the output from the *gcov* utility that, together with the *gfortran* compiler,
analyzes what parts of the program were run and what parts were not:[3]

```
    -:    0:Source:coverage_example.f90
    -:    0:Graph:coverage_example.gcno
    -:    0:Data:coverage_example.gcda
    -:    0:Runs:1
    -:    0:Programs:1
    -:    1:! coverage_example.f90 --
    -:    2:!     Show how to use the gcov utility
    -:    3:!
    1:    4:program test_coverage
    -:    5:    implicit none
    -:    6:
```

---

[3] The numbers before each line indicate how often the line was run. However, the "2" before line 11
should have been "1".

```
  -:    7:    real :: a = 0.0
  -:    8:
  1:    9:    call setvalue( a, 1 )
  -:   10:
  2:   11:    write(*,*) 'Parameter = ', a
  -:   12:
  -:   13:contains
  1:   14:subroutine setvalue( param, type )
  -:   15:
  -:   16:    real, intent(inout) :: param
  -:   17:    integer, intent(in) :: type
  -:   18:
  1:   19:    if ( type == 0 ) then
#####:   20:        param = param * exp(-param)
  -:   21:    endif
  -:   22:
  1:   23:end subroutine setvalue
  -:   24:end program test_coverage
```

The statement that was not run, line 20, is clearly marked. To get this output, use the following commands:[4]

```
gfortran --coverage -o coverage_example coverage_example.f90
coverage_example
gcov coverage_example.f90
```

Line coverage, where the coverage per statement is measured, is the weakest form of test coverage [17]. A more sophisticated form is *branch coverage* and in fact a whole series of coverage criteria exists with different strengths and difficulties to achieve 100 percent coverage. In practice, it is very difficult to reach 100 percent coverage in all but the simplest programs. Still, it is worth trying to achieve as high coverage as practical, because untested code may be sheltering some bug that is waiting to surface.

Branch coverage would reveal that if you change the call on line 9 to

```
call setvalue(a, 0)
```

force the assignment, you miss the implicit `else` branch of the if block. Two tests are required to cover all the branches even in this simple program.

Tools as *gcov*, but also commercial ones like *McCabe IQ*, can help in various ways to measure the coverage or even to design tests to increase the coverage.

Another valuable tool is *static analysis*. The Intel Fortran compiler, for instance, will perform an in-depth analysis of the source code revealing many hidden

---

[4] On Windows, set the environment variable *GCOV_PREFIX_STRIP* to 1000, otherwise, the .gcda file that records the coverage is not produced.

flaws, if you specify the option -Qdiag-enable:sc3. These analyses are costly, though, and therefore not all compilers will take these steps by default.

A slight modification to the preceding program illustrates what this analysis can do. The new source code is:

```
program test_coverage
    implicit none

    real    :: a
    real    :: b

    call setvalue( a, 1 )

    write(*,*) 'Parameter = ', a

contains
subroutine setvalue( param, type )

    real, intent(inout) :: param
    integer, intent(in) :: type

    if ( type == 0 ) then
        param = b * param * exp(-param)
    endif

end subroutine setvalue
end program test_coverage
```

Note the introduction of a variable b and the removal of the initial value for variable a. The output from the compiler is then:[5]

```
Intel(R) Visual Fortran Compiler Professional ...
Copyright (C) 1985-2010 Intel Corporation.  All rights reserved.

coverage_example_3.f90(14): error #12144: "A" is possibly
                            uninitialized
coverage_example_3.f90(23): warning #12301: "B" is set to zero
                            value by default
```

In a short program like this one, it is easy to spot these errors, but in more practical programs you will have a hard time tracking them unaided. It is here these compiler features come in handy.

---

[5] It is necessary to compile **and** link the program because the static analysis is carried out in a later stage.

Appendix B

Caveats

Programming languages – and programming environments – all have their share of surprising features. This appendix attempts to describe the most important ones in Fortran. Not all caveats that appear here are part of the language. Some arise when you use dynamic libraries (DLLs), others are still surprising when you compare Fortran with other programming languages.

B.1 Details of the Standard

Short-Circuiting Logical Expressions In languages like C/C++, or Java, you can rely on the so-called short-circuiting of logical expressions:

```
if ( pointer != NULL && pointer[0] == 1 ) {
    . . .
}
```

The expression consists of two parts: Check that the `pointer` variable is referring to some memory and check that the value at the first location has a particular value. If the first condition is *not* satisfied, it is not necessary to check the second condition. (It would actually lead to a crash of the program.) Therefore, the compound expression is evaluated as if written:

```
if ( pointer != NULL ) {
    if ( pointer[0] == 1 ) {
        . . .
    }
}
```

The Fortran standard does *not* guarantee this, but it leaves it up to the compiler. The reason: efficiency. On modern computers, evaluating both parts and then deciding the outcome can be much faster than the stepwise evaluation that short-circuiting requires. If the expressions get more complicated, the number of tests required to ensure short-circuiting will increase as does the object code.

Saving Local Variables While the Fortran language explicitly states (from at least FORTRAN 77 onward), that local variables in a routine do not retain their values between calls, unless they have the save attribute, some compilers will put them in static memory, because it is more efficient on that platform.

To avoid problems when moving to a different compiler, always explicitly use the save attribute. For instance:

```
subroutine print_data( data )
   real, dimension(:) :: data

   logical            :: first = .true.
   integer            :: count

   if ( first ) then
      first = .false.
      count = 0
   endif

   count = count + 1
   write(*,*) 'Page: ', count
   write(*,*) data
end subroutine
```

This routine may or may not work. It relies on the variable count retaining its value. By using the save attribute, you make this portable and you document the expectations:

```
subroutine print_data( data )
   ...

   logical, save      :: first = .true.
   integer, save      :: count

   ...
end subroutine
```

The variable first implicitly has the save attribute, because of the initialization to .true., but for the sake of clarity, you should use that attribute for its declaration as well.

More on Initialization For programmers used to C and related languages, it may come as a surprise that a statement like:

```
real :: x = 3.3
```

in a subroutine or function is not executed each time the routine is entered. Rather than a short-cut for:

```
real :: x
x = 3.3
```

as it is in C, this statement has a two-fold effect in Fortran:

- The variable x implicitly gets the **save** attribute: It will retain whatever value it has between routine calls.
- The variable x is guaranteed to have the value 3.3 at the **start** of the program.

Which brings another feature, variables in Fortran are not initialized by default. Their value is explicity **undefined**, unless some form of initialization is used or their value is set via assignment.

Double Precision and Evaluating Right-Hand Side There is a very strict principle in Fortran: The right-hand side is evaluated without regard to the left-hand side. The rationale is that is much easier to reason about what a statement means, and, in some cases, there is no left-hand side that could be used to determine the precision or the size of the result:

```
write(*,*) 1.1d0 * 10
```

In this write statement, the precision of the result, and the number that is written to the file, is dictated by the operands alone. The integer is promoted to double precision and the final result is a double precision number.

The first part holds for this assignment as well:

```
real :: x
x = 1.1d0 * 10
```

The expression on the right-hand side is computed using double precision. Only on assigning the result to the single-precision variable x, is it converted to single precision.

This consistent rule presents some surprises:

```
real(kind=kind(1.0d0)) :: x
x = 1.111111111111111111111111111111111111111
```

The value of x is not as accurate as the code suggests: The number appearing on the right may have a lot of digits, but it still is a single-precision number. Therefore, the value of x is the double-precision equivalent of that single-precision value.

Passing the Same Argument Twice Consider the following code fragments:

```
integer :: x, y
x = 1
y = 2
call add( x, x, y )
```

Here is the implementation of the subroutine add:

```
subroutine add( a, b, c )
integer :: a, b, c
b = b + a
c = c + a
end subroutine add
```

Because the dummy arguments a and b are both associated with the actual argument x, you might expect the output to be: x = 2 (twice the original value), y = 4. However, the result may very well be: x = 2, y = 3.

The reason is that the compiler does not need to assume that this aliasing can occur. In particular, it means that in a simple piece of code like this, the value of a can be left in a register (for fast access) and, therefore, b and c are increased by 1, the original value.

However, you do not know if this will in fact occur or not, because it depends on the details of the code and the compiler. Therefore, you should avoid this kind of programming.

If the variables involved have the pointer attribute or the target attribute, then the compiler must take the possibility of aliasing into account. In that case, all manner of optimizations are impossible.

For instance, the fragment:

```
real, dimension(:), pointer :: a, b
a = b
```

has to be evaluated in a way equivalent to:

```
real, dimension(:), pointer    :: a, b
real, dimension(:), allocatable :: tmp

allocate( tmp(size(a)) )

tmp = b
a = tmp

deallocate( tmp )
```

as b might be pointing partially to the same memory as a:

```
real, dimension(100), target :: data
real, dimension(:), pointer  :: a, b

a => data( 1:50)
b => data(26:75)
```

REAL(4)   While many compilers use *kind* numbers that indicate how many bytes a particular type of real or integer occupies, this is by no means universal. **Kind numbers** are simply any positive number that uniquely identifies all properties of the associated type for that particular compiler.

The scheme where the kind number equals the number of bytes already breaks down with complex numbers: The kind number is related to the underlying real values, so rather than four bytes, a `complex(4)` number often occupies two times four bytes. Then, there are computers whose hardware supports two or more kinds of reals occupying the same number of bytes, for instance, one kind adhering to the IEEE 754 format and a native format that is faster for that particular hardware.

An additional drawback of hard coding these numbers is that you cannot easily switch to a different precision: you have to consistently change the "4" into an "8" to get double precision.

Simply put, use portable means, like the `kind()` and `selected_real_kind()` functions to get the kind number.

End-of-file, Output to the Screen, and Others   Values to indicate "End of file" and the logical unit numbers for pre-connected files, such as output to the screen or input from the keyboard, have traditionally been associated with numbers like −1, 6 or 5 respectively. These values, while ubiquitous, are *not* portable.

The best way to deal with them is to avoid specific values altogether ("End of file" is always indicated by a negative number, other read errors are indicated by a positive value, while an asterisk refers to the output to screen or input from the keyboard.) If that is not possible, then the intrinsic `iso_fortran_env` module, introduced in Fortran 2003, contains parameters that can be used instead: `iostat_end` for the "end of file" condition, `output_unit`, and `input_unit` for the respective LU numbers.

Another quantity that may vary from one compiler to the next (it may even be influenced by the compile options) is the unit in which the record length for direct-access files is expressed. This unit can be a single **byte** or a single **word**, and that is often four bytes. The parameter `file_storage_size` in the intrinsic `iso_fortran_env` module gives the size of this unit in **bits**.

External and Intrinsic Routines   According to the standard, user-defined routines are to be declared as *external* routines to avoid possible conflicts with *intrinsic* routines, defined in the standard or as an extension in the compiler. You may be in for a surprise with the following program if you do not know that `dim()` is a standard intrinsic function:

```
real function dim( x, y )
   real :: x, y
```

```
      dim = x + y
end function dim

program use_dim

    real :: x, y
    x = 1.0
    y = 2.0
    write(*,*) dim(x,y)

end program use_dim
```

The solution is either to use an external statement or to put the function dim() in a module.

Mismatches in Interfaces: Assumed-Shape and Explicit-Shape The use of explicit-shape arrays clashes with assumed-shape arrays, as shown in the following example published by Page (2011) on the *comp.lang.fortran* newsgroup (formatting slightly adjusted) [69]:

```
module mymod
    implicit none
contains

subroutine mysub(param, result)
    real, intent(in)  :: param(3)
    real, intent(out) :: result
    print *,'param=', param
    result = 0.0
end subroutine mysub

subroutine minim(param, subr, result)
    real, intent(in) :: param(:)
    interface
        subroutine subr(p, r)
            real, intent(in)  :: p(:)
            real, intent(out) :: r
        end subroutine subr
    end interface
    real, intent(out):: result

    call subr(param, result)
end subroutine minim
end module mymod

program main
    use mymod
    implicit none
```

```
    real :: param(3) = [1.0, 2.0, 3.0], result

    call minim(param, mysub, result)
end program main
```

If you run the program, the three numbers for the `param` array seem to contain rubbish:

```
param=  6.14149881E-39          NaN   3.93764868E-43
```

The problem is the use of an explicit-shape – `real, intent(in) :: param(3)` – instead of an assumed-shape for the array `param`. This kind of mismatch may or may not be caught by the compiler, but if not, it is probably hard to spot in a more realistic program.

Seeding the Random Number Generator The routine `random_number` is very convenient if you need pseudo-random numbers in a program and you do not need to control the quality. Unfortunately, the standard allows the compiler a lot of freedom where the random number generator is concerned:

- There is no guarantee as to the quality, even though most compilers come with a very decent generator.
- There is no guarantee that the generator is initialized with different seeds at each run. Sometimes you will want that to happen and sometimes not. If your program crucially depends on that behavior, you will need to take care of it explicitly.
- Taking care of the proper seeding is not at all trivial. The routine `random_seed` is meant for this. Invoked without any arguments, it resets the random number generator in a compiler-dependent way. It also gives access to the array of values that is used internally by the generator. The actual contents and size depend on the implementation, and you have no guarantee that setting the array to a particular value or values will give a good-quality series of random numbers.
- The behavior of the built-in random number generator in a multithreaded environment like OpenMP, or when using coarrays, is unclear. Ideally, you would get independent sequences but that is not guaranteed.

When you need a high-quality random number generator and detailed control over its behavior, the best solution is to use an implementation that you can control. That is a recommendation that holds for most, if not all, programming languages. Luckily, there is a vast amount of literature on the subject [11], [46].

Opening the Same File Twice Sometimes it is convenient to open a file twice, on different logical unit numbers, so that two parts of the program can process the contents independently. Unfortunately, the Fortran standard does not allow that, not even when the files are opened for reading only. As a consequence, you will have to implement a different solution:

- Stream access allows you to arbitrarily set the reading/writing position in the file.
- Direct access requires you to specify what record to read/write.

Either solution can be used to achieve the effects needed, but they are more involved than might have been possible.

B.2 Arrays

Automatic and Temporary Arrays can Cause Stack Overflow From Fortran 90 onward, you can use automatic arrays:

```
subroutine handle_data( data )
    real, dimension(:)         :: data
    real, dimension(size(data)) :: work
    ...
end subroutine
```

This feature is very useful for creating work arrays of just the right size. The user of your routine does not need to know about the workspace and is not responsible for passing arrays of the right size. Furthermore, the array is created and destroyed automatically, so that you do not need to worry about it either.

There is a caveat, however. If the array gets too large, the stack from which the array is created may well get exhausted, leading to a crash of the program. Try the following code:

```
program check_stack
    implicit none

    integer :: size

    size = 1
    do
        size = size * 2
        write(*,*) 'Size: ', size

        call create_automatic_array( size )
    enddo
contains
subroutine create_automatic_array( size )
    integer                :: size
    real, dimension(size) :: data

    data(1) = 0.0
end subroutine create_automatic_array
end program check_stack
```

If you can expect these arrays to become very large, allocatable arrays are a far better choice. When you allocate these arrays, you can catch the error code and arrange for a graceful shutdown if there is not enough memory.

Array operations are sometimes implemented via hidden temporary arrays, especially if pointers to arrays are involved. It is not immediately clear from the code, but if these temporary arrays are allocated on the stack, then the same problem can occur. Many compilers offer an option to control the behavior. Therefore, small arrays are taken from the stack (which is faster), while large arrays are allocated on the heap (which poses less restrictions on the size).

Lower Bounds Other Than 1 Suppose you use a declaration like:

```
real, dimension(-3:3) :: array
```

and you fill it with the following values: 0, 0, 0, 1, 0, 0, 0.

The function maxloc() will report the maximum at **position 4**, not position 0, as you might expect (array(0) has the value 1 and all other elements have the value 0). This is because the lower bound is not automatically propagated to call subroutines or functions.

This is a compromise. If the lower bound was actually propagated to routines, then code using arrays passed as arguments would need to use the lower bound (and upper bound) consistently:

```
do i = 1,size(array)
    write(*,*) i, array(i)
enddo
```

would need to become:

```
do i = lbound(array),ubound(array)
    write(*,*) i, array(i)
enddo
```

for *all* arrays.

As non-default lower bounds are not that common, it is more convenient to put the burden on programs that actually use non-trivial lower bounds, than to put the burden on all programs.

Array Declarations: dimension(:) Versus dimension(*) The rules for passing arguments to functions and subroutines are simple: Unless the interface to the routine is known explicitly – via modules, interface blocks, or because it is an internal routine – the compiler assumes the FORTRAN 77 conventions.

Therefore, unless the interface to the following routine (which uses an *assumed-shape* array) is known, it is called the wrong way:

```
subroutine print_array( array )
   real, dimension(:) :: array

   integer            :: i

   do i = 1,size(array)
       write(*,*) array(i)
   enddo

end subroutine print_array
```

Therefore, it is called as if it was declared as:

```
subroutine print_array( array )
   real, dimension(*) :: array
   ...
end subroutine print_array
```

and that means at the very least, the size of the array is unknown. In effect, the loop will not run as intended (the size() function may return zero) or the program could crash.

As a rule of thumb, use modules whenever possible. You do not have to consider these interface questions and the compiler can do more checks.

B.3 Dynamic Libraries

Opening a File in a Program and Using It in a DLL or Vice Versa A dynamic library, whether a "DLL" on Windows, a "dylib" on Mac OSX, or a shared object on Linux, is best thought of as a separate program with some special connections to the calling program. Just as two ordinary programs do not share access to files on disk, neither do a program and the dynamic library share that access. The practical consequence is that if you open a file on logical unit number (LUN) 10 in the program, the library does not know anything about that file. If you use LUN 10 within the library, it may be actually be connected to a completely different file. This is caused by the use of LUNs as **global** resources. You can pass the numbers as arguments, but not the connection itself. This even more illustrates the way dynamic libraries work.

Some compilers offer a solution for this and the related problem of memory allocation and deallocation (see the following), but you need to be aware of this behavior.

Allocate Memory in a DLL and Deallocate It in the Program or Vice Versa
Memory allocated in a dynamic library should not be deallocated in the calling program or vice versa. The underlying administrations are independent. This is something to be aware of if you change a **static** library into a **dynamic** one.

As it involves no changes to the source code, only the build procedure needs changed. However, these aspects can be easily forgotten.

Command-Line Arguments Are Not Available in a DLL The intrinsic routine get_command_argument together with two related subroutines give access to the arguments that were given to start the program. This can be very useful, especially because you can use these subroutines anywhere in the program. You do not need to pass them on from the main program, as with other programming languages. However, these subroutines do not always work in a DLL. Notably, it does not work of the most program is not a Fortran program.

Subroutines or Data from the Main Program Used in the DLL The routines and data in a DLL are available to the main program (or other DLLs that link against the first one), if it makes them available. (The method to do this is platform-dependent and it is entirely beyond the Fortran language.)

This is not the case the other way around: a program cannot make its subroutines or data available to the DLL. Only by explicitly passing references to the DLL can they become available. The DLL is created as a more or less separate "program", so it can be used in any context. There is no guarantee that a routine my_subroutine will exist in that context, so the DLL cannot rely on it.

Appendix C

Trademarks

DISLIN is owned by the Max Planck Institute, for Solar System Research, Lindau, Germany.

Doxygen is an open-source program maintained by Dimitri van Heesch.

GNU, gcc, and gfortran are trademarks of the Free Software Foundation.

gnuplot is a plot program developed and maintained by the Free Software Foundation.

Intel Fortran is a trademark of Intel.

Interacter is a trademark of Interactive Services Ltd.

Java is a trademark of Oracle.

Linux is a trademark handled by the Linux Mark Institute.

Mac OSX is a trademark of Apple.

MATLAB is a trademark of The MathWorks, Inc.

McCabe IQ is a trademark of McCabe Software.

MS Visual Studio and MS Windows are trademarks of MicroSoft.

MySQL is an open source project at http://www.mysql.com.

Perl is a dynamic programming language. Its home page is http://www.perl.org.

PGI CUDA is a trademark of The Portland Group and NVIDIA.

PLplot is an open source project at http://plplot.sf.net.

PostScript and PDF are trademarks of Adobe.

Python is a dynamic programming language. Its home page is http://www.python.org.

ROBODoc is an open-source program maintained by Frank Slothouber.

SQLite is an open-source database management, residing at http://www.sqlite.org.

Tcl is a dynamic programming language developed and maintained by the Tcl Association. Tk is a user-interface library that can be used with Tcl and other languages. The home page for both is http://www.tcl.tk.

Xeffort is developed and maintained by Jugoslav Dujic.

Bibliography

[1] S. L. Abrams, W. Chot, C.-Y. Hu, T. Maekawa, N. M. Patrikalakis, E. C. Sherbrooke, and X. Ye. *"Efficient and Reliable Methods for Rounded-Interval Arithmetic."* Computer-Aided Design 30, no. 8 (1998); 657–665.

[2] Ed Akin. *Object-Oriented Programming via Fortran 90/95*. New York: Cambridge University Press, 2003.

[3] Robert Reimann, Alan Cooper, and David Cronin. *About Face 3: The Essentials of Interaction Design*. Indianapolis, Indiana: Wiley Publishing Inc., 2007.

[4] *"Test-Driven Development."* Wikipedia, last modified March 2012, http://en.wikipedia.org/wiki/Test-driven_development, 2010.

[5] *CMake*, accessed March 2012, http://www.cmake.org.

[6] *Coding Standard* accessed March 2012, http://c2.com/cgi/wiki?/CodingStandard.

[7] *"CPU Cache,"* Wikipedia, last modified March 2012, http://en.wikipedia.org/wiki/CPU_cache.

[8] *"Distributed Revision Control,"* Wikipedia, last modified March 2012, http://en.wikipedia.org/wiki/Distributed_revision_control.

[9] *"Factory Method Pattern."* Wikipedia, last modified March 2012, http://en.wikipedia.org/wiki/Factory_method_pattern, 2011.

[10] *Photran – An Integrated Development Environment and Refactoring Tool for Fortran.* http://www.eclipse.org/photran/, 2011.

[11] *"Pseudorandom Number Generator,"* Wikipedia, last modified March 2012, http://en.wikipedia.org/wiki/Pseudorandom_number_generator, 2011.

[12] *TR 29113 Technical Report on Further Interoperability of Fortran with C*, accessed on March 2012, http://j3-fortran.org/pipermail/j3/attachments/20110707/85783ea3/attachment-0001.pdf, 2011.

[13] J. Backus. *"Can Programming Be Liberated from the von Neumann Style? A Functional Style and Its Algebra of Programs."* Communications of the ACM 21, No. 8 (1978) http://www.stanford.edu/class/cs242/readings/backus.pdf.

[14] Gabriele Jost, Barbara Chapman, and Ruud van der Pas. *Using OpenMP: Portable Shared Memory Parallel Programming*. Cambridge: MIT Press, 2008.

[15] Chris Bates. *Web Programming: Building Internet Applications.* Hoboken NJ: John Wiley & Sons, 2001.

[16] K. Beck and C. Andres. *Extreme Programming Explained: Embrace Change.* Boston: Addison-Wesley Professional, 2004.

[17] Boris Beizer. *Software Testing Techniques.* Boston: International Thomson Computer Press, 1990.

[18] *"Fortran Wiki."* Jason Blevin, accessed on March 2012, http://fortranwiki.org.

[19] S-A. Boukabara and P. Van Delst. *Standards, Guidelines and Recommendations for Writing Fortran 95 Code.* http://projects.osd.noaa.gov/spsrb/standards_docs/fortran95_standard_rev26sep2007.pdf, 2007.

[20] John Calcote. *Autotools, A Practitioner's Guide to GNU Autoconf, Automake, and Libtool GNU Autotools.* San Francisco: No Starch Press, 2010.

[21] *"FRUIT."* Andrew Chen, accessed on March 2012, http://www.sourceforge.net/projects/fortranxunit.

[22] Ian Chivers and Jane Sleightholme. *Introduction to programming with Fortran.* New York: Springer, 2006.

[23] *"XML Path Language (XPath)."* James Clark and Steve DeRose, accessed on March 2012, http://www.w3.org/TR/xpath.

[24] Norman S. Clerman and Walter Spector. *Modern Fortran: Style and Usage.* New York: Cambridge University Press, 2012.

[25] *"The Fortran Company."* *The Fortran company,* accessed on March 2012, http://www.fortran.com.

[26] Martyn J. Corden and David Kreizer. *Consistency of Floating-Point Results using the Intel Compiler or Why doesn't my application always give the same answer.* Intel Corporation, 2009, http://software.intel.com/en-us/articles/consistency-of-floating-point-results-using-the-intel-compiler/.

[27] *"Using SQLite with Fortran."* Al Danial, accessed on March 2012, http://danial.org/sqlite/fortran/.

[28] *"Object-Oriented Design Patterns in Fortran."* Victor K. Decyk and Henry J. Gardner, accessed on March 2012, http://exodus.physics.ucla.edu/fortran95/decykGardner07v3.pdf.

[29] *"Debunking the Myths About Fortran."* Craig T. Dedo, accessed on March 2012, http://www.box.net/shared/gksd4706a9.

[30] *"gtk-fortran."* Jerry DeLisle, accessed on March 2012, https://github.com/jerryd/gtk-fortran/wiki.

[31] *"Cache misses."* Kay Diederichs, accessed on March 2012, http://coding.derkeiler.com/Archive/Fortran/comp.lang.fortran/2006-11/msg00341.html.

[32] *"What Every Programmer Should Know About Memory, Part 1."* Ulrich Drepper, http://lwn.net/Articles/250967/, 2007.

[33] *"Xeffort."* Jugloslav Dujic, accessed on March 2012, http://www.xeffort.com.

[34] J. Xia, D.W.I. Rouson and X. Xu. *Scientific Software Design: The Object-oriented Way.* New York: Cambridge University Press, 2011.

[35] Ralph Johnson, Erich Gamma, Richard Helm, and John Vlissides. *Design Patterns: Elements of Reusable Object-Oriented Software.* Boston: Addison-Wesley, 1995.

[36] W. Brainerd et al. *Guide to Fortran 2003 Programming.* New York: Springer, 2009.

[37] *"Junit."* Erich Gamma, accessed on March 2012, http://www.junit.org.

[38] Simon Geard. e-mail message to author, 2006.

[39] David Gelernter. *Generative Communication in Linda. ACM Transactions on Programming Languages and Systems* 7, no. 1 (1985).

[40] P. Goodliffe. *Code Craft, the Practice of Writing Excellent Code.* San Francisco: No Starch Press, Inc, 2007.

[41] *"CUDA Fortran, Programming Guide and Reference."* The Portland Group, accessed on March 2012, http://www.pgroup.com/lit/whitepapers/pgicudaforug.pdf.

[42] Les Hatton. *Safer C, Developing software for High-integrity and Safety-critical Systems.* New York: McGraw-Hill Book Company, 1994.

[43] *"Fossil – Simple, High-Reliability, Distributed Software Configuration Management."* D. Richard Hipp, accessed on March 2012, http://fossil-scm.org.

[44] *"SQLite."* D. Richard Hipp, accessed on March 2012, http://www.sqlite.org.

[45] *"Interval Arithmetic in Forte Fortran, Technical White Paper."* SUN Microsystems Inc., accessed on March 2012, http://developers.sun.com/sunstudio/products/archive/whitepapers/tech-interval-final.pdf.

[46] *"Good Practice in (Pseudo) Random Number Generation for Bioinformatics Applications."* D. Jones, accessed on March 2012, http://www.cs.ucl.ac.uk/staff/d.jones/GoodPracticeRNG.pdf.

[47] *"A Core Library For Robust Numeric and Geometric Computation."* V. Karamcheti, C. Li, I. Pechtchanski, and Yap C., accessed on March 2012, http://cs.nyu.edu/ pechtcha/pubs/scg99.pdf.

[48] B. Kleb. e-mail message to author, 2009.

[49] *"F95 Coding standard for the FUN3D project."* B. Kleb et al., accessed on March 2012, http://fun3d.larc.nasa.gov/chapter-9.html#f95_coding_standard.

[50] *"Funit."* Bil Kleb et al., accessed on March 2012, http://nasarb.rubyforge.org.

[51] *"Collection of Fortran code."* H. Knoble, accessed on March 2012, http://www.personal.psu.edu/faculty/h/d/hdk/fortran.html.

[52] *"Tklib, library of Tk extensions."* Andreas Kupries et al., accessed on March 2012, http://tcllib.sf.net/.

[53] Michael List and David Car. *"A polymorphic Reference Counting Implementation in Fortran 2003."* ACM Fortran Forum 30, No. 2, August 2011.

[54] Arjen Markus. *"Design Patterns and Fortran 95."* ACM Fortran Forum 25, no. 2, April 2006.

[55] *"Ftcl, combining Fortran and Tcl."* Arjen Markus, accessed on March 2012, http://ftcl.sf.net.

[56] *"Ftnunit."* Arjen Markus, accessed on March 2012, http://flibs.sourceforge.net.

[57] *"The Flibs project."* Arjen Markus, accessed on March 2012, http://flibs.sf.net.

[58] Steve McConnell. *Code Complete*, Redmond, Washington: MicrosSoft Press, 2nd edition, 2004.

[59] *"Fortran Refactoring for Legacy Systems."* Mariano Méndez, accessed on March 2012, http://www.fortranrefactoring.com.ar/papers/Fortran-Refactoring-for-Legacy-Systems.pdf.

[60] Michael Metcalf. *Fortran Optimization.* New York: Academic Press, 1982.

[61] Michael Metcalf. *"The Seven Ages of Fortran."* Journal of Computer Science and Technology 11, no. 1 (2011). http://journal.info.unlp.edu.ar/journal/journal30/papers/JCST-Apr11-1.pdf.

[62] Michael Metcalf and John Reid. *Fortran 8X Explained.* New York: Oxford University Press, 1987.

[63] Michael Metcalf and John Reid. *Fortran 90/95 Explained.* New York: Oxford University Press, 2004.

[64] Bertrand Meyer. *Object-Oriented Software Construction.* Upper Saddle River, NJ: Prentice Hall International Ltd., 1988.

[65] John Reid, Michael Metcalf and Malcolm Cohen. *Fortran 95/2003 Explained.* New York: Oxford University Press, 2004.

[66] Steven J. Miller and Ramin Takloo-Bighash. *An Invitation to Modern Number-Theory.* Princeton, NJ: Princeton University Press, 2006.

[67] *"XOTcl – Extended Object Tcl."* Gustave Neumann, accessed on March 2012, http://media.wu.ac.at/.

[68] Suely Oliveira and David Stewart. *Writing Scientific Software.* New York: Cambridge University Press, 2006.

[69] *"Importance of Not Being Explicit."* Clive Page, accessed on May 9, 2011, https://groups.google.com/group/comp.lang.fortran/browse_frm/thread/1a40cc3e6e4546de.

[70] G.W. Petty. *Automated computation and consistency checking of physical dimensions and units in scientific programs.* Software – Practice and Experience, 31, 1067-1076 (URL: http://sleet.aos.wisc.edu/~gpetty/wp/?page_id=684), 2001.

[71] *"Coarrays in the Next Fortran Standard."* John Reid, accessed on March 2012, ftp://ftp.nag.co.uk/sc22wg5/N1801-N1850/N1824.pdf.

[72] *"The new features of Fortran 2008."* John Reid, accessed on March 2012, ftp://ftp.nag.co.uk/sc22wg5/N1801-N1850/N1828.pdf.

[73] Damian W.I. Rouson and Helgi Adalsteinsson. *"Design Patterns for Multiphysics Modelling in Fortran 2003 and C++."* ACM Transactions on Mathematical Software 37, no. 1 (2009).

[74] N.S. Scott, F. Jézéquel, Denis C., and J.-M. Chesneaux. *"Numerical 'health check' for Scientific Codes: the CADNA Approach."* Computer Physics Communications 176 (2007), pp. 507–521.

[75] *"Valgrind."* Julian Seward et al., accessed on March 2012, http://valgrind.org.

[76] *"Version Control by Example."* Eric Sink, accessed on March 2012, http://www.ericsink.com/vcbe/.

[77] *"ROBODoc, Automating the Software Documentation Process."* Frank Slothouber, accessed on March 2012, http://rfsber.home.xs4all.nl/Robo/.

[78] Beverly A. Sanders, Timothy G. Mattson and Berna L. Massingill. *Patterns for Parallel Programming.* Boston: Pearson Education inc., 2005.

[79] *"Doxygen, Generate Documentation From Source Code."* Dimitri van Heesch, accessed on March 2012, http://www.stack.nl/ dimitri/doxygen/index.html.

[80] *"G95."* Andrew Vaught, accessed on March 2012, http://www.g95.org.

[81] Norman Walsh. *DocBook 5: The Definitive Guide.* Sebastopol, CA: O'Reilly Media, 2010.

[82] Eric W. Weisstein. *Pell Equation.* MathWorld, 2011, http://mathworld.wolfram.com/PellEquation.html.

[83] Ewing Lusk, William Gropp and Anthony Skjellum. *Using MPI: portable parallel programming with message passing.* Cambridge: MIT Press, 1999.

[84] *"Pfunit."* Brice Womack and Tom Clune, accessed on March 2012, http://www.sourceforge.net/projects/pfunit.

[85] Wang Xian and Aoki Takayuki. *"Multi-GPU Performance of Incompressible Flow Computation by Lattice Bolzmann Method on GPU Cluster."* Parallel Computing 27 (2011), pp. 521–535.

Index

allocation
  allocatable array, 9, 35, 41, 82, 83, 240
  allocate, 38, 39, 40, 42, 131, 167, 216, 240
  automatic reallocation, 194
  deallocate, 14, 35, 36, 45, 46, 47, 224, 242
analysis
  dynamic, 221
  static, 231
array
  assumed-shape, 221
  automatic, 40, 131
  explicit-shape, 237, 238
  lower bound, 240
  section, 4, 18, 131
  work, 13, 40, 239
  zero length, 19
attribute, xiii, 7, 22, 41, 42, 80, 83, 123, 233
  allocatable, 28, 41, 44, 47
  external, 105, 106, 109, 220
  nopass, 165
  pass, 173, 180
  pointer, 41, 42, 44, 47, 232
  private, 55, 198, 216
  public, 39, 76, 82, 192
  save, 70, 119, 123
  target, 235

binding, 82, 100, 164
bit, x, 7, 10, 17, 22, 30, 71, 77, 78, 92, 113, 124, 143, 188
byte, 126, 236

C++, xiii, 92, 163, 167, 189, 219, 227
calling convention, 79, 81
character string, 9, 36, 37, 60, 77, 82
coarray, x, 208, 217, 238
command-line arguments, 93
COMMON block, 52, 56
compiler, x, xiv, 4, 5, 6, 7, 9, 10, 15, 16, 35, 35, 36, 49, 57, 80, 81, 120, 121, 122, 123, 126, 127, 129, 131, 132, 134, 136, 168, 196, 197, 216, 219, 220, 221, 222, 223, 224, 231, 232, 235, 236, 238, 240, 241

compiler-specific, 9, 121, 131, 238
  optimization, 5, 127, 129
  option, 15, 41, 155, 223
complex numbers, 76, 77, 130, 219, 220, 236
concatenation, x, 39
condition, 19, 119, 123, 124, 128, 130, 135, 138, 181, 210, 232

database, 76, 79, 83, 85, 88, 89, 92, 243
  MySQL, 243
  SQL, 85
  SQLite, 76, 77, 243
derived type, 1, 6, 7, 24, 26, 27, 28, 29, 33, 36, 42, 43, 44, 45, 46, 47, 64, 83, 88, 123, 124, 176, 178, 187, 193
  default assignment, 27
  user-defined assignment, 193
design pattern, 77, 189, 192, 195, 207
dynamic, ix, 21, 168, 170, 187, 192, 221, 232, 241, 243

elemental routine, 7, 15

file formats
  PDF, 92, 243
  PNG, 95
  PostScript, 92, 243
floating-point arithmetic, 136
framework, xi, 114, 115, 118, 119, 120
function
  count(), 4
  intrinsic, x, 9, 12, 27, 78, 84, 126, 128, 161, 167, 170, 196, 236, 242
  present(), 6
  recursive, 5, 32, 39, 184
  size(), 4, 241
  transfer(), 9

Gauss elimination, 115, 135
generic, x, 5, 6, 28, 51, 75, 76, 109, 174, 175, 176, 181, 184, 186, 222
gfortran, xiv, 49, 81, 127, 146, 229, 243
gnuplot, 243

CPSIA information can be obtained at www.ICGtesting.com
Printed in the USA
LVOW10s0021290915

456095LV00016B/179/P